*Broken Systems-Shattered Lives*

# BROKEN SYSTEMS, SHATTERED LIVES

## ABUSE AND DEATH AT THE HANDS OF THE WELFARE SYSTEM

## GARY W. REECE, PH.D.

ISBN:

978-1-950850-55-6 [Paperback Edition]
978-1-950850-54-9 [eBook Edition]

Printed and bound in The United States of America.

Published by

**The Mulberry Books, LLC.**
8330 E Quincy Avenue, Denver CO 80237
*themulberrybooks.com*

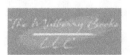

This book is dedicated to the children who enter The Los Angeles County Child Welfare System. Many are abused, too many die, and the system fails to protect and provide needed services. I will tell their stories about the effects of placement on them, the nature of the system they enter, those who are mandated to help and the homes in which they are placed. This is a broken, failed system which profoundly and dramatically creates long-lasting consequences for those families, children and professionals who are a part of the system. Its complexity, bureaucracy and entrenched ways of doing things create a huge obstacle to change.

By looking at the system and how it affects the lives of children who have the misfortune to become embroiled in it, perhaps key problems, issues, and solutions will become evident. Change in any social system is difficult. One as large, intractable, and cumbersome as the Los Angeles County Department of Children and Family Services is formidable. The task is even more daunting when this system reflects and is embedded in a larger societal context replete with political ideologies, economic constraints, values, structure, institutions and historical tradition which creates its own form of inertia.

The book will be grounded and centered in the lives of particular children with whom the author has been involved over the past ten years. Statistics are always abstract. To know the number of children affected by a social system is to miss the trauma, tragedy, and cost in damaged lives and the social cost of these lives to the larger society.

Behind every statistic lies a story. It is these stories I wish to tell. It is hoped that it may raise awareness, inspire, inform, and stimulate the reader to become a part of a movement of concerned individuals committed to change. With this collective mind, together we will create understanding and a vision for transformation. Out of this new vision, perhaps a more enlightened and humane way of protecting and saving our children will emerge.

# A Meditation

## CHRONICLER OF THE WINDS

On that day beneath the unrelenting sun, I discovered the true face of the city. I saw how the poor were forced to eat their lives raw. There was never any time for them to prepare their days — not those who were constantly forced to fight on the outermost bastions of survival. I looked at this temple of the absurd, which was the city and maybe also the world, and it resembled what I saw all around me. I was standing in the center of the dark cathedral of powerlessness.

*Henning Mankell*

## THE LINE

All men live lives enveloped in whale lines. All are born with halters around their necks, but it is only when caught in the swift, sudden turn of death, that mortals realize the sudden, silent, subtle, ever present profile of life. And if you be a philosopher, though seated in the whale boat, you would not at heart feel one whit more of terror, than though seated before your evening fire with a poker and not a harpoon by your side.

*Moby Dick by Herman Melville*

# TABLE OF CONTENTS

# Acknowledgments

This project would never have been finished without the help of so many of my good friends and family. I would especially like to thank and acknowledge my daughter Michele Foster who so generously and graciously volunteered, and competently took on the task of editing and bringing order out of my rambling and fractured prose. To my eternal gratitude, this risky adventure turned into a very pleasant opportunity for us to work together on a project which she flatteringly found challenging and interesting.

Thank you, Michele, for your competence, responsibility, and sense of humor as you hacked your way through the dense forest of my penchant for long and laborious sentences, punctuating only when I pause to think. She also admonished me to never begin a sentence with And. I still don't know why.

I would also like to acknowledge my son Scott Reece who cajoled, coerced, and pushed me screaming and kicking into the "digital age." He encouraged my writing, and inspired me as we sat up and talked until all hours of the night about life in this cosmos and his passion for writing. My friends all know how techno phobic I am. I shocked them when I found my way to social media and I think, onto Face Book and joined several professional discussion groups on line. I still refuse to Twitter. Scott dazzled me with his cell phone, which helped us navigate our way to Yellowstone in a driving rain storm in the middle of the night. He is also a gifted photographer who has attempted to wean me off my old Minolta SLR and teach me how to use a digital camera. I am lucky to have two grown children with such incredible skills who have been helpful to me in this project as well as learning how to be a good father.

To my friends and colleagues overlapping two centuries, Dr. Don Randall, who authored, *Just another Buddhist Christian*, I say particular heartfelt thanks for all the ways his friendship has helped me weather the many crises of my life as I thrashed about and wandered in the wilderness: Finding myself. We spent many pleasant hours camped out under the desert sky talking about the great mysteries. He also read and made helpful suggestions and changes to this manuscript.

There is also another very dear friend, Dr. Rohit Desai, who brings me perspective from his own cultural background, reads my writings, gives helpful critiques, and spots the clichés I am so fond of using. He also has been very helpful with his medical knowledge which supports and affirms me when I my panic over my numerous medical crises.

And then there is my good friend Jack Gebhardt, who is another long time and faithful compadre when we go to the gym, ride our bikes, sit by the lake and tell stories and laugh. He was my sustainer who got me through a cancer surgery, leg amputation, and various other medical crises. He pushed me around in my wheelchair, took me to movies and tolerated my irascible, crotchety old man routine. He genuinely makes me laugh like no other humanoid.

I would be very remiss if I did not mention the foster parents whom I spent 10 long years coaching, supporting, advocating, and being with as they took on the heroic task of raising children with whom they fell in love and suffered along with them in spite of the system and those who made their task so much more difficult.

To my Heroes who allowed me to publish their stories: Patrick, Jeanette, Machelle, and Alex, survivors of the system, I say thank you and I celebrate your courage, resiliency, and strength as you persisted and survived against incredible odds in spite of a system that was mostly a hindrance when it was not outright harming you.

Finally, I would like to pay tribute to a very special couple, Corri Planck and Dianne Hardy-Garcia. They were the foster parents of Sarah Chavez, the two-year-old child they nurtured, loved, helped to thrive only to have her taken from them and returned to the birth family. Six months later Sarah was murdered by her uncle. I helped Cory and Diane through the shattering grief in the months after the time they lost her. In their own words, "So many of you have been so supportive to us over these past few months as we struggled with the loss of Sarah, we remain tremendously grateful for your kindness, friendship and love—it continues to provide us strength to keep fighting for Sarah."

# Introduction

How is an idea born, matured and ultimately brought to fruition as a book? As I reflect on my motivation for writing *Broken Systems* I find that its origins, like a river, have many tributaries. It began with my career change from clinical psychology in the private psychiatric sector and trauma consultation with various entities, to working with abused children in a non-profit foster family agency. The seeds of motivation also stemmed from my natural inquisitiveness. As I encounter situations that raise questions and plunge me into new arenas, my curiosity drives me to find answers. An additional and personal motivating factor is my strong identification with the children who were victimized on a daily basis.

This book's final driving influence is professional. I have studied trauma for the past 40 years. I have spent the whole of my professional career working with trauma victims, consulting with agencies, and conducting critical incident debriefings during community-wide traumatic events. When I made a career change to work with a local Foster Family Agency, it unwittingly placed me in a new environment. This environment challenged me on multiple levels: I had to learn new skills to deal with an unfamiliar workplace, develop new knowledge sets in order to handle unfamiliar situations with families and children, and manage the emotional impact of, and personal identification with, children experiencing horrible life-events.

My career in the private sector of the *child welfare system* has been a 12-year odyssey. On that first day of my new career, I remember feeling totally overwhelmed, lost and shocked by what I encountered. Out of curiosity and a powerful need to understand what I saw, I searched the literature, went to workshops, and talked to experienced colleagues. As my investigation continued and I struggled to make sense of what I was seeing, I began compiling notes and thinking about the families with whom I was working. S I began writing, thinking there were some interesting stories here. Over time, the urge to write became stronger. Then one day an event happened; it became the catalyst for the book. It was the death of Sarah Chavez. Sarah a child whose case I managed was returned to her birth family after being in foster placement for six months--only to be killed by her uncle. After that incident, the momentum increased as my writing was fueled by the tragedy and my anger and a sense of helplessness. I realized, I must tell this story. This book, I realized is my late-career mission. I witnessed too much of the following: Too many children's deaths, brutalized children, Social Workers not doing their jobs, bad decisions that return children to dangerous circumstances, unprepared birth parents lacking basic parenting skills, depressing staff meetings characterized by horrific story-sharing, and finally, too many new mandates and meaningless reports that were never read. The last was the proverbial straw.

No longer could I tolerate the sense of helplessness I felt over the countless children being abused, and it was my desire to understand the severity of their behavior problems which spurred me into action. For my voice to be heard, I began writing, reading, and conducting more research. The ideas began to formulate into chapters. Once the chapters were organized, I began to see the structure, and out of this structure, the narrative evolved. That was when Broken Systems, Shattered Lives, the title, came to me.

Out of an ill-formed sense of anger and frustration came a desire to take action, and out of a compassion for these vulnerable, helpless, impoverished, endangered children, I resolved to do my part to educate, inform, and support other concerned people reading my books and attending my workshops. I wanted to give the children a voice. As the story developed, my motivation was further supported by sources outside the system. It was in those stories that I realized others were paying attention. In particular, Garrett Therolf, Los Angeles Times Staff Writer, wrote many articles chronicling the condition of children in Los Angeles.

My focus on trauma in the lives of children is a somewhat recent development, even though it has a long history. I have devoted the past 30 years of my professional career to studying and working with trauma victims and their families. My interest has been both professional and personal. It began with my attempt to understand and cope with a personal traumatic event which evolved into a career interest. This journey has led me into a variety of situations and encounters with different kinds of trauma victims. As a result, I realize that trauma is a universal phenomenon affecting all people, whether they are groups brought to a standstill by a mass community trauma, or individuals traumatized by violence from strangers. Trauma becomes personal when a family is devastated by the loss of a child. In particular, the most recent national tragedy at Newtown, Connecticut only raises our consciousness to new levels. With the recent onslaught of natural and manmade events -- tornadoes, earthquakes, floods, terrorism, and war -- the tragedies seem endless. We as witnesses are bombarded daily, and out of basic survival needs, we seem grow indifferent, inured by the sheer volume of trauma.

Because of my total emersion in trauma and community involvement, many opportunities have come to me. I have been intimately involved with people at the very moment in their lives when trauma occurred. In those moments, I witnessed their vulnerability and devastation. The experiences I have had have given me the unique opportunity to counsel them as they were transformed by their terrible travails.

One of my more rewarding experiences was as the keynote speaker for a convention for families who lost children through accidents, miscarriages and illnesses. As I shared my story, I was gratified and heartened by people who shared their stories of survival with me. In several breakout sessions, I became aware of how many people have been touched by trauma, their lives hurled off track by unexpected, uncontrolled circumstances. I experienced the comfort and validation that comes from shared stories. This convention became a community of survivors and left an indelible memory which reinforced the belief in the healing power of community through shared grief.

At the convention, they handed out name tags in the shape of an infant's hand with the child's name on it. There were people with one, two and even three names on their tags. At the closing memorial ceremony, attendees went to a table and lit a candle while the name and age of their child was flashed on a screen. My child's name was Nicole, she died in 1971. Sudden Infant Death Syndrome took her life at the age of 6 months. Her death launched my career of searching for healing and understanding. During that search, I walked among the shattered lives of survivors attempting to simultaneously deal with the short and long term effects of traumatic loss.

The complexity of traumatic events is illustrated by my work with a Girl Scout executive whose troop was involved in a multiple-casualty bus crash that occurred a number of years ago. At one point she said to me, "I don't know what to do first. I have dead girls and their families, kids in the hospital, the media swarming all over me and programs to keep running." It was a daunting task made easier by well coordinated, shared community support.

Going from working with groups and individuals who experienced life changing trauma to working with traumatized children seemed like a natural career progression, yet it has been a very difficult one. Perhaps it is because the face of trauma was up close and personal. I was seeing it every day and in my opinion, it was preventable.

Each morning I sit down to breakfast with my copy of the Los Angeles Times. This particular morning a headline jumped out at me: **More Children Die as Reform Falters.** This was dated March 28, 2010. "There have been more than 70 maltreatment deaths over the last three years of children who had been under the supervision of the Los Angeles County Department of Children's Services…The Department of Children's Services is still struggling to implement reforms." This statistic, shocking in its grim reality, refocused my desire to do something about this appalling social tragedy. Each time a story comes out, there is outrage, a flurry of studies, and then nothing changes. I believe there needs to be a response that goes beyond public outcry. There needs to be awareness coupled with a public will and focused endeavor that leads to meaningful change. It also helps when people in places of power lend their voice and oversight to the problem.

In The Los Angeles Times article, County Supervisor Zev Yaroslavsky was quoted as saying that he "suspects the Department of Children and Family Services has failed to acknowledge some recent child deaths tied to abuse or neglect, inaccurately leading the public to believe that the number of children dying under such circumstances is falling." The article goes on to state that statistics released in recent days indicate that six children whose families had previously come to the attention of welfare officials died of abuse or neglect this year, down from 11 deaths by this point last year. Yaroslavsky noted that the department has a very narrow definition of neglect and abuse, citing a recent suicide of an 11 year old boy who hung himself with a jump rope in his foster mother's home in June. The boy, who had spent 15 months in foster care, told a counselor that he intended to kill himself because he was "tired of people hitting me all the time." Just hours before his death, a Social Worker was sent to check on the boy at home and did not remove him.

This was only one glaring example of a failed duty to protect. Zaroslavsky closed by saying "A reasonable person would conclude that this is a case of neglect, even though the county denies it." He goes on to state, "I think the department has an interest in minimizing the number of cases that they put on the list because, frankly, it makes them look better. The Times periodically publishes more articles with the same flavor of outrage and filled with more statistics and deaths. It remains critical of this unyielding and dysfunctional public agency.

The *Los Angeles County Department of Children and Family Services* is a very large organization that has been under siege in recent years with numerous investigations for incompetence, inefficiency, and hundreds of deaths of children in its care. There have been a plethora of recommended changes, and several directors have come and gone. Yet things seem to have remained unchanged. Much of the department's dirty laundry has been exposed for public viewing by the print media. Numerous articles have been written about the department and the findings are very troubling. In an article written by Troy Anderson of the Long Beach Telegram, the context, issues, and controversy which have plagued the department over the last 20 years are well framed:

Up to half of Los Angeles County's foster children were needlessly placed in a system that is often more dangerous than their own homes because of financial incentives in state and federal laws, a two-year Los Angeles Newspaper Group investigation has found.

The county receives nearly $30,000 a year from federal and state governments for each child placed in the system; money that goes to pay the stipends of foster parents, but also wages, benefits and overhead costs for child-welfare workers and executives. For some special-needs children, the county receives up to $150,000 annually.

"Called the 'perverse incentive factor,' states and counties earn more revenues by having more children in the system, whether it is opening a case to investigate a report of child abuse and neglect, or placing a child in foster care," wrote the authors of a recent report by the state Department of Social Services Child Welfare Stakeholders Group.

Since the early 1980s, the number of foster children in California has gone up five-fold, and doubled in the county and nation. About one in four children will come into contact with the child welfare system before turning18, officials say.

This has overwhelmed Social Workers, who often don't have time to help troubled families or monitor the care children receive in foster homes.

The hundreds of thousands of children who have cycled through the county's system over the years are six to seven times more likely to be mistreated and three times more likely to be killed than children in the general population, government statistics reveal.

Officials acknowledge that more than 660 children embroiled in the county's foster care system have died since 1991, including more than 160 who were homicide victims." The service that DCFS now provides is worse than the abuse that most abused children ever experienced. The trauma they inflict on ordinary children is unspeakable."

* For the remainder of this article see appendix A

Today's story has a way of becoming yesterday's forgotten headline. Unfortunately these are not isolated cases and there will be more to take their place. These stories reveal an overall portrait of the plight of too many of our children. It is incomprehensible that more than 660 children in the system in just Los Angeles County have died, with more than 160 being the victims of homicide.

These are our children! They unfortunately have become the wards of the *Los Angeles County Department of Children and Family Services*. Ironically, this child welfare system, is on many occasions, as dysfunctional as the families from whom the children are removed. In every case where there is dysfunction, a mistake, an oversight, failure to detain, a miscommunication, or a failed notification occurs, a child suffers, and often dies.

As I was editing this manuscript for what I thought was going to be the final time, I picked up the Los Angeles Times, again as I was having coffee with a friend. He said, "Did you see this?" (February 14, 2013, ironically Valentine's Day.) This time the headline: **Blind Leading the Blind,** another article by Jason Song and Garret Therolf. I, of course immediately grabbed the paper and read the article which led off with:

> A stifling bureaucracy and inept work force have crippled Los Angeles County's child protective agency resulting in a system that allowed children to remain in unsafe homes, sometimes to die at the hands of their caretakers, according to a confidential county report.

This was apparently a new investigation, conducted by an independent counsel for the Board of Supervisors which looked at 15 recent child deaths and a torture case. They found:

> In all but two instances, investigators found that caseworker errors began with the agency's 1st contact with the children and contributed to their deaths. This report is the harshest assessment of the DCFS in recent memory, echoing complaints from child advocates that the county has rejected for years.

The report goes on to document a list of departmental problems:

- The decision to place the least experienced workers in the most crucial job: Assessing danger to children. According to the report workers get 160,000 child abuse calls a year and the workers, "Are just doing their time."

- They found that the Supervisors are poorly qualified and often disregard policy creating a situation of "The blind leading the blind."
- Workers are rarely held accountable for egregious errors. The results have been preventable deaths if Social Workers had just taken basic steps to assess the risks.

Among cases reviewed, there was only one firing, apparently for falsifying a report, and the only other serious discipline was a 30-day suspension. The report was written by Amy Sheik Naamoni who was hired to help guide reform efforts. She found that many of the department's errors were rooted in its strategy to keep children with their families and avoid detention by putting them in foster homes instead. A new director has been hired to help facilitate the reforms: Phillip Browning is going to embark on a reorganization plan with new assignments, training and procedures. Browning said his goal was to restore common sense and critical thinking to the child welfare network. These will be in response to the report which recommended a 4-year blueprint for reform, "The first comprehensive effort in a decade."

In summary, the report found general lack of skill and poor supervision in which Social Workers became blind to dangerous family situations. A tendency to place the least experienced or trained personnel in The Emergency Response Unit, was also cited. The report further stated that investigations relied on bureaucratic rules, not common sense and close observations. The voluminous rules and procedures led to paperwork and relentless attention to following thousands of pages of policies which superseded *hands-on social work*. Lowell Goodman, Union Spokesman, said, "Even the finest Social Workers could not perform their best efforts in this system."

Browning has promised to streamline policy manuals and raise standards across the department. He has also promised to upgrade the Emergency Response Team with higher paid workers. He stated, "This is going to be hard work." A very keen insight!

What I find so fascinating about this "latest review" is that it sounds strangely like the last promise to reform I have been reporting on in this writing. And that was 3 years ago. Each time the promised reforms come after another shocking case of unimaginable brutality to a child. The promise of reforms comes and goes, and the children still continue to die.

Every year, over 800,000 children in this country are removed from their homes due to abuse, neglect, domestic violence, or parental drug and alcohol problems. At any given time, over half a million children are in foster care. These children have been removed because they have experienced multiple threats to their safety and security and are subjected daily to trauma which affects their health and development. These children are vulnerable and their physical, emotional, psychological, and social well-being is at great risk. Those who languish in the system in long-term foster care have a dismal record of achievement. They struggle because of their psychological and mental health issues and lingering effects of trauma and learning problems. As a result of all these factors, they do not find success in their school endeavors. Also, because of their unstable and often impoverished living situations, they do not acquire the most rudimentary social skills and motivation to succeed or plan for the future.

Many of these young people are ill-prepared for adulthood and lack a safety net to support them in times of need. They struggle to acquire adequate housing, food, and education. This book directly addresses, through case examples, the impact on children removed from birth families and placed in the child welfare system. *Broken Systems, Shattered Lives* is written 1) to raise awareness of the plight of children in the system 2) to expose the dysfunction of the system 3) to identify the long-lasting social and psychological effects of dysfunctional families cause traumatic effects which resulted in the placement process 4) to suggest the necessary remedies for treatment, and 5) to provide insight and information to teachers, Social Workers, and foster parents that will help them in their work with these children.

The approach I have taken in telling this story is to weave together cases of actual children in the system that I have worked with over the past 12 years. It tells of the devastating effects of multiple placements, indifferent Social Workers, brutal birth parents and a system that dismally fails to serve the best interests of abused and neglected children. It also tells the stories of caring families who take these children into their homes and in doing so also experience the traumatic effects of placement on the children. I believe that unrecognized and untreated trauma and loss in children leads to nothing being done about it.

When I began my work with these children, I was shocked by the level of abuse children suffer at the hands of those who should be protecting them. As I encountered the foster care system for the first time, I was amazed at the extent of dysfunction throughout all levels. I also wondered how the system could be this terrible and if anyone was aware of how bad it actually was. Eventually, I wondered if anyone cared. The stories in the Times at least indicted there are attempts to bring these matters to public attention.

I also questioned how these children could suffer at the hands of adults with such apparent societal indifference. I thought "Why isn't something being done?" I believe it is because the children are an invisible, voiceless and powerless minority. A minority in Los Angeles County which is disenfranchised, discriminated against, abused, neglected, and, in some cases, killed. Even though they have legal representation, their rights are often superseded by rights of other groups (primarily their parents). In many ways the problem continues because it is invisible, below the threshold of public awareness.

I am using the term *disenfranchisement* in this context to mean "any group, person, relationship, loss or event which is not valued or sanctioned by society." Disenfranchisement happens for many reasons. Historically, the foster-parent child relationship has long been viewed as something less than valuable. As a consequence, it has often been poorly supported by social agencies. Because of the new emphasis on placement permanency, foster parenting is even more attenuated. Because of their ambiguous and often temporary role in children's lives, lack of agency support and intrusion in their lives, foster parents are frequently underestimated, ignored, or devalued. The placement effects on this disenfranchised group of children are made worse because the children are not valued and their loss or trauma is not seen as significant. Consequently, what was lost is not valued and the view of the trauma is minimized.

Another ramification of disenfranchisement is that minimal resources are provided to help foster families deal with the emotional impact that fostering children has on their lives. Frequently, by the single act of taking a child into their home, foster parents unexpectedly become at risk for emotional and psychological distress as they struggle to cope with the demands of foster parenting. Foster parents often experience an unanticipated reaction when they relive their own childhood traumas while dealing with and caring for their foster children. Finally, as a result of the huge cuts in state and federal funding for these programs, disenfranchisement occurs and is often seen as an unfortunate but necessary budget decision. It is common knowledge that the first programs to receive cuts are typically in the areas of health, education and welfare. This cutting cycle has been particularly virulent since the national and state budget calamity of 2008. "Special needs children" in placement are a unique population. Their special needs and circumstances exist because they have experienced multiple traumas which resulted in their placement: physical and emotional abuse, domestic violence, sexual abuse, neglect and abandonment. They have also experienced trauma from being removed and placed. What is not given credence is that entering the system results in serial trauma. This trauma comes in the form of going to court, losing control of their lives, having a cumbersome and impersonal bureaucracy determine their fate, and being handed over to total strangers who are responsible for meeting their needs for safety, security, and nurturance.

As a consequence of being removed to "protect them," the children begin a journey characterized by sequential victimization. They often bounce from one court-ordered placement to the next, and are placed with other children whose plight is similar to their own. Sibling groups are often split up. Group homes, residential facilities, foster homes, and temporary holding facilities become the tapestry against which the drama of their victimization is played out: first victimized by inadequate and often incompetent-impaired parents, and then victimized again when their primary attachment is disrupted by their removal. The victimization continues as failed placements result in being moved from one placement to the next. Then, as if they have not suffered enough, because of the court-ordered reunification plan, they are forced to see the offending parent in a weekly visit or series of visits, thereby creating a situation that leads to secondary trauma. Imagine what would happen if a rape victim was required by law to spend several hours a week "visiting" her rapist. The effect on children is similar.

Well-meaning court and dependency workers and well-meaning caregivers, often ill-equipped to help these wounded children heal and normalize their lives, participate in this cycle of instability. The net result is a serial form of trauma where children are caught in a cycle of victimization which terrorized them and renders them helpless, with little say regarding their future. The children in this system flounder and struggle to survive against overwhelming forces. Each time the system fails, the misery and wounding of children is compounded. In my view, it is a trauma epidemic, a shadowy force that is the tip of the social system iceberg.

Trauma for these children has many levels. The first level is formed from family living conditions that led to removal of the child. Already experiencing sufficient trauma to be deemed "in need of protection," these children begin a long and tumultuous saga through a fragmented, unwieldy, overburdened, and impersonal children's justice system. Removal from the first level and placement in this system constitutes the second level of trauma, which compounds the initial trauma. This is due in part because the system lacks the necessary resources, technical proficiency and interagency coordination to provide families with needed services and support. In today's climate of budgetary crises, the necessary mental health services are no longer available to provide the crucial help needed to allow these children to recover from their ordeal. In short, they are not well served by this system, the very system mandated to serve and protect them. In a perverse way, they have become a new social group victimized by discrimination.

The body of knowledge regarding trauma has evolved considerably over the past few decades. Starting with the primitive notion of battle fatigue and war shock, it has broadened to include individuals, groups, first responders, and individuals who have been subjected to all manner of sudden and horrific events. During my career, *traumatology* has become a sub-specialty and is so refined that its pernicious effects are now investigated at a neurological level.

In my career as a psychologist I focused largely on the effects of single event trauma on adults. Twelve years ago when I made a career change to work with a foster care agency, I saw an opportunity to bring my clinical skills and accumulated knowledge of trauma to the population of children placed in the foster-adopt system. As I entered this new and very foreign, world I experienced a kind of culture shock. The first shock was seeing so many children with emotional damage. As I handled case after case of children placed with our foster family agency, I noticed a repeated constellation of symptoms in these children. Unlike the adults and adolescents I was accustomed to working with in the private mental health sector, the children seemed, to my surprise, to have a whole range of multiple disorders -- primarily symptoms of Attention Deficit and Post Traumatic Stress. They also had combined attachment, mood and behavioral disorders. I wondered how this could be.

The second shock was the discovery of an underworld of violence and the horrible things parents do to their children. The third shocking discovery was the dysfunctional nature of the system serving the children. These shocking discoveries have consumed my attention and professional curiosity. Pursuing and understanding the connection between the above three factors with the unifying theme of Trauma and Loss has been my purpose.

Through my observations, a thread of commonality became glaringly obvious amongst these children's stories: a history of disruption permeated by parental neglect, abuse, addiction, and homelessness or domestic violence, followed by removal from the home and placement in a large system. That these children experience these horrendous events when they are the most dependent and vulnerable added to the intensity of the trauma.

As I continued, trying to make sense of what I was seeing, there came a more gradual discovery. I found that what I had learned about trauma in the lives of adult survivors was an inadequate model for understanding the complex behavior-psycho-emotional-social problems in the lives of the children I served. An even more disheartening fact was that trauma had very deep roots, even beginning before birth and then continuing, becoming embedded in the family dynamic of tragedy.

These children have genetic histories where there may be a long family history of mental illness and addiction. Add drug abuse during pregnancy, poor prenatal care, maternal stress, and domestic violence to the mix and one can see that children are suffering from complex and ongoing trauma. Hence, the complexity of the problem and how this dramatically increases the odds against a good start in life seriously tilts in a negative direction. This book is a recounting of my encounters with the foster-adopt system and my relationship with the children I have come to know, understand and love, and the families that have taken them into their homes. I believe my search for understanding is best told and illustrated through the stories of these children. Their stories speak loudly of the trauma, the confusion, life-long scars, chaos, and uncertainty of having lives thrown completely off their developmental track through the accident of birth and placement. I have come to the conclusion that in order to grasp the complexity of the problem, it is best viewed in its entire context as a matrix of interlocking processes: Pre-placement trauma compounded by placement trauma and the ongoing trauma of being subjected to dysfunctional systems working against each other. My inevitable conclusion: *Broken systems lead to shattered lives.*

This is a social and national tragedy which, in the context of our larger national concerns goes unnoticed. That is why I refer to these children as *disenfranchised.* They and their problems are overlooked. Not valued, they are the invisible, shadow population who only become visible as adults when they commit crimes, produce more children, are plagued by drug abuse and homelessness, and fill our jails and mental institutions. It is a well known statistic that 70% of the prison population has been in the foster care system. And 80% of children in the foster care system go on to become homeless when emancipated from the system.

This epidemic of family and societal failure is a major cost to our society as a whole through incarceration and/or homelessness and through over-burdening of other social support systems. It is estimated that 50-70% of the children passing through the juvenile justice system have experienced trauma directly through drug exposure during and after pregnancy. Following birth, these children have acquired mental health disorders. In my experience, all of the children who have been removed from their homes have experienced significant losses which, if untreated, have the potential to become major impediments to functioning adulthood.

Study after study confirms that early abuse and neglect have lifelong-effects which impair a person's ability to have healthy relationships. Children who have been abused are more self-destructive, prone to addiction, likely to divorce, more likely to be involved in criminal activity, and have serious attachment problems as well. It is cliché to say that adult abusers were abused children, but it is nevertheless true.

The unrecognized effects of removal from their families of origin and the attendant trauma and loss are the greatest hurdles to successful adjustment and recovery for children dependent upon social services. I once attended a conference in which David Sanders, former director of *Los Angeles County Department of Children and Family Services,* said "As an agency we do a good job of protecting these children from harm but we do not do a good job of raising them. This is a massive failure." In light of recent revelations about the deaths of children in placement, it appears we are not even doing a good job of protecting them. He believed that the solution was to prevent children from entering the system in the first place. "Family preservation and reunification should be the goal," he said. However, there are many families ravaged by mental illness, homelessness, poverty and addiction who cannot, nor should, not be preserved. To return certain children to their families of origin often has had tragic results.

Ultimately, children entering foster placement experience many different kinds of trauma: the original traumatizing event which led to the attention of welfare workers, the disruption of their primary attachment bond, and the resulting traumatizing events of placement. Compounding these traumatizing events is another profound event—the grief associated with each loss. Traumatized children seldom have time to heal from their trauma let alone grieve their many losses: family, neighborhood, friends, toys, pets, and their home. This combination results in double jeopardy for the children.

It has been my experience that the events of removal, placement and adjustment to foster care are largely overlooked as far as the traumatizing consequences are concerned. For example, I attended at conference in Los Angeles on death, grief, and trauma in the lives of children. During one presentation on traumatized children, I asked the presenter about the effects of foster placement. He said that was not within the scope of their study.

My reason, again for this book, is that placement in foster care is a major cause of trauma in the lives of children, and that children who are subjected to these traumatic events do not receive the recognition or specialized form of care they so desperately need. In fact, I have seen that the event of placement is treated as a non-event. Frequently, the child is removed and placed with little regard for its impact. When the anticipated adjustment, developmental, and learning problems occur, the most minimal forms of intervention are seldom provided. Because the children often find it difficult to adjust, they are blamed, given seven day notices, and stigmatized as "difficult." Care is inadequate, foster parents are poorly trained and inadequately supported, and services are difficult to obtain.

Psychological care for these children is often sporadic and not integrated into the total care of the child. And because of the recent economic calamity, services are being more severely curtailed. Foster parents are often viewed as ancillary to treatment and not kept informed of the direction and reason for treatment. When treatment is given it is often by practitioners who are not trained in specific forms of trauma treatment. Though *Permanency* is the new code phrase in the child welfare system, it is seldom achieved without great effort and serial episodes of impermanence. Many fractured families come into the system and receive many different forms of support and services in order to preserve the family. The children are left in these families while they try to overcome their multiple problems. Other forms of permanency are also being advocated and the net result is a system in a state of flux where the children suffer. Again, broken systems lead to shattered lives.

That all of this creates uncertainty, confusion, anxiety, and disorientation is a powerful understatement. I have long been aware of how troublesome, painful, and overwhelming the entire experience of placement can be and how frequently lifelong wounds are created. Out of personal experience working with particular trauma victims, I have come to the following conclusions to be further discussed in the following chapters:

- The results of trauma are complex and often long-lasting if not addressed and the profound effects of trauma on developing children need to be fully understood.

- Grief and mourning of those losses cannot be addressed until the primary trauma is first worked through.

- In order for healing to take place, the trauma triggers must be uncovered, memories regained, feelings re-

- experienced, meaning made of the experience, and control restored.

- Children need a healing environment which is safe, stable, consistent, and secure, a nurturing world of significant attachment with caring adults that allows for recovery from the effects of trauma and loss.

- The process needs to take place within a healing context established by a system that facilitates, coordinates, and supports the children and those who care for them.

- The process must place the wellbeing of the children first

The rest of this book contains discussions on the following topics:

- Chapter 1 is devoted to the process of placement as it is worked out by the two major institutions involved.

- Chapter 2 explores the effects of disrupted placement.

- Chapters 3, 4, and 5 discuss the effects of pre-placement trauma, placement trauma and loss, mourning and ways to safeguard the children after placement occurs.

- Chapter 6 looks at a case in which the system worked very well and had a positive outcome.

- Chapter 7 reveals how the system breaks down completely when I explore the Smith family's journey through the system.

- Chapter 8 discusses what happens when one county Social Worker does everything she can to sabotage the placement.

- Chapter 9 analyzes to the impact the system has on the families with whom the children are placed.

- Chapter 10 is dedicated to all the children who died because the system failed them.

- Chapter 11 tells the stories of survivors in their quest for healing and establishing a secure sense of self. These stories are told in their own words.

- Chapter 12 summarizes and concludes with suggestions and a discussion regarding issues and possible solutions

The cases documented will illustrate the many problems with the system: inadequate or lack of communication, poorly-trained and inexperienced staff, and supervisors, failed, outdated policies, little meaningful assessment of case circumstances, and hasty decisions made that ignore the best interests of the child. Following these decisions, an unnecessary sequence of multiple placements occurs in which trauma and abuse compound daily. These are problems that urgently need to be addressed. Too many children are lost and/or permanently impaired by indifference or poorly-applied, ineffective solutions. This project is a quest to illuminate these problems and through understanding, discover remedies.

To the children who have experienced life changing crises in their lives, I offer this effort to reach out and touch your lives. I want you to know that there are adults who are working hard, who care, and are trying to make it a better and safer world for you. This journey begins by looking at the process of placement and analyzing the structure and function of the Department of Children's Services, Family Law Center, Adoptions, Foster Care families, the Foster and Family Adoption Agencies (FFAAs), and the children who bear the brunt of placement.

*For reasons of privacy and confidentiality, all the names of individuals in case studies are fictitious so that they may remain anonymous.*

# Chapter 1

## A PERILOUS JOURNEY

When a child enters the Los Angeles County Child Welfare Department, a journey begins which often follows the path of unforeseen consequences. These mixed outcomes reflect the hoped-for benefit of removing a child from danger. However, as it has been all too frequently documented, the journey may have tragic and sometimes fatal consequences. The psychological harm with an overlay of physical danger makes the journey even more hazardous, because the child is literally ripped out of the home by a complete stranger and then placed in one tenuous situation after another. The point of origin is typically a home characterized by hazardous conditions, some of which are the result of poverty and homelessness. The result of being in this type of home is neglect, abuse, violence, chaotic living situations and dysfunctional parents. Once the child is removed from the original home, the child's life is changed forever.

When removing a child, the goal is to protect the child from danger; hence the name Child Protective Services. On this journey the child, who has nothing to say about what happens regarding planning or future placement, will be in the care of strangers: The child's fate is determined by strangers, the child is living with strangers, governed by strangers, and that child is separated from family, neighborhood, and friends. This journey is akin to falling down the rabbit hole in *Alice's Adventures in Wonderland*.

> The rabbit-hole went straight on like a tunnel for some way and dipped suddenly down, so suddenly that Alice had not a moment to think about stopping herself before she found herself falling down what seemed to be a very deep well... when suddenly, thump, thump! Down she came upon a heap of sticks and dry leaves, and the fall was over...

There were doors all round the hall, but they were all locked, and when Alice had been all the way down one side and up the other, trying every door, she walked sadly down the middle, wondering how she was ever to get out again.

Lewis Carrol - *Alice's Adventures in Wonderland*

The foster child's strange world is a very large Wonderland. It is a bureaucracy covering the entirety of Los Angeles County. It is divided into 8 Spas or Regions: Palmdale-Lancaster to Compton, Pomona, West Los Angeles and Long Beach. Each Region has multiple offices like Spa 6- Vermont, Compton, and Wateridge, and Spa 3- Pasadena, Glendora, and Pomona. These are large, geographically-related offices which serve a population of millions of citizens. Each region is run by a Regional Director, or if the Spa is large, it may have more than one Assistant Regional Administrator (ARA), several supervisors, Social Workers, investigators and a large support staff of clerks. To understand a typical Spa office, visit Metro North, a large office building with multiple floors. After you search in vain for parking and pay $6.00, you have to search for the right floor, where there may be a maze of 100 cubicles with a Social Worker, files, phones and chairs for interviews. Once there, you encounter families and their children waiting in reception areas for appointments with their case workers. There are also several rooms with toys set up for family visits. The noise is pervasive and because of the bustle of people moving about, it has the ambience of a zoo or a three ring circus. Each Social Worker carries a case load of approximately 25-30 cases.

Within each office there are several subdivisions: Family Reunification Services, Emergency Response Teams, Adoptions, Independent Living Programs, Foster Homes, Shelter Care Homes, Group Homes and Residential Facilities, and Investigators. This whole kingdom is governed by the Los Angeles County Board of Supervisors with a massive budget supported by the Federal Government to the tune of several billion dollars. Beneath the Board is another level of committees, directors, and panels who are supposed to be overseeing the functions of this *kingdom*. Presently there are approximately 20,000 children in care at any given time. This figure is down from a high of 60,000 noted a few years ago. In

Jane interviewed her as well. Jane observed tracks on her arms from intravenous drug use, and several visible scars from bullet wounds. Jane removed the child due to "conditions of clear neglect in an unsafe environment."

Again, she found a child living in appalling conditions, experiencing neglect and inappropriate contact with adults engaged in criminal activities. Jane had to remove and detain the child. During transportation to Jane's office, the child was frightened, confused, and feeling the loss of her personal world, mother, and all that was familiar in order to be protected from circumstances into which she was born. This inevitably set up a sequence of events which would alter the trajectory of her life forever.

These examples of typical home visits illustrate not only the plight of special needs children, but also the daily travail of a job in which individuals carry out their prescribed roles in a large agency dedicated to protecting endangered children. The job carries with it the risk of exposure to dangerous environments and individuals, while being tasked with protecting children who have been abused, tortured, battered, neglected and, in countless ways, injured by the hapless adults in their lives. Seeing this kind of absurdity, brutality and indifference to the painful plight of vulnerable, innocent children on a daily basis has a powerful impact on the psyches of all who work in this system. It is a system rife with social travesty. It is a cycle of repeated ignorance, banal repetition and helplessness bordering on ultimate futility that wears down the compassion of even the best-intentioned worker. It is the cumulative effect of relentless stress, physical exhaustion, large case loads, the daily grind of running around the huge city of Los Angeles, and trying to deal with an extremely dysfunctional population of birth parents. This is the price paid by well-meaning and caring individuals who stand between the children and their abusers.

In addition to the myriad of rules, policies and procedures that fill rooms full of manuals, all of these factors comprise Jane's world. Several other job expectations compete for her time as well. Going to go to court and testifying regarding the conduct of a case or defending a decision made in the field, all the while being berated by lawyers during testimony add to the stress level. Additionally, being second-guessed at every turn while under public scrutiny further compounds the ongoing stress. While performing these duties, Jane has to attend numerous poorly-run meetings with no clear agenda.

As one can see, prioritizing and juggling all of these demands takes an enormous emotional toll on Social Workers like Jane. Each of them finds her own way to deal with it, but professional burnout is a legitimate issue, and becoming cynical and indifferent is a perpetual reality. These were just some of the reasons Jane finally resigned after 18 years. She said that the final straw was being unable to handle public indifference, parental brutality, suffering of children, and sexual abuse perpetrated by adults. It became too much for her. She said, "One can only see so much suffering before it really gets to you, and then your hands are tied by the courts and crazy decisions made by lawyers and judges. Add to that, the ineffective and broken system and *Alice in Wonderland* is a very good metaphor for what is going on."

## A System on the Firing Line

Because of Jane's familiarity with the system and depth of experience, I asked her to conclude our conversation by offering an assessment of the problems encountered in today's department. The following observations were offered by Jane in an interview in which she reflected on the well-publicized and ongoing problems of the DCFS, the issues that need to be changed in order to provide a more effective organization.

Her first observation is that we must always keep in mind that Los Angeles County is geographically the largest and most diverse county in the country. It is also the largest in terms of sheer size of the bureaucracy and the number of clients served. Added to the geography is the factor that many different regions exist, making it hard to coordinate their activities. Jane said, "Each Spa often operates as its own little kingdom ruled by its chiefs. There can be quite a large difference in the way they apply policy and set procedures."

She also added, "There are so many moving parts, that this creates an environment that cannot help but have numerous opportunities for things to go wrong. To wit, police, sheriff and other law enforcement agencies interface with birth families, Social Workers, and the Children's Law Center." All of this is under the jurisdiction of the Los Angeles County Board of Supervisors. Below them in the hierarchy are several layers of management, boards, and committees who set and implement policy.

As of this writing, a new director had just been hired, and per Jane, "[no one] knows which direction he will want to take the department. There have been a series of changes, and it's like playing musical chairs in the last few years with several department heads coming and going."

In addition to the size and complexity of the issues in the department, Jane emphasized the individual role of the county Social Workers and the enormous responsibility they carry in the decision-making process in the field that affects the very structure and stability of families and their children. "Going to a home in an often dangerous neighborhood, encountering who knows what horrific circumstances and finding a child in terrible condition because of abuse, neglect or family violence is very difficult... People in the public domain do not understand nor are they able to comprehend what awful things people do to children and the utter mindlessness, depravity, and lack of caring exhibited by parents. Confronting this daily was the final reason I left the department."

Jane added, "It is very hard to go into a home and remove a child, knowing what comes after removal. I had to take the child to the office, often on a Friday evening, and find a placement for the child, and very often it is while you have six other screaming emergencies. It can get very hairy at times." Jane feels that the life of the individual Social Worker is made more difficult by the size of the caseload and the volume of paperwork each case entails. Some become embittered and cynical and stop caring as a defense against the continual onslaught of tragedy. Others do the minimal requirements just to get by, quit, or go on medical leave. However, there are many that do their jobs conscientiously and work to save lives.

At the level of the individual Social Worker, Jane feels more training is needed. Some children in distress are not identified because the Social Workers have little training in recognizing developmental issues, attachment problems and mental health issues. She added that abuse of children goes undetected because some birth parents are very skilled at hiding that abuse. Due to the limited time the Social Worker has in the home, it may not be possible to thoroughly assess the child. Jane recounted a story in which both child and birth mother were in her office and she suspected the child had been abused, but the evidence was border line. To verify, she had a colleague talk to the mother while she took the child to see a doctor in a neighboring office who specialized in abuse. The doctor took a look at the child and then confirmed Jane's suspicion, "Yep." she said. "Definitely a failure to thrive!"

To handle uncertainties like this, Jane's suggests more training and the partnering of new Social Workers with mentors. This would help with assessment and critical decision making. It is important because, in some of the most notorious cases, serious abuse was not detected even though "reputedly the Social Worker was making regular home calls."

So much of the work comes down to judgment calls. As one County Board Supervisor said, "People just need to do their jobs." In some of the other cases it comes down to Social Worker attitudes, biases, or prejudices. According to Jane, some Social Workers have a definite preference and bias toward "keeping families together at all costs." This bias is then reflected in reports and recommendations that lead to some children being returned inappropriately to dangerous homes. This is also noted in some judges who "have a bias toward family reunification and then rule against strong recommendations to the contrary."

One issue repeatedly occurs because of the very structure of the families from which the children are being removed. Jane stated that a very high percentage of the homes are single parents, typically single women. In these homes, the violent boyfriends, often not observed in the home or even known about, are the perpetrators of the abuse.

Jane's assessment of the department comes down to the following: The overly large size of the department, inefficient bureaucracy, a billion dollar budget, too many moving parts, poorly or inadequately trained workers, lack of clinical skills, large case loads, too much paperwork, and the pressure to place without adequately matched or properly assessed child/foster home fit (too often the placement occurs before the Social Worker has been able to obtain a cogent family history crucial to successful placement). Ultimately, Jane believes that considering the incredible mix of variables such as poverty, a wide-ranging socio-economic factors, mental illness, substance abuse, domestic violence and intergenerational dependence on the welfare system, the current outcomes are to be expected.

If the problem of dealing with injured children within a large department governed by all kinds of procedures is not difficult enough, it becomes even more problematic when the children, Social Workers and birth parents have to interface with a different world called the Children's Law Center, a topic to which I now turn my attention.

### The Children's Law Center Los Angeles

The average person in Los Angeles is probably unaware of the Children's Law Center (CLC). What is it and how does it work? The CLC was founded in 1990 with six attorneys hired to represent children alleged to be victims of neglect and abuse. At that particular time there was no right to counsel for children in dependency hearings and no recognized standards for representation. According to a public information brochure, the general area of practice was often referred to as *Kiddie law*. Initially, it was simplistic and unsophisticated. There were few, if any, legal service providers whose sole purpose was dedicated to representing children.

Things have changed considerably in the past 20 years. The CLC is now the second largest law office in the country. It is the sole provider of legal representation to almost all of Los Angeles

County's 24,000 abused or neglected children. The CLC mandate is to represent each and every child appearing in court every day. It must deal with young children in life-changing circumstances. It must make decisions regarding where a child will live and with whom, reunification plans, visitation schedules and how much contact will be allowed with family and siblings.

CLC is a massive structure located in Monterey Park California. It houses a variety of necessary services: Education, mental health, substance abuse, crossover experts, investigators, support and technical services. As needs have been identified and as crucial services changed to meet demand, the department has continually adapted and grown. Investigators now go to homes, and visit children in foster and group homes and in juvenile halls and hospitals.

The goal of the CLC is to ensure safety, asses the child's needs and progress and link families to necessary services. The Agency also ties to facilitate healthy family relationships and help older youths transition to independence. The goals are huge, complex, and accompanied by massive responsibilities, often with very mixed outcomes and occasional failures. Over 5,000 children age-out of the system every year. Because so many children aged-out of the system find themselves on the streets, jobless, homeless and often incarcerated, Congress passed a law extending the eligibility age from 19 to 21. This law was passed in 2009 with far-reaching changes. It also changed the manner by which children are aged-out of the system. By passing this law, CLC hopes to dramatically improve outcomes. The program now includes many supportive services for the aged-out group, like supervised independent living centers and college dorm or shared apartment living while still receiving support.

With such humble beginnings, CLC has evolved into a huge organization with a 275- person staff of lawyers, paralegals and investigators representing 28,000 children. Some startling statistics about foster children and youth have been provided by CLC.

- Foster care youth are 25% more likely to endure:
  - *Homelessness*
  - *Poverty*
  - *Compromised health*
  - *Unemployment*
  - *Incarceration*

- Only 54% will earn a high school diploma

- 2% will earn a BA or higher

- They are 84% more likely to experience premature parenthood, thereby perpetuating a cycle of intergenerational abuse.

- They are 51% more likely to be unemployed

- 30% will be on public assistance.

Studies from the American Academy of Pediatrics raise concerns regarding children entering the foster care system. They find that foster care youth experience a greater degree of chronic health problems, more developmental delays, and psychiatric disorders. They believe these higher numbers are the results of three factors:

1. The amount of abuse

2. Placement trauma

3. The fact that while children are in care their health needs are often neglected.

Another shocking statistic is that 20 children died between 2007 and 2008. Statewide there were 65 deaths in one year. These numbers may be low due to confidentiality laws hiding actual numbers of children who die in care. In 2006 there were 78,278 children in foster care statewide. It is an unfortunate statistic that an average foster baby will be in three different homes before the first birthday. Not only are these statistics eye-opening, but even more concerning is the economic cost. The County receives nearly $30,000 from both federal and state governments. Some special needs children may receive $150,000 annually.

One other statistic bears noting. Minorities comprise 85% of children in foster care. Clearly foster care is poverty-driven. For example, a major reason for referral is the ubiquitous category of *neglect*, a euphemism for poverty-related conditions. A common complaint is "The home is dirty and cramped, with lack of money for food, clothing and medical care." Another major reason for removal is single mothers who leave their children unattended while at work or who keep an older sibling out of school to care for the younger child.

Some critics complain that the vague definition of neglect leads to unbridled discretion and, combined with lack of training, a dangerous combination is placed in the hands of Social Workers charged with deciding the fate of families. Another criticism is that the child abuse hotline itself is an instrument of abuse: Some people reporting abuse do it for revenge, are malicious neighbors, spouses involved in divorce, angry lovers or the children in care turning in bogus reports.

### Entering the system

Children under the age of 18 enter the system through referral. The sources of referrals are varied. Calls may come into the child abuse hotline anonymously, or referrals may come from mandated reporters such as teachers, doctors and other health care providers. All of these "mandated reporters" must, by statute, report suspected abuse. Newborn children are referred at birth if they test positive for drugs in their systems. DCFS Social Workers are a major source of the referrals because the ER workers receive calls that must be investigated. Regular CSWs also remove and detain children for "reasonable cause" which means that, in their judgment, the child is determined to be in imminent danger. They may also detain if the child is found to be left unattended.

In rare instances, CSW's may come across a case where the birth mother voluntarily relinquishes a child at birth or at a later date if she feels she cannot take care of the child. In other cases a CSW may encounter a situation where that child is not necessarily in imminent danger but there are sufficient facts to cause concern. In this case a dependency petition is filed, at which time the parents are ordered to appear for an initial hearing where the court will determine whether detention is necessary.

## What happens to the cases?

There is no simple answer to this question because a number of issues are at stake. For example, if an action is to be taken, the court must determine if there are any other actions pending in other courts; (e.g. a parent is charged with a criminal act or the minor child is out on probation). If there are actions in other courts, all court actions stop pending dependency court action. The CLC has superior jurisdiction over all issues involving child custody. All proceedings of the court are kept confidential to protect the identity of the child. Access to records is only given to parents, guardians, district attorneys, and Social Workers. Any agency providing services also falls under the mantle of confidentiality.

Once the child enters the system, a complicated procedure commences. There are a number of players in the whole drama. The County has representation and bears the burden of proof in all dependency action. Then, the CLC with its army of professionals gets involved. It is a legal services organization devoted to representing children in the dependency action. As of 1996, the CLC only represents the child, not the parents. The children are considered separate parties.

The CLC has three separate offices with approximately 30 lawyers in each firm. They are assigned cases as they come into the Court. Also, panel attorneys are appointed to represent parents. Clearly, this is a complicated process with multiple functions and players. As one judge remarked to me, "With three lawyers involved, I have a wonderful opportunity to be appealed from every direction."

Multiple people support the entire process. Court reporters transcribe the proceedings, bailiffs, and sheriff's department employees protect the court from possible violence, and court clerks keep the paper work moving while taking all the orders the court hands out and formalizing them into "minute orders."

Additionally, there are hearing officers in 22 court rooms. The children who are appearing also have to be picked up for the court hearings by drivers who transport them from their homes to court. Imagine a waiting room outside these courts in which families, their children, and lawyers all meet and talk over what is going to happen. It is a very noisy, busy place. In addition to the waiting room, there is a play room where children wait to be seen or united with their families. Trying to coordinate all of these rooms, personnel and activities is a monumental task.

After making a referral, the Department of Children and Family Services (DCFS) has three working days, excluding weekends and holidays, to review the case and decide either to release the child back to the custodial parent with no court involvement, or file a petition on behalf of the child requesting a writ which declares the child a dependent of the court under their supervision. If a petition is filed with the court, notice must be sent to the child's parents or guardian alerting them to the date, time, and location of the Detention Hearing. The petition is a document detailing factors that led to the charges sent to Juvenile Court. The language is specific and descriptive, containing allegations that the CSW believes can be proved by evidence. The petition process frequently causes delays, either because the notification was not performed, the party could not be found, or the paperwork went to the wrong address.

## The Petition

When a case arrives at one of the CLC law firms, an attorney is assigned. The ER worker writes an application for petition and detention. This is usually written by a Social Worker specializing in drafting legal petitions. If more than one child is detained, the name of the oldest child becomes the case name. The case also lists the names of the parents and all other siblings. The petition is the key document. It contains a description of the various kinds of abuse and neglect discovered. It includes various specific categories:

- Physical harm
- Neglect
- Emotional damage

- Sexual abuse
- Severe physical and sexual abuse of a child under the age of 5
- Death of a child
- Abandonment
- Voluntary relinquishment
- Cruelty
- Abuse of a sibling

All of the above categories have very specific language with definitions of the specific charge(s). These definitions can be several pages. In the court's opinion, if the charges are found to be sufficient to detain the child in protective custody, a series of events follows. First, the child is taken to a certified-licensed foster home or to the home of a relative who is deemed safe and responsible. At the hearing, the judge then decides and makes orders regarding visitation, frequency and monitored status of the birth family visits. The child is then placed in temporary custody. Separate lawyers are appointed at the detention hearing: County counsel, birth parent counsel, and the child's attorney. The next step is the Pretrial Judicial Hearing.

## Pretrial Judicial Hearing

The next step involves entering and being processed through the system, and may take from two weeks to two months. It is called the *Pretrial Judicial Hearing*. Essentially, it is a trial to review evidence, make a plea and, if there are allegations, deny them.

Following the Pretrial Judicial Hearing is the *Adjudication Hearing*. This is where a judge will hear witnesses, accept or allow evidence and make a determination about the facts or truth of the allegations. If, in the judge's mind, the facts are substantiated the child is held. If dismissed, the child is released.

If the child is held, there is a *Disposition Hearing*. This hearing pertains to matters of the child's custody, where he or she is to live, and the Reunification Plan that the parents must follow to regain custody. Once the Reunification Plan begins, it is monitored and DCFS submits progress reports on that plan. This plan is dependent upon the nature of the complaints brought against the parents. For example, if the complaint involves domestic violence or drug and alcohol abuse which led to physical abuse and neglect, the judge typically orders the parents to take a parenting class and attend a drug and alcohol program, either in-patient or out-patient, depending upon the severity of the abuse problem. Parental compliance with the plan is very difficult to verify and is often another cause of delays and hearings.

The Reunification Plan also stipulates the number of weekly visits, their length, and monitor status. Of late, the courts have been pushing reunification by ordering visits three times weekly for two hours per visit. The judge also specifies the location of the visit. Typically the visits start out as monitored visits, and if successful, progress to unmonitored status. The monitor may either be a designated DCFS monitor, an aide that specifically performs this role, or a member of the foster care agency. These members are Foster Care Social Workers.

As demonstrated, the birth family visits are a huge factor in the foster care process, particularly if the placement is a "concurrent placement," meaning there is a dual plan for the child. With this dual plan, if the reunification plan is successful, then the child will be returned to the custodial parent. Conversely, if the parent fails to comply with the plan, that failure will lead to termination of the visits, and ultimately termination of parental rights. This is called the *.26 Hearing*. This hearing process is complicated, fraught with much drama and is highly stressful for all concerned: The children, the foster parents, the birth parents and Social Workers. The difficulties will be discussed at length in following chapters.

Every six months, Review Hearings are held to monitor the status of the Reunification Plan. This continues until the child is returned or parental rights are terminated and the child is placed on the official adoption path. If there have been multiple offenses by a birth parent (usually a mother who has several children in the system), or the birth parent has tested positive for drugs and her child is born drug-positive, it is common for the child to be "fast-tracked for adoption." With the federal push for permanency through adoption, parents with children under age three will only have 6 months to stabilize their lives. With older children, the parents have twelve months. Personally, I have not seen many cases resolved within 6 months or even 12 months. Typically the cases can linger on for years.

In all cases, only the courts have the ability to terminate parental rights and set a permanency plan. The CSW must submit an appropriate permanency plan that is also reviewed every 6 months. This is the typical process. However, in my experience, there is seldom a *typical* case. Birth family visits are missed, birth parents enter and leave drug rehab, they fail to complete their prescribed classes, and there are relapses, appeals, and difficulties with the children reacting badly to the visits. All of these factors have a negative cumulative effect on the child.

Additionally, failure by a DCFS worker to complete requisite reports, file late reports, or not to notify a parent about a hearing is also problematic. All of these factors lead to numerous delays which can drag on for months and even years. The net effect is that the child and foster parent are left in limbo, filled with stressful uncertainty and helplessness, all of which is mandated by CLC.

If the court orders termination of parental rights, the parent has a right to file a *388 petition* within 60 days. It is a difficult time for children and foster/adopt families waiting anxiously for the whole process to be over. They are living in a state of suspended animation in which they wait and wonder if they are going to be able to have a child. Sometimes, after months and years of having custody, they are ordered to return the child to the birth parent. As you can imagine, it is a very wrenching and traumatic event to have a child returned to the custodial parent after bonding with the foster parent, particularly if he is still feeling endangered by the custodial paraent. I have witnessed these heartbreaking scenes too many times. It is most difficult when the court orders reunification even when all concerned parties believe that it is not in the best interest of the child. In some cases it has resulted in the death of that child.

In 1998, the California State Legislature introduced the concept of *Concurrent Planning*, previously mentioned as a placement option. With Concurrent Planning, adoption is the most preferred plan. In today's Court, a child is placed in a foster home that is eligible for both foster care and adoption. Most of the homes now have dual certification. The permanency options are basically adoption, legal guardianship and long-term foster care. Under Legal guardianship, the legal rights of the birth parents are suspended and the guardian becomes the legal caretaker and under long-term foster care, a child will remain in the foster home until age 18.

All of the above proceedings are subject to the 388 Hearing, the most common appeal vehicle by which DCFS, a parent, or other party may petition the court to change custody, or nullify/modify custody or a visitation plan. The burden is on the petitioning party.

Finally there are a whole host of agencies, acts and motions pertaining to children governed by the CLC. For instance, there is the Indian Child Welfare Act, created because Native American children fall under a separate set of rules. This often becomes a complicating factor if a child is found to have traces of Native American blood. Another mitigating factor is when the parentage of the child is in question. It is called *alleged or presumed father*. Tests have to be taken to prove or disprove this issue, all of which cause delays and allow for legal maneuvering. Many adoptions and placements have been delayed until the heritage and parentage of a child can be verified.

Additionally, there is an Info line. The Info line dispenses all pertinent information and makes referrals to various agencies. Additionally, the CLC also must monitor Special Education and have in place a School District Liaison officer in each district to deal with foster children. There are also matters related to dispensation of Social Security and undocumented children, while the regional centers oversee the mental and physical health of the children served. Regional centers also provide services to children in the system known as *Special Needs Children*.

As one can see, the CLC is a large organization charged with protecting the legal rights of its clients, but it is also involved in overseeing a large, complex, interrelated number of services. It is tasked with protecting the legal rights of the children and parents and interfaces with numerous law enforcement and social service agencies. In sum, the CLC is large, cumbersome, and complex. As a summation, I will comment on issues that are vital to understanding the effects of the CLC's interaction with the DCFS and how that interaction affects the children with whom I have worked.

## Unanswered Questions

In order to get a feel for how it functions I attempted to contact and set up a series of interviews with a representative of CLC. Their literature "encourages inquiries and public interest" about their functions. I contacted them and had a gracious and welcoming conversation with the public information coordinator. She proposed to let me sit in on hearings and she even suggested that she would find an attorney so that I could "shadow" a case. I was very impressed with this offer. She said that she would call me after she made the arrangements. I waited for two weeks for this to happen. Then I called and left several messages. My call finally was returned two months later with an apology and I was referred to a lawyer who was to cooperate with me and give me an inside look at the workings of the court. I had three conversations, via e mail, and informed the lawyer, who was concerned about confidentiality, that I was not interested in specific cases, but in learning how judgments were made regarding reunification. When I disclosed my interests in this area, my calls were not returned and the promised arrangement never occurred. I can only conclude that the person I spoke with must have found out that I was writing a book which might be critical of the CLC. Or, as was my experience while working with the system, the lawyer was just too busy to return calls. In any case I did not get the desired inside look I had hoped for. Therefore, I must rely on my own perspective formed through personal experience with clients and appearances as an expert witness testifying on behalf of my clients.

In general, my experiences with various representatives of the minors, families and the court left me with an impression that they are very difficult to reach, i.e., they seldom returned phone calls, and when contact was made, they did not provide meaningful information due to supposed confidentiality. It is interesting that this *confidential* information could have been legally shared as I was a part of the team and sharing is supposed to be encouraged to provide the best possible outcome for the children involved. In essence, lack of information, lack of communication, and lack of cooperation had negative implications for the child in question. The net effect was that, either poor decisions were made on the basis of poorly shared information, or decisions were based only on knowledge gained from one member of the team, (usually a Social Worker who had a variety of motives and agendas) Moreover, in my experience, when and if information was given out it was done with reluctance and often the FFA worker and the foster parents were the last to know about crucial decisions.

Often times, when the court decided to reunify, it gave the order and the foster family was the last to know. They were suddenly ordered to take the child back to a Social Services office, having no legal recourse, or preparation. This left them feeling shocked and frustrated, and the child was moved again without any thought to the mental health implications of the decision.

I realize that the CLC has a huge responsibility when it intervenes in the life of a family and makes decisions which have tremendous implications for the future of that child and family. I also realize that it is burdened by a huge number of cases it processes each day. There are a large number of services and departments to oversee, and a large number of people working with each case. That there are myriad possibilities for things to go wrong in a complex and large bureaucracy is a given. The complexities of interacting social systems are daunting. All of these factors make the job of the CLC very difficult. That being said, I believe that there needs to be greater weight given to the physical, mental and emotional well-being of each child under its jurisdiction.

When children are removed because they are in danger, the physical danger is often given higher weight and is most often the primary reason for initial removal. Ironically, when the judge sees that the physical dangers are no longer present, the child is often returned without regard to his or her mental health and stability, the mental health and stability still being a major risk factor.

During my time as a FFSW, there are three questions that were never answered. These questions constituted my need to interview someone from the CLC. The first is basic. Why are the birth parent legal rights given a higher priority than the mental health needs of the children? This is epitomized during the disposition hearing, when CLC has a major decision to make. At this time, custodial placement of the child and identifying the conditions of the family reunification plan have major impacts on the case. At issue here are the legal rights of the parents versus the well-being of the child. My experience has been that parental legal rights trump the rights of the children who should be protected from future harm.

My second question is, why are the birth parents not subjected to more stringent mental health-competency assessments before reunification?

My third question is why are the opinions of mental health, adoption and foster care professionals not given more weight in determinations on reunification? In my view, if these three questions were given a higher priority during decision making, the number of tragedies occurring daily may be reduced significantly.

I believe it is important to understand how the CLC and the DCFS functionally interface, how each must interact and function in a mutually dependent fashion. It is this dual bureaucracy, with its powerful impact on and great control over families that is the issue here. Again, it is best seen through the cases they manage. It begins where the child enters the system.

## Detention

The journey through the system begins when someone makes a phone call - a mandated reporter like a teacher, a nurse or a doctor, or a neighbor or family member (it should be noted that over half of the reports of abuse and neglect are unfounded).

Nevertheless, each report must be investigated. If the child is detained, a chain of procedures is set into action. The first, after finding a place to "park" the child, is to have a detention hearing within 72 hours. This is mandated by law to protect the rights of the parents. If the decision is made to detain, the child is taken with the CSW to her office to begin the process of finding an immediate placement in a foster home. There is a regulation that prohibits the agency from keeping a child overnight in an office. Because of this, there is a lot of pressure to place the child, especially since many of the referrals take place late at night, at hospitals, or on the weekends. In those cases, it is often difficult to find someone willing to take the child at a moment's notice.

This particular difficulty was highlighted in an article in the Los Angeles Times (July 12, 2011): A a Los Angeles County Social Worker accused his managers of routinely housing children in a regional office building without sufficient meals and bedding while trying to keep the news from their bosses.

The problem apparently stems from a chronic shortage of foster homes throughout the area, with fewer families willing or able to care for the most problematic children. The situation resulted in children spending nights in offices, sleeping on the floor or in car seats. "In some cases the treatment that these children receive comes very close to the child abuse from which they are escaping," the Social Worker said. This highlights the peril and precarious nature of the child's dependence on the adults passing the child along through the system. Remember, while this is happening, the child's sense of security and safety is at risk.

The County has contracted with some individuals to provide emergency respite when no home is immediately available. This is often where the process gets very complicated because the Social Worker may not have a coherent family history for the child.

Entrance into the world of Child Protective Services changes everything for a family and their children. Once children are placed, strangers have control over their lives. From that moment forward, they have entered a complex and bewildering system. The very act of placement becomes a defining moment; their new reality has a tremendous impact, where everything changes for the family as well as the child. Their physical and emotional development, how others perceive them, the nature of their relationship with their family, their self-esteem, and their legal status before the law are all impacted. Welcome to Wonderland, Alice:

> Alice tried another question, "what sort of people live about here?"
> "In that direction," the cat said, waving its right paw round, "lives a Hatter: and in that direction," waving the other paw round, "lives a march Hare. Visit either you like: they're both mad."
> "But I don't want to go among mad people," Alice remarked.
> "Oh you can't help that," said the cat, "we're all mad here. I'm mad, you're mad."
> "How do you know I am mad?"
> "You must be," said the cat, "Or you wouldn't have come here."
> Alice was not much surprised at this, she was getting used to queer things happening.
>
> —*Lewis Carrol*—*Alice's Adventure in Wonderland*, pg 85

In an instant, the child is defined by placement. The spurious title is *Special Needs*. There are also numerous negative labels that are assigned to the family as well. This is a defining moment for all concerned. Once a family enters the world of The Children's Law Center and the Child Welfare System, the family has an entirely new social status: *Bad Parent*. How does the family then explain their new status? They are labeled with terms like *Neglect* and *Child Abuser*. These labels really stick, particularly if there has been an accusation of a criminal act against a child. Then the police are involved and this changes the status of the parent again. Sometimes the CSW is unaware of a parent's criminal background due to a breakdown in communication, and ends up going into a dangerous situation to remove a child. If the alleged act was done by a father, then the mother must keep him out of the home and he has to have his case resolved before he can be a part of visitation. Again, it is all very complicated.

Once the referral is made, the machinery is set in motion: Detention, a pre-release hearing within 30 days and a disposition hearing within 60 days. Then the creation of a permanency plan comes, which may mandate various programs and set up a series of birth family visits. It is at this point that the permutations and possibilities for children to experience the true uncertainty and peril of their position come into play. As mentioned, the CLC has been recommending multiple visits per week, lasting two or three hours. There are all sorts of regulations governing the birth family visits, such as rules for cancellation, for termination of the visit, what the birth parent may or may not say to the child during the visit, and criteria for determining whether or not the parent is "under the influence." There are also cases where phone visits are ordered, with more rules governing this as well. Missed visits and foster parents having to listen in on phone calls all may have an effect on the birth family's degree of compliance or progress. The reason this is crucial is because it may lead to the next step, A *Termination of Parental Rights* hearing. This is the pivotal moment in placement for the family. I have been involved in heart-wrenching meetings where the birth mother was informed that her children were being permanently taken from her and placed for adoption. In some cases, if there are no suitable homes for the child to be placed for adoption, they may languish in long-term foster care or be placed under legal guardianship.

As it can be seen, the process is fraught with an infinite number of things which can go wrong. Murphy's Law of "what can go wrong, will go wrong" is operative here. To reiterate, each time something goes wrong, children suffer.

## Birth Family Visits

After Detention, the next opportunity for agency interface occurs when the CLC orders family visits, where the child is placed in another position of jeopardy. By ordering multiple visits per week and visits of several hours at a time, the court sets the stage for keeping the child in a continual state of distress and possible repeated secondary trauma.

I have witnessed scenes where the child is brought for a visit, is fearful and clinging desperately to the foster parent and begging not to have to see the parent. In one case the child, when placed in the room with the parent, stood at the door, crying and begging to be let out for the entire visit. In other cases, the children have stated that they do not want to see the parent and the court forces them to have the visit anyway. The birth family visit issue will be discussed at greater length in future chapters. This issue of trauma due to birth family visits is certainly central to the constant battle to keep children from harm while the CLC creates an environment of peril.

Birth parent rights and visits with their children are an integral and significant part of the whole process of placement. How it is implemented often adds to the distress and prolongation of the child's stay in limbo. Since visitation is part of the Family Reunification Plan, it is mandated by the CLC and all minute orders must be strictly adhered to. Many times visitation orders appear nonsensical in that they may be legally correct, but the outcome can be disastrous and even fatal. In chapter 9, I detail several cases when children die as a result of decisions made by the CLC. In other cases, the outcome, while not disastrous, exposes the child to threat. For example, an order for an unmonitored visit to a parent who is clearly schizophrenic and probably impaired in her ability to care for that child should not be given, because it places that child at risk. In another case, the visits to the birth mother had to take place in an alcohol and drug treatment facility located 40 miles away from the foster home. The visit required an entire day to pick up the child, transport the child to the facility, monitor the two-hour visit and return the child to the foster home. In yet another case, the Family Reunification plan required the foster parents to transport the child to multiple visits, sometimes several times a week, while dealing with the emotional, psychological and behavioral aftermath of the visits. To add to the distress, these parents have no legal standing before the court. They must comply with all mandates and live with the anxiety of not knowing from one moment to the next if their child is going to remain with them or be removed without warning.

In sum, there are many complications, issues, and difficulties when providing a seemingly simple setup for a birth family visit. Birth family visits are the arena where several crucial issues collide. The first principle for this visit is preservation of the parents' rights before the law. Society has stepped into a family's living room and made a judgment that they are unfit parents and that a child is in imminent danger. Having made that judgment, one or more children are removed and placed in custody. These parents have the right to dispute the judgment and are afforded a means to regain custody. Therein is the purpose of the Disposition Hearing and Reunification Plan. The problem develops in the ability of the legal system to guarantee the safety of the child. The crucial questions are: What constitutes 'safety?' Where is the concern for the child's mental health? As the process is currently playing out, parental rights take precedence over the child's mental health. Ordering contact between abusive or neglectful parents and the child places a child in a position of re-exposure to an abusive or neglectful parent and the possibility of experiencing a traumatizing scenario over and over again, thereby creating secondary trauma.

There are other dynamic factors at play besides the effects of the visits upon the child. The logistics of the visits, the impact of the visits on the caregiving family, the amount of time involved in setting up the visit, and the relationship between the members of the system. All of this must play out under the supervision and governance of The Children's Law Center. What is crucial is that it all takes place when the ER worker makes a decision to remove the child from what is deemed to be a dangerous environment.

## Family Reunification

Another major issue arises when the CLC decides to reunify the family. There is nothing simple about family reunification. There are often frequent appeals filed to change or challenge the court order and as a result, these may cause a continuance because one party does not show up, a Social Worker "forgot" to file appropriate paper work, or a parent was not properly notified. One can certainly see how this complicated process involving so many agencies and legalities takes an agonizing toll on the children and is highly disruptive and taxing to the lives of the foster-adopt parents. Clearly, it is a case where cooperation must take place, and in fact, is probably the area of greatest need and danger where the safety of the children is most at risk.

There have been several notable cases in which the court ordered reunification and the child died at the hands of the family after reunification occurred. What is troubling is that the reunification took place against the recommendation of the Social Workers and mental health professionals responsible for case management. In spite of abundant evidence that this was a dangerous and unstable family situation, the child was sent home with disastrous results. There needs to be better case review and assessment before such important decisions are made. Also, before a Reunification Plan is put in place, there should be assessment of the family on a psychological level to determine whether the family has a possibility of rehabilitation and the requisite abilities to provide a stable, safe, secure, and viable home situation. Paperwork showing completion of a parenting course or a drug rehabilitation course is not sufficient evidence of parental competence. The combination of mental illness, poverty, and drug addiction is a deeply embedded and complex condition that requires far more education than a few classes.

In sum, detention, placement, birth family visits, and family reunification are tasks performed by the CLC. This is a huge responsibility with grave consequences. The impact on families and their children is life-changing. The psychological ramifications of leaving children in abusive homes must be balanced with the psychological costs of removal. As we have seen, all decisions result in suffering. Damaged children maturing and leading dysfunctional adult lives have enormous societal costs that are incalculable. Many of these problems can be traced to larger societal problems of poverty, drug addiction, homelessness, and mental illness. There are no easy solutions. Scapegoating is easy because it is a target-rich environment. Careful assessment of the numerous problems must be performed, and cooperation and thoughtful analysis by the many agencies involved is required. An informed citizenry must also be involved because it involves the welfare of our children for whom we all bear collective responsibility.

This entire book has been written to show how the system functions and to allow the reader to get a sense of the dynamics of life in the system for a child, the effects of disrupted attachment, and the role it plays in traumatizing children. As one can see, much of the drama is played out in the struggle between the birth family and its place in the whole legal framework of family preservation and reunification.

Since the effects of removal and the impact on the mental well-being of wards of the court are clearly life-changing decisions, I have written extensively on the effects of placement and disrupted attachment on a child's development and now turn my attention to that discussion.

# Chapter 2

## LOST CHILDREN
## TRAUMA AND DEVELOPMENT

Before I began my work as a Psychologist/Foster Care Social Worker within the foster/adopt children's world of the Department of Social Services, I spent 25 years in the private psychiatric field. I became weary of doing psychotherapy 50 hours per week and was frustrated at the direction the mental health delivery systems were going. As a response, I decided to investigate alternative career options. As part of my search, I looked into teaching and consulting, but finally decided to try a whole new arena. Little did I know that the arena I chose was in far worse shape than the field in which I practiced. My first few days in this new job were shocking and disorienting. I witnessed things I had never seen before and ventured into parts of LA County that I had only seen on the evening news. I saw a 3-year-old boy jumping up and down on his bed for three hours in a raging tantrum. I tried to take another 3-year-old boy to a family visit and found that I had to hold onto him the whole time as he lacked impulse control- if he saw a rock, he would throw it, and he would take off running, or hit someone.

I encountered foster parents overwhelmed by bizarre behavior that they could not understand. For instance, a 7-year old girl hoarded a cache of food under the bed, a 5-year-old boy destroyed brand new toys just given to him, and a 4-year-old boy physically assaulted his foster mother and then totally destroyed his room. There were reports in the *Los Angeles Times* of children being beaten and starved to death. It was dismaying to me to encounter these new realities in a world where my experiences only scratched the surface of the horrors lurking below.

One very troubling, unexpected reality for me was witnessing deep levels of psychological disturbances previously seen only in adults and adolescents. I had an extensive background in clinical psychology and was well equipped to deal with severe psychiatric disturbances in adolescents and adults, but this world was entirely different. I found myself dealing with deeply disturbed children at the same time as I navigated an unfamiliar variety of job functions and role expectations. I soon realized clinical psychologists were required to do things differently than Social Workers. For example, instead of approaching problems as a clinician, I was required to do a clothing inventory for four children in one foster home. I sat on the floor with piles of clothing and counted socks, underwear, shirts, shoes and pants. The ostensible reason for this was to make sure that the foster parents were spending at least $50 per child per month on clothing. The foster parents also had to have receipts to prove it. It appeared that I had become an accountant! This "necessary procedure" seemed to me to be demeaning to the family, as well as personally embarrassing. This was only one of the many adjustments I had to make in my new role.

I also had to do home inspections and make sure there was enough food in the house and that the house was safe. There are hundreds of policies defining a "safe" foster home, and I had to learn each of them and fill out a pink sheet that covered various safety concerns and categories which had to be reviewed: family fire drills performed; knives, drugs and toxins properly locked up, etc. There was a log for all medications that had to be meticulously kept, noting each time a pill was dispensed, even an aspirin. There were even rules about new people staying in the house. If they stayed over two weeks, they had to be "Live-Scanned" and finger printed. On one occasion, I was reprimanded and the agency had to pay a fine because the family's natural teen-age son turned 18, and a certain rule states that, because he was still living there, he needed to be finger printed even though nothing else in the living situation had changed. Parents are also supposed to keep meticulous logs on the child's behavior and keep records of changes in weight and height. They were also expected to make doctor and dental appointments and have the concerned professional fill out all paperwork. Most of the time they forgot and considerable time was spent chasing paperwork.

To me, it felt like I had entered a strange new and surreal world where everything was somehow off-kilter. It was as if I had fallen down the rabbit hole into The World of Alice in Wonderland:

> *Alice took up the fan and gloves, and as the hall was very hot, she kept fanning herself all the time she went on talking: "Dear, Dear! How queer everything is today!*
>
> *And yesterday things went on as usual. I wonder if I've been changed in the night! Let me think: was I the same when I got up this morning? I almost think I can remember feeling a little different. But if I'm not the same, the next question is, who in the world am I? Ah, that's the great puzzle!" And she began thinking over all the children she knew, that were of the same age as herself, to see if she could have been changed for any of them.*

—Lewis Carroll -*Alice's Adventures in Wonderland, Pg. 21*

I had, naively and unknowingly, entered what felt like a foreign country—a strange wonderland of experiences known as the Child Welfare System. It had been there all along, this *parallel universe.* Each day on the job led to more revelations: A special language to learn and a huge system with multiple players and levels of bureaucracy consisting of Social Workers, birth families, children, and a court system ruling over it all. I found myself transporting children all over L.A. County to visit their parents, and supervising parent/child visits at various agencies after picking the children up at their foster homes. It was a surreal experience. I could not believe the horrible things parents had been accused of doing to their children. One on occasion, I placed a 6-month-old infant with multiple bone fractures (arm, leg, and skull fractures). Another time, I encountered a shaken baby at an intensive care unit at Children's Hospital who was in a vegetative state, blind, deaf, and in a coma. I could not believe how wounded and damaged the children were. What was most disturbing was that these were not *extreme* cases, but appeared to be the new norm.

The awakening was complete when I realized how difficult it was to get anything done. I had been led to believe that each child had an integrated service plan with all related professionals interacting for the benefit and wellbeing of that child. This was laboriously laid out in the quarterly reports I was required to write and submit to the DCFS. With time, the dawning realization was that a huge difference existed between what was on paper and what was happening in the reality of my daily grind. I was shocked at how dysfunctional the system was: Social Workers not doing their jobs and not answering their phones, lawyers refusing to return calls, and foster parents with no legal rights trying to help the children traumatized by the entire ordeal. My most heartbreaking and frustrating observation was the CLC seemingly making decisions that endangered the children and resulted in cruel and often tragic outcomes.

To illustrate how difficult the transition into this new world was for me, I cite the following example that occurred early in my work experience. He was a Hispanic boy about 18-months of age. The case got my attention in particular because, when I visited him in his foster home, he appeared to be mute and not yet walking. He was manifesting several areas of developmental delay, but did not exhibit any diseases or overt trauma.

Due to my lack of experience, I failed to pick up on these problems because the foster mother always had him sitting in a high chair during my visits. Eventually, I learned that I had to look at children more carefully and critically during my visits. Finally, on one visit, I saw him crawling on the floor and noticed the obvious delays: He was not walking or talking. I wondered what was going on.

These types of problems became of primary interest to me as my journey into the foster care system evolved, the months and years passed, and the number of cases mounted. I began to see that these disorders tended to cluster in a very recognizable set of symptoms. In working with these children and families impacted by social services, I noticed the same recurring behaviors and problems in the children. The cluster of problems included developmental delays, autism, Post Traumatic Stress Disorder, Attention Deficit Disorder, Reactive Attachment Disorder, Sensory Integration Disorder, Major

Depression, and Oppositional Conduct Disorder. These major diagnostic categories, identified in the children's section of the Diagnostic and Statistical Manual of Mental Disorders (DSM IV), were on display and often within a single child. Their development was being seriously affected, and in some cases dramatically delayed. I could clearly see that there was a connection between the chaotic conditions which led to placement, and the continuance of that chaos after placement. Something was profoundly affecting the development of these children.

This led me to further explore these connections I was making. Through a workshop, I was exposed to the work of Daniel Siegel, and that exposure birthed a perspective that lead me to an entirely new way of looking at the experiences of the children with whom I was working. On one visit in particular, I became fascinated by the play of a 4-year-old girl. The visit took place on the patio of the foster home and the foster mother and I watched her play with the door of a toy stove for 45 minutes. She opened and closed it obsessively with total disregard to me and the foster mother. She was exhibiting one of many signs of autistic behavior. Ignoring and not orienting toward the foster mother was another.

For me, a turning point was the discovery of an important work, *The Developing Mind* by Daniel Siegel, who theorizes that the relationship between experience and brain development is how the brain becomes wired. "The structure and functioning of the developing brain are determined by how experiences, especially within interpersonal relationships shape the genetically programmed maturation of the nervous system." (Pg. 2). This insight was eye-opening to me. Early in my education theories I learned about the role of nature and nurture, but Siegel's theory was one that integrated the two positions. As the years progressed, the insights kept forming. I discovered the work of Allan Schore. His seminal work, *Affect Regulation and Disorders of the Self* totally shifted my perspective and created a whole new paradigm. He wrote "In short, development is transactional and is represented as a continuing dialectic between the maturing organism and the changing environment." (Pg.72). The implications for this are enormous for our understanding of early childhood development. Siegel, elaborates further:

> Through understanding the connection between mental processes and brain functioning, we can build a neurobiological foundation for the ways in which interpersonal relationships—both early in life and throughout adulthood—continue to play a central role in shaping the emerging mind. (Pg. 3)

This new information from Siegel and Schore, coupled with my knowledge gleaned from 20 years specializing in trauma, allowed me to make the connection between early childhood experiences and development. Since these children had less-than-desirable beginnings, the pieces of the puzzle began to fall in place. What I was witnessing were levels of trauma and varieties of trauma with which I had never before dealt. Trauma, as I have seen and experienced, is one of the most powerful and unpredictable factors that can dramatically alter the trajectory and order of any life. Thousands of lives every year bear the imprint of trauma. Imagine how much more lasting and scarring trauma can be for the weak, vulnerable, and defenseless: our children. What I was discovering was that when a child is traumatized, the effects on development are profound and often last a lifetime.

In the remainder of this chapter, I will chronicle how my approach as a clinician working with adults and teens was transformed by the study of the effects of trauma and child development. I will also describe how this field has evolved from its historical beginnings to my current understanding of how complex, sequential and ongoing trauma profoundly affects the bodies, minds, and lives of children.

## Trauma and Development

In order to advance my knowledge, I researched a number of important areas of child development: The brain, normal growth, family interaction and the emerging field of neurobiology as it investigates infant brains and nervous systems. These studies raised the question of why early life events have an inordinate influence on everything that follows. This, from the time of Freud to the present, is one of the fundamental questions posed by behavioral scientists. The emerging partial, as determined by neurobiology is that <u>the infant brain is designed to be molded by the environment it encounters.</u> (Schore, Pg. 72)

Since graduate school I have had a particular interest in the ways *identity* develops, and how it is affected by crisis and the impact of trauma on our sense of self. My doctoral thesis focused on the work of Jean Piaget who wrote extensively about the development of Cognitive Schemata (maps). In my thesis, I made a relation with the work of Erik Erikson's developmental stages and John Bowlby's work on attachment. This interest proved to be a helpful foundation when, years later, I came full circle through my work with the children. I came to understand how their worlds were shaped and their development affected by the most difficult circumstances and environments. Only recently have I become aware of work being done in understanding the biological significance of the underpinnings of our personalities, that nebulous entity we call the *Self.* For me, the foundation of this growing perspective on brain function was the critical role that experience plays in brain growth and development. In the introduction to *Life Story Therapy with Traumatized Children*, Bruce Perry writes:

> It is the very part of our brain that is most uniquely human, the neocortex that allows us to store, sort, and recall our past as we construct the narrative that becomes the pathway from the past and it is also the neocortex that envisions our pathways to the future. The neocortex allows humans to tell time, to create complex symbolic representations and associations that have transformed into various forms of language; in music, art, writing (all inventions of our past) we are able to tell our story where we came from and how we belong. (Pg. 9)

This groundbreaking work is foundational for our understanding of the areas of brain function which are the basis of complex cognitive activities. It has led to further work on the effects that trauma has on development and how disruptive trauma can be to these functions. The ramifications of this are considerable. First, let us look at trauma and its effects on children's development. Then we will look at the implications this has for all who deal with the problem: professionals, institutions which form the structure of placement, and the parents who face the many challenges of taking a special-needs child into their families.

## Trauma A Historical Perspective

From an historical perspective we have come a long way because our understanding of trauma has been constantly evolving. Over the past thirty years, that understanding has grown immensely through its origins in studies of combat victims suffering from shell shock and battle fatigue. This led to the concept of Post Traumatic Stress Disorder (PTSD). Trauma and shell shock during World War II in particular led to the study of the brain and the effects of shock. Over time, war trauma studies progressed to the investigation of single-event trauma of various kinds, primarily with adult victims. These studies have gained further refinement through observations of large-scale disasters and of veterans of more recent wars in Iraq and Afghanistan. Eventually, investigations into the neurological factors involved in trauma have made great strides over the years. In more recent history this research now includes the effects of trauma on children. When individuals, adults or children are traumatized, they experience *speechless terror* where the experience has left them unable to make sense of what has occurred, but they retain an indelible memory of pictures, smells, touch, taste and sound. These are the essential features of PTSD.

This recent interest has fine-tuned our knowledge when understanding the experiences of children subjected to various kinds of trauma. This has led to a variety of treatment programs for traumatized children. For example, the University California Los Angeles, has a trauma program for children suffering the traumatic loss of parents. There is also an excellent neurologically-based program; The Child Trauma Academy in Houston Texas (Bruce Perry, M.D., Ph.D. Director). Moreover, internationally acclaimed programs exist, such as The Child Trauma Intervention Services in Melbourne, Australia (Richard Rose, Director). These programs, to name a few, have evolved as research progressed and one thing became clear. There are major differences between adults diagnosed with PTSD and children subjected to various traumas. As a significant outcome of the work done at the Trauma Academy in Texas, the neurological effects of trauma are now being explored and refined with new medical technology. In this regard, Perry notes the serious consequences of early life disruptions on development. I was intrigued by the way he linked trauma, neurodevelopment and personal narrative:

> The neurobiological consequences of the destruction of narrative for a people are devastating. It is the same with individual maltreated children. A fragmented, damaged, discontinued personal narrative puts an individual child at risk. A child that is lost within her own family, community, and culture is neuro-developmentally vulnerable. Without a life story a child is adrift, disconnected, vulnerable... Sadly most mental health interventions with the maltreated children do not pay attention to the child's story. (*Life Story Therapy with Traumatized Children,* Pg. 10)

What do we mean by *trauma*? Historically, trauma has generically defined catastrophic experiences as events which render an individual helpless and subject him/her to horror or death. Gradually, it has been given greater definition and specificity. It is now broken down into categories: single-event, serial, sequential, complex, multiple, and simple. What we are finding is that children raised in dysfunctional environments experience all of the above kinds of trauma on a daily basis. This leads us to more fully understand the primacy of the early environment and in particular the role parents play in their child's dysfunction. Each specific kind of trauma affects a child differently. Consequently, children who have experienced trauma are vulnerable to a wide variety of lasting consequences which show up as problems in development and behavior.

## The Effects of Trauma on Development

What are the effects of trauma on development and what are the specific mechanisms at work when a child is traumatized? These were the basic questions I pursued. As my level of awareness increased, I pushed my research efforts to find answers to why children are so profoundly affected by trauma; specifically the kinds of trauma experienced and what short and long term effects of early trauma and life-disruption exist. The answer may be known intuitively, but let us explore some of the research in order to 1) understand the impact of trauma and why it is bad for children, 2) understand which areas are most affected. For the sake of simplicity, we need a working definition.

The research consensus defines childhood trauma as *those events in childhood that produce a sense of helplessness, anxiety, shame, humiliation, and/or abandonment for which there has been no satisfactory repair from a caregiver.* When such an event occurs, it results in a breach of the crucial parent-child relationship. Though children are often rendered helpless by daily interactions between themselves and their caregivers, not all result in trauma. What are particularly disturbing to children and of lasting effect are what Siegel refers to as *attunement failures* between parent and child. According to him, these failures are always, by definition, *small-t traumas,* or life events that are more common experiences and are upsetting, but on the surface are not thought of as traumatizing. If they are repetitive, fixed and rigid, there is no way to process the negative emotion that the trauma creates, and the effects become cumulative leading to disturbances (breaches) in the relationship. Siegel says small-t trauma is split off from consciousness and stored in largely inaccessible memories in the child's unconscious (implicit memory system). When the child and his/her environment are out of balance and become disconnected in such a way that no repair takes place, small-t trauma occurs, resulting in anger, fear and eventually defensiveness.

What are the necessary and sufficient conditions that lead to a traumatized state of mind? In both the case of adults and children, the key ingredient seems to be a state of helplessness and separation in the face of actual (or perceived) danger, resulting in a state of victimization and alienation. A traumatized state then occurs when a child is unable to respond effectively to a situation; this inability to respond is, in turn, signaled by anxiety and/or panic, as no apparent way to restore harmony or the relationship seems to exist. We can see then, that children are much more vulnerable to the experience of helplessness because of their dependence on caregivers. Bessell A. van der Kolk underscores the primary role of parents in protecting children and helping to maintain a stable and secure environment:

> The primary function of parents can be thought of as helping children modulate their arousal by attuned and well-timed provision of playing, feeding, comforting, touching, looking, cleaning and resting—in short by teaching them skills that will gradually help them modulate their own arousal. Secure attachment bonds serve as primary defenses against trauma-induced psychopathology in both children and adults. <u>In children who have been exposed to severe stressors, the quality of the parental bond is probably the single most important determinant of long term damage.</u> (*Traumatic Stress*, Pg. 135)

The focus is now further refined and is thus aimed at small and even large trauma experiences processed in the parent-child dyad. However, when there is impairment of parental empathy, these effects are not processed interpersonally but are stored. Again, what is significant is that these events are often not one-time occurrences: daily repetition leads to a kind of serial trauma perpetrated by the very people who are supposed to be protecting and nurturing these children.

By linking trauma with development, an entirely new perspective for understanding the short and long term effects of trauma is presented. Siegel, Lillas, Schore, van der Kolk and Perry, along with many others, have created a new model for understanding how the human brain becomes organized in a way that is integrated, self-regulating and capable of complex cognitive tasks and behaviors necessary for healthy adult functioning. They have even found the particular areas of the brain that are responsible for organization and integration. There are a number of areas of the brain involved that make this happen:

> A growing body of current evidence shows that the neural circuitry of the stress system is located in the early developing right brain, the hemisphere that is dominant for the control of vital functions that support survival and the human stress response. Because the stress coping strategies are deeply connected into essential organismic functions, they begin their maturation pre and post-natally, a time of right brain dominance...Attachment experiences of the first 2

years thus directly influence the experience-dependent maturation of the right brain. These include experiences with a traumatizing caregiver, which are well known to negatively impact the child's attachment security, stress coping strategies, and sense of self.

(*Dysregulation of the Right Brain*, Allan Schore, the Australian and New Zealand journal of Psychiatry, Pg. 29)

Connie Lilllas, an expert on infant mental health and parent-child relationships, further expands on the connection between experience and brain development and why the early years are so critical.

What we do for infants in our care may play a bigger role in shaping their lives than our efforts would for any other group of children. We know this because a child's brain grows more during the first three years of his or her life than any other; growing to about 80 percent of adult size by three years of age and 90 percent by age five.

### *A Quick Lesson on Brain Functioning...*

Our brains are filled with millions of neurons (also called nerve cells) that send messages to each other via synapses. The neuron together with the synapse forms a pathway for transmitting information, allowing each area of the brain to communicate with the others. It is this communication that allows us to do everything from recognizing letters and numbers to forming friendships.

We are born with all of the neurons that we will ever have – it is the *synapses* or connections between those neurons that are constantly being formed throughout life. However, it is during the *first few years* that we are genetically programmed to produce an explosion of synapses. What we know as "brain development" is actually the wiring and rewiring of the synapses. And, because the brain operates under the "use it or lose it" rule, those synapses that are constantly used, remain. Those that aren't are "pruned" away. Every experience, from riding a bicycle to reading a book, or learning a new song excites certain neural circuits and leaves others inactive. Those that are consistently turned on over time will be strengthened, while those that are rarely excited may be lost. In a "normal" child, this is an efficient method of brain development – get rid of the excessive synaptic connections to make the remaining circuits work more quickly and efficiently.

However, in an abused and/or neglected child, synapses may be pruned away that are neglected, but not unimportant. The small owner of these lost synaptic connections will find him or herself struggling to do what would come naturally to another child.

Unfortunately, the brain becomes less plastic as we age and pruning ends – this means that we have a window of opportunity for certain connections to be made. Once that window closes, specific opportunities are lost. (*Infant/Child Mental Health,* Connie Lillas and Janiece Turnbull, Pg. 56)

These recent theories are based on the assumption that the structure and functioning of the developing brain is determined by how experiences, especially within interpersonal relationships, shape the genetically-programmed maturation of the nervous system. There are indeed critical periods for development. Current workers in the field of developmental traumatology now agree that the overwhelming stress of maltreatment in childhood is associated with adverse influences on both behavior and brain development, especially the right brain which is dominant for coping with negative feelings and emotions and for the all-important skill of stress regulation.

By looking at the effects of trauma on development in this new framework, I believe we will be able to have a more complete picture of what a child within children's services undergoes when removed and placed in a surrogate home. It will reveal not only how he/she is affected, but also why he/she struggle and what roadblocks exist to recovery. Perhaps, we will then be able to devise better strategies for ameliorating the effects of trauma and placement on a child's development. When we do this, we will be able to pinpoint specific parental conduct that is deemed detrimental.

Connie Lillas describes and lists the effects of these experiences caused by being in the foster/adopt system:

Children under 5 represent 39% in care, the presence of biological vulnerabilities within a context of unstable or absent emotional care takes a serious toll on the immune system: 80% of foster care children have at least one chronic health condition, 25% have 3 or more major health problems, more than 59% have developmental delays, 80% have been exposed to substance abuse in-utero, and 49% have low birth weight. The result is that these children are biologically more vulnerable, are more difficult to care for, have multiple placements and have been exposed to multiple risk factors.

In sum they are biologically and psychologically vulnerable. Couple this with birth parents also being vulnerable because of substance abuse, domestic violence, depression, homeless, and mental illness: This is a prescription for predictable failure. (*Infant/Child Mental Health*, Pg.129)

This growing body of research on traumatized children reveals a wide range of effects over a broad continuum. The degree of trauma is a function of type, intensity, perpetrator, age of the child at the time of the trauma, and frequency of abuse or neglect. We now know with certainty that the effects of trauma create developmental delay, and often result in the child being frozen emotionally at the age when the events happened. Allan Schore writes in *Healing Trauma* regarding his view on relational trauma: "The concept of trauma, which is by definition psychobiological, is a bridge between the domains of both mind and body." (Pg 109) This view of trauma makes it a very utilitarian concept; the bridge that allows us to understand complex relationships between environment, development, cognitive functioning, social behavior, and adult functioning.

This bridge has led to a whole new perspective on the devastating effects of childhood trauma, a perspective based on an understanding of how the brain becomes organized, leading to the formation of our basic sense of self and critical areas of brain function. What we must keep in mind is the ambient nature of trauma-- what happens when the first thing a child encounters at birth is not a warm and welcoming environment but a trauma:

The fact that such trauma is "ambient" clearly suggests that the infant is frequently experiencing not single episode or acute but "cumulative and chronic unpredictable traumatic stress" in his very first interactions with another human. (*Dysregulation of the Right Brain*, Allan Schore, the Australian and New Zealand Journal of Psychiatry, Pg. 20)

At birth, as we are now coming to understand, a child's brain is not completely formed and in very complicated ways it is profoundly affected by interaction with the environment. Understanding the basic assumption that children are not miniature adults leads to making critical distinctions between adult and child trauma. The first distinction is that children are more dependent and therefore more vulnerable. Secondly, during the process of developing, trauma has been found to profoundly affect that process because children are born with incomplete systems programmed genetically to develop in a predictable, experience-based sequence. Trauma interferes with this normal sequencing.

## Trauma and Attachment

Siegel enhances the view of the importance of early childhood experience and parenting with this comment regarding the relationship between experience and development:

> The central thesis of my work is that the early social environment, mediated by the primary caregiver, directly influences the final wiring of the circuits in the infant brain. These circuits are responsible for the future social and emotional capacities of the individual. The attachment relationship thus directly shapes the maturation of the infant's brain and the human stress response. (Pg. 112)

Siegel's work and that of others underscores the importance of attachment and that failure to understand these attachments leads to *the problem of the unrecognized and persistent effects of trauma and loss.* Failure to recognize these effects leads to subsequent difficulties in children struggling to adjust to placement without proper support. When not recognized and accounted for by those responsible for their placement, it has very tragic consequences. It is this lack of knowledge that leads to well-intentioned foster-adopt parents being overwhelmed and feeling inadequate when dealing with the task of caring for foster children. It also explains how they find themselves encountering behavior and situations for which they have little preparation and background—knowledge that would enable them to cope with children entering their homes. The behaviors they find most difficult to moderate are behaviors which are emotionally driven: temper tantrums, poor impulse control and volatile emotional mood swings; behavior which appears to be totally out of control--dysregulated. Finally, this lack of knowledge and subsequent interventions leads to the lack of comprehensive services to ameliorate the developmental problems of the children in their care.

There are critical brain centers that are responsible for memory, information processing, emotion, motivation, and judgment. These centers, all linked with neural pathways, are designed to lead to integration and organization responsible for development of a sense of self. Sudden, unexpected changes or elevated stress lead to the phenomenon known as *dysregulation*. In children this may be seen as episodes in which the child seems to fall apart at the slightest amount of change or over-stimulation. This occurs because the child has not acquired the capacity to regulate strong emotions or cope with the stress of a change in routine.

## Dysregulation

Once again, Schore takes us to a new level by discussing the importance of regulating affect, in particular, understanding that children so obviously out of control and volatile are not the exception, but the norm.

> It has been said that the most significant consequence of the stressor of early relational trauma is the lack of capacity for emotional self-regulation, expressed in the loss of the ability to regulate the intensity and duration of affects....In light of the essential role of the right hemisphere in the human stress response, this psychoneurobiological conception of trauma-induced stress response clearly suggests affect dysregulation is now seen to be a fundamental mechanism of all psychiatric disorders. *Dysregulation of the Right Brain*, Allan Schore, the Australian and New Zealand journal of Psychiatry, (Pg. 11)

Regulating emotion refers to the general ability of the mind to alter various components of emotional processing. In many ways, the self-organization of the mind is determined by the self-regulation of emotional states. How we experience the world, relate to others, and find meaning in life is dependent upon how we regulate our emotions. Again, we come to this fundamental observation that the connection between experience and the emotions generated from those experiences alter critical areas of brain systems.

The area of the brain involved in emotional processing is the *limbic system*. The limbic system is centrally located in the brain and plays a vital role in coordinating the activity of higher and lower brain structures. The limbic region is commonly regarded as the emotional brain because it mediates emotion, motivation and goal-directed behavior. It is located in the middle brain and is comprised of the amygdala, hippocampus, thalamus and hypothalamus. The amygdala plays a key role in the way memories are stored and internalized based on sensory and emotional effect. The hypothalamus regulates body temperature, hormones and glands and is a major mapper as it gives the brain a sense of self through multiple layers of integration. The thalamus connects areas of the cerebral cortex with the spinal cord and other regions of the brain in order to assist sensory perception and movement.

The hippocampus filters and sends memories to the cerebral hemisphere for storage and can retrieve memories from storage when needed. The hippocampus is considered the cognitive mapper. It gives the brain a sense of self in space and time through multiple layers of integration. This process of the hippocampus functions through the *narrative mode*. Narrative is a part of social discourse and is inherently social. Narrative is also neurobiological, as it facilitates the integration of coherence within the mind. This is how the various layers of brain function are tied together and organized, and the narrative mode of cognition is fundamental to the mapping process. This may be the very heart of our autobiographical narrative and the way the mind attempts to achieve a sense of coherence, tying the past, present and anticipated future together. The capacity of the mind to create such a global map of the Self across time and various contexts is an essential feature of being human. What holds it all together is our *narrative*, or life story. It is easy to see that when our personal story or narrative is disrupted through trauma or placement, there is a cascading effect in brain neurology, our sense of self and our behavior with others. The narrative, when disrupted early in development, produces adverse effects evident in the child's behavior. It is frequently said that when you know a child's history, her behavior makes perfect sense. This is how the notion of narrative pulls all of these ideas together and furthers our ideas about the development of a coherent identity.

Siegel states, "Neural integration is fundamental to self-organization, and indeed to the capacity of the brain to create a sense of self." (Pg. 302) Over-arousal of the central nervous system also leads to changes in arousal levels, information processing, hyper-vigilance and irritability, and learning problems. These may be the permanent results of chronically high stress levels.

> What this means is that a process that links distinct circuits not only creates a new form of information processing, but also establishes a more complex, integrated network that influences its own capacities. Integrated systems, by virtue of their coordinated activities, establish their own characteristic features...As we will see, such neural integration becomes a central process that is directly related to self-regulation. (Pg. 304)

## The Stress Response System

Neural integration and self-regulation are key factors that, when affected by over-arousal of the autonomic nervous system, result in disruption of the integration and organization of centers related to the development of a sense of self. Research indicates that the neurological circuits are directly affected by the residual effects of prolonged stress, resulting in chronic over-arousal of the autonomic nervous system, which then creates a significant effect on several important neurological centers in the brain: Amygdala, hippocampus, limbic system, frontal cortex, and other vital information processing centers. (Siegel, Pg. 330)

The dynamic relationship between emotional arousal and interaction of the various related brain areas can be understood through the functioning of the stress response system. When we are under a high level of stress, the autonomic nervous system is triggered in association with the endocrine system, causing the release of stress hormones that prepare our brain and body to respond to a perceived emotional or physical threat. Rose comments on the effects of constant threat as it pertains to current and future learning:

If trauma is constant, and threat is real and dangerous, the brain utilizes what resources it can provide to respond to protect the whole. This constant heightened response involves the child's concentrating on the threat and her perception of it: However, the brain has already selected where it is required to respond ant this means that healthy development in the brain is not underway. Important learning does not take place as the brain is on guard and the trauma is the focus of learning. (*Life Story Therapy with Traumatized Children*, Pg.49)

Because of threat, more specifically, constant, persistent threat, high levels of stress hormones may produce higher daily base line levels of hormone release. Chronic stress inhibits neuronal growth in the hippocampus which is involved in memory. "Excessive stress hormone release appears respectively to impair the hippocampal and amygdal contributions to memory processing." (Siegel, Pg. 50) The value of these findings is present in research done in the last 10 years concerning memory of traumatic experiences. Through this research, the reason that traumatic experiences may remain outside of awareness and suddenly be triggered by something in our current experience intruding upon the survivor's internal experience can now be understood.

Regulation of extreme emotion, like that experienced through exposure to trauma, becomes the pivot point for dealing with said trauma. Why is self-regulation fundamentally seen as emotion regulation? "Emotion, as a series of integrating processes in the mind, links all layers of functioning." (Siegel, Pg. 275)

The importance of regulating powerful emotions, then, is critical for healthy development of the brain, cognition, memory, and even the developing sense of self, all of which are dependent upon on the appraisal and arousal process of the mind. Again we come back to the critical relationship with the caregiver. Siegel notes that achieving self-organization, the pinnacle of psychological maturation, occurs within emotionally-attuned interpersonal experiences. Therefore emotional regulation is at the core of the self. (Pg. 274)

This principle cannot be stated too often. In my work with abused children who have been placed, my central observation was that these children were easily upset and had a great deal of difficulty regulating themselves. In other words, they were volatile, and had difficulty regaining a calm state. This, of course, led to the newly-found parental surrogates having the same difficulty of regulation (i.e., controlling out-of-control emotions and behavior). Much more will be said about emotional regulation as related to attachment in the following chapter.

## Developmental Trauma Disorder

In retrospect, all of this information was coalescing for me as I managed my cases. The information helped me to make sense of my observations by synthesizing the various perspectives. It has been a rather steep learning curve. I began to understand how these children were severely affected by early trauma. Based on what I was learning, I developed a framework that allowed me to understand what I was seeing. I had discovered a whole new diagnostic category that was being used by Van der Kolk. Here is Van der Kolk's position on childhood trauma, indicating how trauma leads to a separate diagnostic category for children:

> A history of neglect, physical and or sexual and earlier onset of maltreatment was directly related to symptoms of emotional dysregulation. Symptoms of emotional dysregulation are also at the core of a construct called *Developmental Trauma Disorder*, in children and adolescents reflecting the complex adaptations to prolonged psychological trauma in childhood.(*Life Story Therapy with Traumatized Children*. Pg. 46)

*Developmental Trauma Disorder*: That was clearly what I was seeing in these young children. How this was related to parental abuse was the next link in my understanding. These findings indicate that brain development, organization and integration are directly dependent on interpersonal experience. The actual development of the neural circuitry is dependent upon the type and quality of interpersonal relationships. This last factor has been given considerable emphasis in the last few years by work done on attachment.

> Indeed, current studies in developing traumatology now conclude that the overwhelming stress of maltreatment in childhood is

associated with adverse influences on brain development. This maltreatment specifically refers to the severe affect dysregulation of the two dominant forms of infant trauma-abuse and neglect. (*Dysregulation of the Right Brain*, Allan Schore, the Australian and New Zealand journal of Psychiatry, Pg.11)

To recapitulate, if we step back for a moment, we can see this is why trauma is so devastating to a young and developing child's brain. Trauma disrupts, distorts, delays and in some cases totally derails the developmental process, all because the child is, (1) young, (2) vulnerable, (3) developing, and (4) totally dependent on caregivers. Research now clearly shows that emotion serves as the central organizing process within the brain, thereby determining the ability of the brain to make sense of experience, integrate events, interpret the data and then adapt to future stressors. Hence, overwhelming emotion via a traumatic stressor and its concomitant hormonal and neurological effects is the reason trauma has not only temporary, but also long-term effects on development. These profound effects have lasting consequences on emotional regulation, attachment security, stress coping strategies, and basic sense of self. These are wide and encompassing areas of psycho-social development and function. As van der Kolk notes on the role of trauma, specifically attachment patterns:

Recent research has shown that as many as 80% of abused infants and children have disorganized/disoriented attachment patterns, including unpredictable alterations of approach and avoidance toward their mothers. . . Thus early attunement combines with temperamental predispositions to "set" the capacity to regulate future arousal; limitations in this capacity are likely to play a role in long term vulnerability to psychopathological problems after exposure to potentially traumatizing experiences. (*Traumatic Stress*, Pg. 186)

These children who enter the system are not just suffering from trauma. They are suffering from *Multiple-Complex-Serial Trauma*. We can only conclude that this phenomenon accounts for the myriad effects we see manifested in their behavior. Van der Kolk observes, "The lack or loss of self-regulation is the most far-reaching effect of psychological trauma in both children and adults." (Pg. 187)

Abused children are struggling to cope, adapt, and survive in circumstances which would overwhelm the defenses of any adult. These conclusions are now confirmed by the neurobiological theorists: van der Kolk, Siegel, Schore, Lillis et al. They are unanimous in their belief that the brain is dynamically related to environmental forces and that in order to develop normally; it needs a stable, consistent, nurturing environment. When this environment is disrupted by abusive or neglectful experiences, very serious developmental consequences occur. These results are all encompassing:

> The lack of development or loss of self-regulatory processes in abused children leads to problems with self-definition (1) disturbances of the sense of self, such as a sense of separateness, loss of autobiographical memories and disturbances of bodily image (2) poorly modulated affect and impulse control including aggression against self and others, and (3) insecurity in relationships such as distrust, isolation, suspiciousness and lack of intimacy. (*Traumatic Stress*, van der Kolk, Pg. 186)

In my work, I saw the entire trauma spectrum on a daily basis. This was a different world than the world of single event adult trauma I had been working with up to this point. It was clearly tied to parental abuse. In fact, the specific parental attachment behaviors that were likely to be at fault have been described by Lillas, who gives us a list of parental behaviors that lead to dysregulation in children. Below are a few of the behaviors she observed in her studies on parent-child interactions.

- Parent constricted emotionally
- Parent hostile-critical to child's emotions
- Parent anxious, intrusive or distracted
- Parent overly hostile in punishment
- Parent withdrawn, not present
- Parent impulsively changes themes in play
- Parent vacillates between being permissive and overly harsh or rigid
- Parent physically abusive

- Parent too controlling or parent sets poor limits

- Parent does not exhibit pleasure or delight (*Infant/Child Mental Health,* Pg. 94)

These kinds of parental behaviors set up patterns that become a part of the emotional memories generated through every-day encounters. They eventually become linked in the child's nervous system with other patterns of sensation and arousal which are reinforced through daily repetition and become styles of interaction. In short, they become the attachment paradigm.

## Trauma Defenses/Dissociation

Conclusions from the research are irrefutable: chronic stress and trauma have a direct effect on the organization of the brain, the self, and the ability to function socially through adaptation. This is the essence of adult functioning, namely, the ability to learn, self-regulate, profit from experience, and adapt to changing social conditions. It is no stretch to then include a byproduct of trauma or the numbing of emotions--fear, rage, terror, shame, and humiliation too overwhelming to process. When faced with overwhelming fear or terror, something must be done to survive, to cope. This leads to a psychological defense I have frequently observed in young children, a phenomenon known as *dissociation.* Present in both adults and children, it is often more pronounced in children. When dissociation occurs, there is an inability to feel or recall the trauma. This defense can be deceptive; and it often leads observers to think that the individual is unaffected by the event. All too frequently when a child is placed, the foster parent often observes "how she seems to be smiling and pleasant" when introduced into the home. Lenore Terr, in her insightful book *Too Scared To Cry*, noticed in children:

> At the moment of terror, young children tend to go on behaving almost as usual, even as their psychological underpinnings are being torn asunder...Seldom are there tears. Instead there is an immobility of expression, a failure to move the mouth, a lack of animation in the eyes. The face of horror in childhood is grave and relatively immobile, it may look dazed, but it rarely looks

hysterical....The terror lingers even if the event is happily resolved. (Pg. 34)

Dissociation results from the failure to integrate experience. It is caused by an overwhelming event that leads to fight, flight, or in the above case, freezing. Freezing leads to dissociation which often appears in a child as a trance-like state. In essence, it is the inability of the self to take in and make sense of overwhelming experiences. For survival sake, the experience must be blocked out. The physiological response is to shut down in order to manage a surge in energy in the system caused by too much arousal. Schore precisely describes this phenomenon:

> In the present period we are also seeing a parallel interest in developmental research on the etiology of the primitive defense that is used to cope with overwhelming affective states — *dissociation.* From the perspective of developmental psychopathology, an outgrowth of attachment theory that conceptualizes normal and aberrant development in terms of common underlying mechanisms, dissociation is described as offering potentially very rich models for understanding the ontogeny of environmentally produced psychiatric conditions. Disorganized-disoriented insecure attachment, a primary risk factor for the development of psychiatric disorders, has been specifically implicated in the etiology of the dissociative disorder. Neuroscience is now delving into the neurobiology of dissociation, especially in infancy. It is currently thought that dissociation at the time of exposure to extreme stress signals the invocation of neural mechanisms that result in long-term alterations in brain functioning. This principle applies to long-term alterations in the developing brain, especially the early maturing right brain, the locus of dissociation, withdrawal and avoidance, and a spectrum of psychiatric disorders. (*Dysregulation of the Right Brain*, Allan Schore, the Australian and New Zealand journal of Psychiatry, Pg. 12)

The following example puts this in perspective and grounds it. I observed a monitored family visit. The birth mother was diagnosed as schizophrenic and had been living on the streets. She appeared for the visit with her mother and mother's her husband along with two other siblings. They all rushed into the room to visit Mikey, a 2-year-old boy. The birth mother's father picked him up, hugged him and then passed him around the circle of family members like a sack of potatoes. As this was going on, I observed that Mikey went totally limp and developed a glazed stare in his eyes. The grandfather noticed that "Mikey didn't look right." I told him that Mikey was receiving too much stimulation and that he needed to be held by just one person. Mikey was totally overwhelmed by all of the touching, jostling, noise, and impact of too many people to interact with, even though they were all very "glad to see him."

Schore and others conclude that trauma, when experienced early in an infant's life and in relationship to his caregivers, has profound and often lasting effects that cover the entire gamut of human neural development. Early relational trauma has a significant negative impact on the experience-dependent maturation of the right brain, which is in a critical period of growth during dyadic attachment experiences. The effects are:

- *Cognitive:* Memory impairment, information processing difficulties, distorted sense of time, learning difficulties, loss of academic skills, and impaired ability to concentrate.

- *Emotion (affective):* Inability to regulate emotions, avoidance, depression, guilt and shame, feelings of helplessness and powerlessness, negative self-esteem and frozen or blocked emotion. In addition, children often exhibit uncontrolled rage, extreme emotional volatility with low frustration tolerance, and an inability to soothe or comfort themselves.

- *Behavioral:* Increased aggression, oppositional behavior, regression with bed wetting and soiling, muteness, repetitive play, sexualized behavior, suicide attempts, chemical dependency, self-destructiveness, risk taking, poor impulse control, and anti-social behavior.

- *Physiological:* Over-arousal of the Autonomic Nervous System leading to hyper-vigilance, and a host of neurological effects.

- *Attachment:* In addition to all of the above, there are also the difficulties related to attachment. Children who have been traumatized have difficulty trusting, experiencing intimacy, and the ability to have satisfying long-term relationships.

All of the above effects have been classified as a diagnosis which is called, *Developmental Trauma Disorder*. These effects are a dynamically active part of the child's ongoing experience. It is this topic to which I next turn my attention: he role and function of attachment, both in healthy development and in the traumatic impact of disordered attachment.

# Chapter 3

## ATTACHMENT
### SECURE / DISRUPTED / DISORDERED

In Chapter 2, I established that the fundamental role of parenting is to establish an attachment bond between caregiver and child. When this goes awry and becomes traumatizing, it has far-reaching consequences for development. In essence, the attachment figure is intended to be the source of protection, soothing, connection, and joy. In order to understand the implications for early development, we need to take a more comprehensive look at attachment in all of its critical functions and its foundational role in the development of a functioning human being.

What is attachment, how does it occur and what important psychological functions does it facilitate? Attachment is the very foundation of being human. As such it is a biological, psychological and social process. It is essentially an inborn survival mechanism and is based in the survival mechanism of all species. The dependent, vulnerable, offspring need protection and nurturance in order to survive. Fundamental to attachment is personal safety. Once safety is assured, other aspects of childhood development are manifested and evolve. The central purpose for attachments is to provide a context and mechanism in which the child is sheltered and contained while developing to the level of being capable of independent functioning.

It is vital to understand that the developing mind functions best under conditions of perceived safety. Without safety, the child is continually struggling to reduce threat and create safety through the basic stress responses of flight, fright or freeze. If safety is assured, then a child is free to explore the world and development proceeds normally. Perceived safety is the foundation to all development, and parental behaviors incompatible with providing that sense of safety, security and cohesion directly impair the developing child's ability to contain and regulate emotion. When unable to govern shifting states of needs and states of mind, the child faces an attachment dilemma--a state in which coherence is difficult and there is no satisfactory solution. This leads to a lack of integration in building a life story or *cohesive narrative.* In short, whatever threat disrupts the narrative process creates a state that is potentially traumatizing. In general, loss or trauma may have a negative impact on a child's expectations of the future and directly shape his maps of the world and prospective memory. In this regard, Siegel writes: "Unresolved parental trauma or loss can lead to disorganized/disoriented attachment. The result is that the child enters repeated chaotic states of mind." (*The Developing Mind* Pg. 294)

The attachment mechanism operates quite simply through a thousand daily transactions between parent and child. As the parent responds to the infant's needs on a daily basis, a subtle but powerful bond begins to develop. Attachment is a continuous interaction, a dyad based on reciprocal behavior with the infant signaling needs initially through distress signals and an emotionally sensitive caregiver responding to the signals. When this occurs, attachment is increased. If there is a failure through lack of attunement or neglect/abuse/intermittent or inconsistent care-giving, attachment is likely to occur less effectively. In this case it may lead to insecure attachment. Trauma is the basis of factors leading to narrative disruption.

These emotional transactions, repeated experiences of attachment behavior, become encoded in neurological networks in the brain leading to organized patterns of behavior. In particular, the parental response provides aid which reduces distress in the form of physical discomfort or uncomfortable emotions such as fear, anxiety, sadness or frustration. Effective responses which reduce distress allow the child to feel soothed, and eventually create a secure haven in which to retreat when upset. This leads to what Bowlby, the father of attachment research, calls a *secure base.* He developed his theories as a psychiatrist during World War II, when he worked with children from London who had been moved to the countryside for their safety. He writes of his observations about grief in infancy and early childhood:

> Let us turn first to the data that originally gave rise to this study, observations of how a young child between the ages of about twelve months and three years responds when removed from the mother-figure to whom he is attached and is placed with strangers in a strange place. His initial response, readers of earlier volumes will recall is one of protest and of urgent effort to recover his lost mother. He will cry loudly, shake his cot, throw himself about, and look eagerly towards any sight or sound which might prove to be his missing mother. This may with ups and downs continue for as long as a week or more. Throughout it the child seems buoyed up in his efforts by the hope and expectations that his mother will return. Sooner or later, however, despair sets in....He is in a state of unalterable misery. (*Attachment and Loss*, Pg. 9)

With these keen observations the direction of knowledge about child development was altered forever and our knowledge of attachment behavior in infants was given a foundation and framework of understanding. Secure attachment appears to be a strong indicator of emotional resilience. In the case of loss of a loved one, especially an attachment figure, the mind is forced to alter the structure of its internal working models to adjust to the painful reality that the self can no longer seek proximity of, and gain comfort from, the caregiver. As Bowlby observed, it may then be in a state of despair, of unalterable misery.

Attachment, then, is the basis of psychological and social development, and we have now come to understand it is also the key to brain organization. As we have seen in chapter 2, it also serves as a function of survival, because the child must seek proximity in order to feel safe and protected from harm, abandonment, starvation and protection from predators/strangers. Siegel notes that attachment is highly keyed to threat:

> For these reasons the attachment system is highly responsive to indications of danger. The internal experience of activated attachment system is thus often associated with the sensation of anxiety or fear and can be initiated by frightening experiences of various kinds, most notably separation from attachment figures. (Pg. 68)

Attachment is most crucial in the first year of life, although it does continue throughout the entire life cycle. Attachment information is recorded in an unconscious memory file which is stored in the *implicit memory system.* Implicit memory occurs before the development of formal language. This becomes the stress processing mechanism. It is because of this mechanism that the effects of attachment are ever-present in both overt and in subtle ways. Robert Neborsky explains the attachment stress response mechanism this way:

> Our brains have in them inherent trauma processing systems. These are a function of secure attachment. If a child is disturbed by an environmental effect, he or she returns to the attachment figure for comfort. Comfort takes many forms, both overt and covert. On the overt level, mothers pick up their children, hold them and distract them, etc. On the covert levels, processes like mirroring affect or containment behavior and vocal and tonal synchronization (reassurance, soothing talk, and singing) until the child is soothed and returns to a calm state. . .It is clear that this process becomes internalized and becomes autonomous—operates without mother or father present and works at an unconscious level. *(Healing Trauma,* Pg. 286)

This bond of attachment serves several major functions and is the basis for learning very complex social skills: a sense of trust and worth, the regulation of emotion, a working model of the world, how to soothe and repair attachment breaches, a method of self-regulation, and ultimately it is the attachment paradigm or a guide for all subsequent relationships.

First, through effective care-giving the infant learns a basic sense of trust. The child learns that she is safe, secure, and cared for. The primary developmental gain at this stage is a sense of trust and worth. In his works on child development, Erik Erikson has written that the first and most primary developmental stage is the stage of trust vs. mistrust. He describes it as a state of "hallowed presence" (Erikson, *Identity Youth and Crisis*). Children who are neglected often feel unwanted, and therefore unworthy. This has a profound effect on the developing sense of self. Daniel Hughes writes:

The infant discovers who he/she is—the original sense of self-in the eyes, face, voice, gestures and touch of her mother and father. Her self-discovery involves the discovery of the impact that she is having on her parental figures." (*Building the Bonds of Attachment*, Pg .7)

As part of this world-building process, parents are modeling many important behaviors. As a model, the parent is teaching the child how to modulate emotions. Learning to feel, express, and contain complex, powerful emotions is no easy task and the ways we experience our emotions are not biologically given. Though the primary emotions of anger, fear, and pleasure are biologically based, their mode of expression is largely socially determined. Regarding the function of emotion, Siegel observes:

Emotions are what create meaning in our lives, whether we are aware of them or not...As the intertwined, dynamic nature of emotions and environmental encounters unfold, each of us continually emerges and defines ourselves (Pg. 139).

Emotion, then, is a fundamental part of attachment relationships in the early years and throughout each person's lifespan. The earliest forms of communication are about primary emotional states. These emotional states are the *music of the mind* which create the fabric of our lives and our relationships with others. It is the difference between the world of emotion as viewed in joyous color and the world stripped of joy as black and white and experienced as depression.

Another gain in the attachment process is building a working model of the world through the process of *mapping,* or neural connections that provide a sense of order and meaning. According to Piaget, infants are cognitive theorists in a continuous process of mapping their worlds and then revising them through the process of accommodation and assimilation—they continue to modify the maps with new information. This process is called *equilibration,* or continually seeking harmony and balance even in the face of tumult and the distress of changes in the attachment dyad (Piaget, *the Psychology of the Child*).

As children grow and develop, they are constantly engaged in the process of making sense of their world through construction of these maps of complicated neurological connections called *schemata.* These maps include identification of how the physical universe works. For example, a young child plays the game of dropping something on the floor, with the parent, in exasperation, picking it up and the child dropping it again. Through this game, the child learns about gravity. The child also learns how to engage the parent and through this continual daily engagement, learns *a working model of the world.* This model is both physical and social.

Also involved in this complex matrix of maps are the essential features of socialization: The child learns the rules of the game in this world and, when functioning properly, socialization teaches the child that he/she is valued, that adults behave in a predictable and trustworthy fashion, and that the world is safe and secure (object constancy). Most attachment experts agree that this working model of the world is essential to healthy adult functioning and is the basis for becoming an integrated, fully-functioning, autonomous adult. These social schemata help us make sense of the world and help us to live with a sense of meaning, purpose and significance. In essence, these maps guide our daily behavior. When they do not function properly (e.g. the child learns abusive, neglectful and violent rules for behavior), the outcome will be quite different.

This is most true in the case of trauma, as we have seen; where the basic assumptions regarding the world are violated. These basic assumptions are: 1) The world is safe-stable-secure, 2) the world is just, 3) the world is predictable and 4) the world of people is trustworthy. When these assumptions are shattered because of trauma, it can be devastating. How many times have we witnessed stunned survivors of a tragedy being interviewed, and hearing them say, "How could this happen," "Why," and "Why me"? Standing amidst their shattered world they cannot make sense of what has just happened. For developing infants, this experience is even more shattering because the child's world is only in the formative stage, and instead of healthy assumptions he learns a quite different world view.

It is easy to see, then, why attachment is so critical to all development and why disruption of this bond leads to faulty brain development, predictable changes in self image, attachment style, behavioral problems, and inability to regulate emotions. When the child becomes tied to the attachment figure by thousands of attachment bonds, feelings, thoughts, interaction patterns, expectations, roles, communication structure, safety, security, identity, and all social behavior, the natural progression of development has occurred. These innumerable bonds, having become the working model of the world (attachment paradigm), are all sustained by these powerful attachment bonds. The very self of the child is developed, nurtured and shaped by the daily interaction patterns of those closest to the child and embedded in the familial environment.

Attachment is the key. It is the process, the psychological system which is responsible for our very survival. In sum, the attachment paradigm leads to the development of a child's ability to:

- Deal with threat and cope with stress.
- Know how to be soothed and eventually to soothe him/her self
- Make sense of the world through a working model of how the world works—cognitive map development
- Communicate and regulate emotions and eventually contain big emotions and impulses
- Enter comfortably into dyadic relationships—intimacy-social relatedness
- Develop a basic sense of self-identity
- Form a conscience through establishment of empathic/compassionate connections

Since the primary function of attachment is preservation of safety and security, let us look at what happens when a child is subjected to threat. How does this system function to preserve our mental equilibrium and health when we are exposed to threat? Stability and our survival depend upon our ability to regulate and modulate emotions triggered by threat. First, the threat must be perceived in order to respond effectively. Secondly, in our response to threat, we must be able to isolate the source of danger and appraise the level of threat. Finally, we must find an effective means to mobilize a response to the threat in order to preserve and restore our equilibrium. If a child is not able to master these tasks, it is highly probable that he/she will be frozen at that level of failed adaptation. This freeze creates an attachment paradox--an apparent situation without solution. It functions in this manner: When a child is upset by parental behavior, the natural instinct is for the child to seek proximity or closeness for safety. What happens, however, when the supposed source of safety is also the source of terror? This situation creates conflict or ambivalence in a child in which the child is filled with conflicting needs, the need for safety through proximity and the need for safety through avoidance. What is the child to do? The equation then becomes Proximity = Closeness = Fear/Avoidance.

In this situation, the child struggles to adapt and cope by reducing the threat and anxiety. Siegel tells us that the insecurely attached person must constantly recruit other sources of comfort within or outside of self when under threat conditions. These are in the form of defenses or addictions...The person's impaired capacity to metabolize stress will eventually lead to instability, an inability to adapt, or some form of rigid, fixed response pattern.

Rather than create secure attachment as effective caregiving is supposed to do, neglectful or abusive parenting creates what is known as *disorganized attachment*. This kind of parenting is often transmitted inter-generationally as parents raised in violent, frightening and maltreating families transmit their fear and unresolved losses to their children through neglectful, insensitive or abusive care and lack of love and affection. When the infant is placed in an irresolvable paradox: closeness and contact with the parent triggers fear rather than safety, or closeness to the parent both increases the infant's fear and simultaneous need for soothing, contact and comfort (Levy, *A Handbook of Attachment Interventions*, Pg.11).

The inability to cope or adapt to this loading of stress is the source of many of the maladaptive behaviors seen in both young children in placement as well as adults who suffered prolonged trauma as children. Addiction, self-destructive behavior, depression, dissociation, dysregulaton, anti-social behavior, lack of attachment, and violence are just a few of the possible outcomes of the unresolved infant's attachment paradox. When operative, acute trauma violates a child's sense of control, thereby leading to a surge or discharge of extremely intense emotions of grief/ anger/fear. This surge activates inborn defenses, or attempts to restore homeostasis and adaptation. In the infant or young child, responses to acute overwhelming fear result in states of emotional detachment or dissociation. These experiences then reside in implicit memory like a preverbal image of feelings. According to Neborsky, "Understanding this process is crucial to successful work with trauma victims. The emotions associated with childhood trauma (relational failure, abuse or neglect) are either repressed or dissociated in an unconscious file" (Pg. 284).

These files remain even into adulthood where they can be reactivated by new trauma or intimate relationships. It is these states which I refer to as unhealed wounds, because when one of these files is reactivated, it is like opening Pandora's Box, leading to a flood of emotion, an indication that a wound has apparently not healed. "These failed stress responses produce impairments to achieving self-regulation and integration of the self state; it, in these ways, damages the individual's deepest sense of self and the ability to regulate internal states" (Siegel, Pg. 295).

## Emotional Attunement

Achieving self-regulation and integration of the self-state is a difficult task under optimum conditions. Basic trust, world-building, emotional control and processing are all accomplished through the developing attachment bond. The means of learning this is through *emotional attunement*. Through emotional attunement, a child learns to sense and feel his/her own emotions and, most importantly, the emotions of others. This is the basis for empathy. Daniel Hughes observes:

Affective attunement, defined as the inter-subjective sharing of affect is central to the development of a secure attachment during the first year of life...These experiences, the original dance of humanity are the reciprocal interactions between the mother and infant that serve to regulate the infant's early affective life, develop deep interests and begin to create the meaning of self/other as well as the events and objects of the world." (Pg, 21)

Psychological attunement drives the attachment process by acting as a mechanism that maximizes and expands positive affect and minimizes and diminishes negative affect. Either through exhaustion, poverty, drug use, intergenerational abuse, or mental illness, parents who fail to be appropriately attuned, or fail to repair inevitable breaches in attachment (regulatory failure) will create in their children attachment problems most likely ranging from insecure to ambivalent or disordered attachment. When these children are removed and placed in another home, they take with them whatever attachment paradigm they acquired, including their learned coping defenses.

Critical to psychological development is the learned ability to soothe and/or heal oneself. Through the process of attuned attachment a child, by being soothed when in distress by the sensitive caring responses of the caregiver, is learning the complicated process of dealing with distress. This is the function of caregiving: a sensitive response to a child who sends out distress signals. Through the process of repetition and the daily experience of being soothed by another, the child eventually will internalize this process (i.e. self-regulation). We know this has been accomplished when the child is able to contain difficult emotions, and respond to her own distress by finding a way to soothe herself. On the other hand, if the child is under a constant state of anxiety due to daily trauma the effects will be harmful. Rose notes:

If trauma is constant and threat is real and dangerous, the brain utilizes what resources it can provide to respond in ways that protects the whole. This constant heightened response involves the child's concentrating on the threat and her perception of it: however, the brain has already selected where it is required to respond and this means that healthy development in the brain is not underway. Important learning does not take place as the brain is on guard and the trauma is the focus of learning. (Rose, Pg. 49)

## Self- Regulation

Children with attachment issues due to abuse and interrupted attachment bring with them issues related to trust and control, manifested in a tendency toward dysregulation, as discussed in chapter 2. We know that it is most difficult to experience intimacy if one does not trust another and does not know how to resolve conflict, heal a relationship breach or work through hurt feelings and resentment. In the child's new home it is incumbent upon the parental surrogate to establish a climate of safety, consistency, security and positive affect, or a new affect regulatory environment. It is extremely important to help a child regulate emotion while maintaining the relationship. For the child, it is important to help them understand that frightening emotions do not lead to the feared consequence of abuse, shame, humiliation or abandonment they likely experienced in the past. As with the birth parents, it is also true in surrogate parents that the ability to be attuned and regulate emotion and behavior is primarily dependent on the surrogate parents' own learned abilities from childhood. The age-old maxim is, if you can regulate your own emotions, you will be less threatened, frustrated, or disturbed by extreme behavior and emotional dysregulation in your own children.

## Dysregulation

It is the topic of dysregulation which has led to a new and exciting direction in research led by Allan Schore. He conceives that the basis of attachment is affect regulation and that the emotional state of the maternal figure is primarily responsible for the security and durability of the attachment bond. This is the manner in which the self comes to regulate its own processes, consisting in part in the regulation of emotion. For children in placement this is a major problem. Poor impulse control, rage, emotionally driven states, and volatility are all features of children who have had their lives disrupted by placement. Siegel notes:

> Our skills at regulating emotion allow us to achieve a wide range and high intensity of emotional experience while maintaining flexible, adaptive, and organized behavior. The process of emotion

regulation—and dysregulation—can involve any of the basic levels of emotion: physiology, subjective experience and behavioral change. (Pg. 156)

The eventual regulation of emotion creates what psychologists refer to as *the self*. It is clear that emotion is vital to being an integrated self, as well as one who can function in relationships with others. Emotionally disturbed behavior, whether in an individual, relationships, or between countries, creates high levels of distress and eventually chaos.

In recent years, an integration of psychological and biological models of human development has shifted attachment theory to a *self-regulation theory*. Because of this, researchers now believe secure attachment depends on the mother's regulation of the infant's internal states of arousal. As Hughes has said, it is a process of "co-regulation." In other words, the attachment relationship functions to mediate the dyadic regulation of emotion. When the attachment transactions are dysfunctional, this leads to regulatory failure and distress and, when this occurs, repair is crucial in order for the reestablishment of equilibrium. The critical determinant is the level of attunement the mother has to the infant's various emotional states. This kind of synchrony leads to a release of neurotransmitters critical to brain development and social bonds. As seen in the previous chapter, "The right brain stores internal, working models of the attachment relationship. It processes emotional and social information—the functions are as diverse as enabling empathy, humor and many of the capacities that are fundamental to human subjectivity" (van der Kolk, *Traumatic Stress*, Pg. 53).

Schore goes on to further emphasize this critical role:

The mother functions as a regulator of the socio-emotional environment during early stages of post natal development which can alter brain activity levels. The limbic system is developing rapidly in the 1st year. Attachment communications specifically impact limbic and cortical areas of the developing right cerebral brain." (*Dysregulation of the Right Brain*, Allan Schore, the Australian and New Zealand Journal of Psychiatry, Pg. 13)

The implications of emotional regulation are crucial for parenting. We have all observed how relationships become destabilized or fractured when feelings get hurt. In foster care it is even more critical to understand how parental emotional states affect the emotional states of the child. When a parent fails to respond in a sensitive or attuned manner, it leads to a disturbance in the child's emotional state, and if left unresolved can lead to disruptions or a breach in the relationship. This is frequently manifested in difficulties with emotionally-driven behavior. These disruptions must be repaired, and in spite of the child's outrageous behavior, the foster parent must be able to be present in the face of the child's anger, anxiety, sadness, shame or rage and help the child to regulate these affective states. If they are successful, this will lead to a stable and satisfactory condition of self-development and social relationships.

Schore's contributions on affect regulation are foundational for understanding the crucial dynamics between the parent child dyad, emotional regulation, and neural–brain development:

> The self-organizing of the developing brain occurs in the context of a relationship with another self, another brain. The primordial relational context can be growth facilitating or growth inhibiting, and so it imprints into the developing right brain either resilience against or a vulnerability to later forming psychiatric disorders. (Schore, *Affect Dysregulation & Disorders of the Self*. Pg. XV)

In simpler terms, the consensus has been established that development represents the emergence of more complex forms of self-regulation over the lifespan and that the attachment relationship is critical because it facilitates the development of the brain's self-regulatory systems.

Schore's contribution has shifted and refined our focus on attachment and how it is formed to the critical role that *affect regulation* is to healthy development. Not only that, but he has also established how this takes place. "The experience-dependent growth of the infantile nervous system whose components are undergoing a growth spurt of organizing, disorganizing and reorganizing in the first years of life is linked with the specifically affective experience taking place in the caregiver-infant dyad." (Schore, Pg. 5)

We now know that the quality of the parent-child interaction related to affect regulation takes place within the rituals, routines, and caregiving exchanges that are constantly taking place within the days and nights of the first few years of life, and that it is the tone, the quality of that interaction as the caregiver seeks to regulate the child's comfort, that is the defining variable. Responding to cries of distress, the mother seeks to restore calm and comfort, security and safety of her infant. At stake is how the infant communicates through various affective states: discomfort, growing agitation, anger, relief, and return to calm are all being regulated by an attentive mother. However, the emphasis becomes even finer. It is not just touch, and soothing, holding, bathing, and feeding that are used to communicate. Schore and others are now focusing on the most critical aspects of the interaction: the eye contact between caregiver and infant.

> These mutual gaze interactions represent the most intense form of interpersonal communication, and in order to enter into this affective communication the mother must be psychologically attuned not so much to the child's overt behavior as to the reflections of his internal state. (Schore, Pg. 7)

It was Bowlby in 1969 who established that vision is central to establishment of a primary attachment to the mother, and imprinting is the learning mechanism that underlies the attachment bond formation. Furthermore, attachment is more than overt behavior. It is internal, "being built into the nervous system as a result of the infant's experience of his transactions with the mother."

I witnessed a very powerful demonstration of this phenomenon at a recent workshop on attachment. At this workshop Present Connie Lilas showed a video that demonstrated the mirroring effect of the mutual gaze as the infant became acutely attuned to the mother's face for cues. The mother was instructed as she held her child to present an absolutely impassive, expressionless face to her 9-month-old infant. As she did this for approximately one minute, the infant moved from calm to slight discomfort as he read his mother's face. Then his agitation gradually increased as he gazed at her stone face, until he finally broke out into a full-blown cry filled with fear and distress, complete with flailing arms and kicking legs. When the mother relaxed her facial expression into one of warmth and concern, the infant immediately began to settle down. This demonstrated the important role in affect regulation of the maternal, mutual gaze.

As a result of this moment-by-moment matching of affective direction, both partners increase their degree of engagement and facially expressed positive affect. Neglectful and abusive interactions by birth parents are well documented. These behaviors may be the result of depression, drug abuse, poverty, or prior histories of abuse in their families of origin. They include a parent leaving the child unattended in a car seat placed before a television set or with a bottle propped up in the mouth or leaving an infant in the crib so long he develops a flat spot on the back of the head; a father poking his head into the room where the baby is lying and crying, saying "shut up or I will give you something to cry about;" a mother so worn down by taking care of too many children she does not come to the infant who is in distress; the enraged parent holding and shaking the infant because he won't stop crying. All of these behaviors have a profound impact on the child and are prime examples of poor affective regulation and attunement failures. These behaviors set the stage for the direction of the child's nervous system development and lay the ground work for future major psychiatric disorders.

To review, because infants inevitably seek the parent when alarmed, the frightening parent places infants in an irresolvable bind (the attachment paradox) wherein they cannot approach the mother, and shift their attention or flee. These infants are utterly unable to generate a coherent strategy to actively cope with their frightening parents. This leads to attunement failure which, if not repaired, leads to regulatory failure. It comes back to the critical role of the caregiver. Schore states that at ten months, 90% of maternal behavior consists of affection, play and caregiving. In sharp contrast, the mother of the 12-17 month old toddler expresses a prohibition on the average of every nine minutes. In the second year the mother's role now changes from caregiver to a socialization agent, as she must now persuade the child to inhibit unrestricted exploration, tantrums, and bladder and bowel functions. He for the first time is running into someone who rather than trying to soothe him and keep him comfortable is now becoming an obstacle, an inhibitor, a controller of his behavior.

In other words, in order to socialize her child, she must now engage in affect regulation not only by soothing and comforting, but also behavior regulation which leads to negative and heightened affect (frustration). In this conflict, he loses the pleasure of freedom and the pleasure associated with all of these activities. This now becomes an arena for attunement failure, regulatory failure and possible breaches in the attachment bond. If these breaches are not healed or overcome, this will lead to serious consequences. As we can see, the growing and developing infant becomes increasingly mobile and autonomous with increased expectations toward socialization in that the child must now use the toilet instead of a diaper, and must eat with a utensil instead of fingers. Then there are the admonitions: Don't break mommy's treasured collection of plates, don't hit your sister, don't scream in the house, stop running, stop torturing the dog, stop jumping on the couch, quit fighting with your sister, etc. In other words, emotional regulation includes eventual behavioral regulation. Many of these prohibitions are given out of frustration, anger, exasperation, and high levels of emotional arousal. "How many times have I told you?" "Don't make me come up there!" The child is beginning to encounter frustration about his highly narcissistic desires and motivation. While all this is happening, parents also have their own emotional regulation issues. This is where the difference between healthy emotional regulation and abusive or neglectful regulation occurs. This makes the next factor important for the attachment process: *Regulatory repair*.

### Regulatory Repair

Schore underscores this important process: "As a result of the interactive mis-attunement of socialization experiences, the toddler is suddenly and unexpectedly propelled from an ongoing accelerating positive affective state into a decelerating negative affective state, a stressful state." (Pg.17)

Prolonged states of distress, fear, anger, and shame are states he has not learned to self-regulate. In early development, effective parents have provided much of the necessary modulation and regulation of the child's distressed states, particularly helping him to transition from distress back to calm. This transition is an important part of development of self-regulation. It involves and highlights the central role of stress recovery in affect regulation. The caregiver's role as emotional regulator is once again emphasized by Schore:

> If the caregiver is sensitive, responsive and emotionally approachable, especially if she reinstitutes and reenters into synchronized mutual gaze visual-affect regulating transactions, the dyad is psychobiologically reattuned, shame is metabolized and regulated, and the attachment bond is reconnected. This repair is important to future emotional development. The key to this is the caregiver's capacity to monitor and regulate her own affect.... negative affect is reduced when the parent continues to maintain affective engagement with the child who is experiencing negative affect, thereby communicating tolerance of negative affect in both. (Schore, Pg. 19)

There are key elements to emphasize during regulatory repair: 1) the dyad is reattuned, 2) shame is metabolized, 3) the attachment bond is repaired, and 4) the child remains engaged with the parent. My observation when working with birth parents is their singular inability to remain engaged in a manner which produces positive experiences of joy and playfulness, and their responses to correcting behavior are often harsh, punitive, or angry, which produce the spiraling experience of distress and negative affect (principally a sense of shame). These socializing behaviors lead to more attunement failure and eventual regulatory failure that ends in a breach in the attachment bond.

As these authors have noted, Lillas, Siegel, and Schore, this serial attunement failure is what leads to such disordered behavior. What is critical is the devastating effect it has, not only the child's behavior and psychological sense of self, but also on brain development. The continual experience of negative affect has the net effect on the brain of creating high levels of stress hormones and neurotransmitters which then go on to affect the development of key areas of the brain.

> Success in regulating smoothness of transition between states is a principal indicator of the organization and stability of the emergent and core self.....I suggest that the orbitofrontal system is an essential component of the affective core. This prefrontolimbic region comes to act in the capacity of an executive control function for the entire right cortex, the hemisphere which modulates affect, nonverbal communication, and unconscious process for the rest of the lifespan. (Schore, Pg. 23)

Siegel answers the question: why is self-regulation seen as fundamentally emotion regulation? Emotion, as a series of integrating processes in the mind, links all layers of functioning." (Siegel, Pg. 275) He defines the process thusly:

> Emotion regulation refers to the general ability of the mind to alter various components of emotional processing. The self-organization of the mind in many ways is determined by the self- regulation of emotional states. How we experience the world, relate to others, and find meaning in life, are dependent upon how we come to regulate our emotions." (Siegel, Pg. 275)

Current researchers now contend that if children grow up with dominant experiences of separation, distress, or fear and rage, they will go down a bad pathway, and it is not only a bad psychological pathway, but a bad neurological pathway as well.

To summarize, in this discussion we have learned:

- An integration of psychological and biological models of human development has shifted attachment theory to an affect regulation theory.

- Secure attachment depends on the mother's regulation of the infant's internal states of arousal.

- Her responses, tactile, facial, visual, and gestural communication via her appraisal of her infant's internal arousal and affective states regulates them, and communicates them back to the infant.

- The mother must be attuned to the infant's states in order to regulate affect.

- The attachment relationship mediates the dyadic regulation of emotion.

- The disruption of attachment transactions leads to regulatory failure and distress.

- The primary caregiver is not always attuned.

- Repair is crucial and it must lead to reestablishment of equilibrium.

- Resilience in the face of stress is an ultimate indicator of attachment security.

- This synchrony leads to release of neurotransmitters which are critical to brain development and social bonds.

## Attachment Style and Personality

As research on attachment studies evolve, it has focused on parental patterns in correlation to various kinds of attachment. Generally, attachment styles are categorized into secure attachment, anxious attachment, ambivalent attachment, and disorganized attachment. This may be regarded as an attachment continuum from secure through severely disturbed attachment behaviors. Schore emphasizes how critical the mother's participation is in the interactive regulation during episodes of psychological attunement, misattunement, and reattunement. He argues that this participation not only modulates the infant's internal state, but also indelibly and permanently shapes the emerging self's capacity for self-organization through the process of regulatory recovery.

Again, he notes how different the affective experiences of the caregiver-infant relationships are between the securely and insecurely attached dyads. If regulatory failure occurs and severe breaches in attachment are the result, or multiple placements have occurred, then a condition called *Reactive Attachment Disorder* may be the outcome.

Schore has found that the affective experiences of the caregiver-infant relationship are quite different in securely and insecurely attached dyads. (Pg. 26) For instance, he found that the mother of the securely attached infant permits access to the child who seeks proximity at reunion, and shows a much stronger tendency to respond appropriately and promptly to his/her emotional expressions. When this availability is shown consistently, it leads to engendering an expectation in the secure infant that, during times of distress, the primary attachment object will remain available and accessible. This, of course, has been learned through continual testing and reinforcement of the mother's constancy.

Basically, in the securely-attached child we find that the child seeks proximity as noted by playing separately and then occasionally returning to the parent for contact. He feels secure enough to leave the presence of the parent and is confident that the parent will be there when needed. The securely-attached child is also easily soothed. What kind of parenting creates this condition? Parents who are securely attached, emotionally available, perceptive and responsive to their child's needs produce securely-attached children. The research is overwhelmingly clear on this: an ultimate indicator of secure attachment is resilience in the face of stress which is expressed in the capacity to flexibly regulate emotional states via the mother's interactive regulation of affect. The child then becomes able to *auto-regulate*.

The next question in research about personality/attachment style is: What are the long term structural and functional consequences to those infants not fortunate enough to have optimal, "good enough" care-giving during those critical developmental periods? Schore's research again is quite extensive in responding to this question:

> The mother of an insecure-avoidant infant exhibits very low levels of affect expression, presents a maternal pattern of interaction manifested in withdrawal, hesitancy and reluctance to organize the infant's attention or behavior. This caregiver typically experiences contact and interaction with her baby to be averse and actively

blocks access to proximity seeking attachment behavior which is exhibited by pushing away or withdrawal. This can only be experienced as an assault from his haven of safety. (Pg. 27)

In her research, Lilas found similar results in parental behaviors. Parents who are emotionally unavailable (insensitive, rejecting, unresponsive, not present, hence, not tuned in) produce children who are avoidant of attachment. Parents who are inconsistently available and responsive-often self preoccupied with their own needs, have ambivalently attached children. In essence these parents are sending strong covert messages through their behavior: stay away from me, don't bother me, you are not wanted. As a result of these messages of rejection, the infant does not appear happy or sad when the mother leaves or returns. Schore found in similar behaviors on return, the child actively avoids the mother, or in her presence ignores her through avoidance of her gaze, rather than seeking comfort from her interaction: When reunited with the mother, he actively turns away, looks away and even seems deaf and blind to her. (Pg. 27)

In stark contrast, Schore compares the maternal behaviors of the securely-attached child to that of the parent who produces Disorganized/Disoriented attachment. He writes:

> The good-enough mother of the securely-attached infant permits access after a separation and shows a tendency to respond appropriately and promptly to his or her emotional expressions. She also allows for the interactive generation of high levels of positive affect in shared play states. These regulated events allow for an expansion of the child's coping capacities and thus security of the attachment bond is the primary defense against trauma-induced psychopathology. (Pg. 281)

In contrast to this healthy scenario of the attuned, present, consistent, appropriate mother who creates a calm, stable, and secure child are the parents who are violent, aggressive, and or abusive, who are both a source of fear and need for security. They have children who are disorganized in their attachment. This is because the child, when seeking proximity, receives a danger signal. The child does not know whether to flee the danger, detach, or just shut down. Very often he does all of this. In other words, the attachment dynamics are quite different. For one, the communication of emotion so central to the attachment dynamic is distorted, and because the mother's attachment is disorganized, she provides little protection against other potential abusers of the infant, such as the father or a boyfriend. According to Schore, this mother:

> ...Is inaccessible and reacts to her infant's stressful emotions inappropriately and /or rejectingly, and shows minimal or unpredictable participation in the various types of affect regulating processes. Instead of modulating she induces extreme levels of stimulation and arousal, and because she provides no interactive repair the infant's intense negative states last for long periods of time. Prolonged negative states are toxic for infants and although they possess some capacity to modulate low intensity negative affect states, these states continue to escalate in intensity frequency and duration. (Pg. 282)

The only way, as we have learned, for the child to respond to these overwhelmingly negative states of emotion is to either dissociate or to remain in a state of fear-terror, dysregulated hyper-arousal, or confused or contradictory behavior patterns which directly affect the production of stress hormones. thereby impacting key brain areas. Disorganized attachment is also found in research that highly correlates it with later hostile/aggressive behavior. Again, the child left in the attachment paradox, instead of finding a haven of safety in relationships, is placed in a situation of being alarmed by the parent, and can neither approach, shift its attention, nor flee. Hence we begin to see early warning signs of disruptive behavior, temper tantrums and aggression that persist beyond the first two or three years. In essence children maltreated in infancy are more likely to be more aggressive, assaultive, and engage in self-destructive behaviors. They tend to be angrier, hyperactive, distractible, inattentive and non-compliant in pre-school and kindergarten. Their behavior is likely to be regulated less easily and they may be seen as volatile and easily upset. Schore observes that the later consequences of maltreatment are linked specifically with exposure to parental shame-humiliation and are all too frequently accompanied by early child abuse which eventuates in dissociated rage.

This is demonstrated in research with 9-year-old boys, exhibiting psychopathic tendencies, who have difficulty in processing emotions such as sadness and fear. This research also shows that boys can become more aggressive under conditions of "threat to the self." In short, one researcher pointed out that dysregulated and disorganized mothers are giving their toddlers the early training for when they grow up and become violent. They do this by ignoring their child's signals of anxiety or ridiculing his signals of vulnerability and need for comfort. They are consistently rough and bossy with the child as well. "Paradoxically, when the boy does strike out, the mother is at a loss to put an effective stop to his behavior." (Schore, Pg. 286)

In sum, the dysregulated, indifferent, neglectful, shaming, and rejecting maternal behavior toward her infant leads to dire predictions for her developing child's future behavior. In this parent-child attachment pattern lie the seeds for the disturbed, aggressive, oppositional, and potentially violent adolescent and adult.

To illustrate the complexity of emotional regulation and attachment styles and how it becomes the dominant factor in personality development persisting into adulthood in the form of adult personality disorders of the self, I offer up a case from my experience as a psychotherapist. The client was a 50-year-old musician, generally regarded as a child prodigy and genius as an adult pianist. He was raised in a home with a working father and a mother who suffered from Multiple Sclerosis. She was quite ill in the first few years of his life and, because he was a hyperactive child, she did inappropriate things to control him, like lock him in the cellar for hours at a time, or tie him into a swing. At other times, she invited him into her sick bed along with all the medical paraphernalia. The only way he found to cope with this inappropriate, abusive environment was to play the piano, which he did very well and for which he received a lot of childhood attention and praise. She died when he was a teenager.

How did this early trauma affect him? As an adult, he has had severe problems with regulating his emotions and behavior. He has abused drugs and alcohol and developed a serious gambling problem that cost him thousands of dollars. He also suffered from volatile mood swings and poor impulse control. The most pronounced feature of his pathology, as one might expect, was his relationships with women. He was totally incapable of commitment, resulting in a divorce. His pattern of behavior was to seduce one woman after another in serial relationships. He would usually be with three women at a time, all of whom were insecure and dependent, and who happened to be talented musicians as well. As one might surmise, this created very dramatic times of chaos as he managed to let each of the three women know about the other two. Each would demand commitment/loyalty and would become intensely jealous of the other women in the triangle.

At the age of 50, he was still reenacting his childhood trauma, and continuing to make a mess of his life, and squandering his enormous talent through his self-destructive behavior. The relational trauma of childhood was still functional, and his self-regulatory behavior learned in childhood was still operative. His ambivalent relationship with his mother (attachment paradigm) determined his relationships with women, and his inability to regulate his emotions, soothe himself, and control his behavior led to a wildly chaotic and troubled life, which left him deeply dissatisfied and depressed and financially bankrupt as well. Clearly, his early trauma set the course for the rest of his life. Unhealed wounds, a shattered life, and the failure of parents to nurture this talented, creative child resulted in an adult who was still stuck at the emotional age of a 3-year-old. The sad and ironic part is that most of his childhood abuse was never reported, and had this parental behavior been known, he would no doubt have been removed and placed in surrogate care. Standards were much different 40 years ago.

Today, the maltreated, abused, neglected, and rejected child is often removed from the maltreating, abusive home and placed in a system that often continues this cycle of abuse. The removed and placed child is then forced to deal with new environments filled with new challenges and threats, placed once again in an attachment paradox—to relinquish his parents and adapt, to dissociate, to become overwhelmed or dysregulated…what is the child to do? In effect, removing the child places the child in very unfamiliar territory, one for which she has no adequate defenses. It is another unsolvable paradox. The child normally would seek proximity for comfort, but having been abused, she knows there is no comfort to be gained. She cannot flee the threatening parent, but in the case of placement she is removed only to be faced with entirely new circumstances. How does this new trauma affect attachment behavior and subsequent development?

## Placement: Strange Situation

Removing a child from danger seems like a no-brainer, but the very act of removal becomes another form of trauma-- placement trauma--and subsequent events after placement add to and become part of the ongoing traumatizing circumstances. This results in secondary trauma experienced by children of placement. The secondary trauma occurs on a daily basis, when they are removed, or changed from one placement to another. In many cases, the child is removed and replaced with little thought for the implications or consequences of subsequent placement. When this occurs, several other things make it less likely that the possibility of secondary trauma will be resolved: little information is shared regarding the child's history, few foster parents are trained in dealing with treatment of trauma, and the professionals involved in the system are not adequately prepared to intervene in this injurious process.

To illustrate, there is an experiment in attachment research known as the *Strange Situation*. It was pioneered by Mary Ainsworth, a psychologist who wanted to understand what happens to a child temporarily separated from his mother and left in a strange situation. The experiment is structured so that the mother and child are playing in a room with toys. The mother gets up and leaves while there is a stranger in the room observing. When mother leaves, the child predictably cries (protests) and begins to search for mother, then panics when she cannot be found, and is then unable to be soothed by the stranger. The child is only soothed (ceases crying) when mother returns and picks up the child. When children are removed from their homes, it is a replication of the *strange situation*, but magnified several times over.

In the case of placement, the child remains in the strange situation with an unfamiliar caregiver for an indefinite period of time, sometimes permanently. The child experiences abandonment terror and remains in this highly-charged emotional state for some time. Being in a perpetual state of fear and having that compounded by a state of helplessness equates to big T-type of trauma. The child is removed, creating a shock, followed by a sustained, overwhelming experience of fear and loss with an inability to resolve the fear through the reconciliation process, and resulting in the child's customary defenses being unable to resolve the situation. The child, therefore, remains in a state of perpetual helplessness and fear.

Placed in a strange home, cut off from family and friends and living among strangers are all traumatizing experiences that have corresponding losses. With each traumatizing loss there is accompanying grief that must be acknowledged and dealt with. Primary trauma, attachment trauma, and placement trauma all may be exacerbated by continual exposure to insensitive caregivers and social welfare professionals who, through ignorance or insensitivity, continually serve as triggering agents for residual secondary trauma. The consequence of trauma has serious and long-lasting effect.

As can be seen, children placed in the foster care system have many experiences that profoundly affect their development. Historically, and all too often, this has gone unrecognized. Children are removed and moved about as if they were commodities or mere packages.

I recall one experience when a Social Worker brought a child to our agency with three Hefty bags full of assorted clothes and toys, signed the requisite forms, handed the child over to us and walked out. During this rather perfunctory procedure, very little information was given regarding the child's history at that time. In this case he was a 2-year-old boy who had been living with his sister and grandmother. The CSW was accompanied by the 13-year-old sister. The Social Worker deposited the child and his belongings and left with the sister without saying goodbye, preparing the child by talking to him, giving us any pertinent information, or even acknowledging the possible impact of leaving this child with total strangers.

As might be expected, the little boy went into immediate panic, the classic response to abandonment as described by Ainsworth: Crying (protest) and frantically trying to follow the sister as she left (search), followed by being distraught for several hours, and finally falling asleep from exhaustion (resignation and despair). The new foster parents, with whom we had arranged placement, came and took him home with them. They did a tremendous job of comforting him in the next few weeks. They even sat up with him at night because he was frightened by being with strangers and having nothing familiar around him. To his frame of reference, he had been abandoned. Confused and terrified, he longed for his family. In one life-transforming moment, he had lost everything: Family, neighborhood, cultural identity, safety, security, his home and familiar surroundings. He was entering a new world; a new reality with different rules, people, and for him, a transformative event. Though this was a memorable case, it was by no means unusual. This little boy had entered the AS-IF world where things are not as they seem, like a Mad Hatter's Tea Party:

> There was a table set out under a tree in front of the house, and the March Hare and the Hatter were having tea at it: a Dormouse was sitting between them, fast asleep, and the other two were using it as a cushion, resting their elbows on it, and talking over its head. "Very uncomfortable for the Dormouse," thought Alice, "only as it's asleep, I suppose it doesn't mind." The table was a large one but the three were all crowded at one corner of it: "No room! No room! They cried out when they saw Alice coming. "There's plenty of room!" said Alice indignantly, and she sat down in a large arm chair at one end of the table. "Have some wine," the March Hare said in an encouraging tone. Alice looked all around the table, but there was nothing on it. "I don't see any wine." She remarked.
>
> —**Lewis Carroll** - *Alice's Adventures in Wonderland, Pg 89)*

There is no way any child could be prepared for this overwhelming, life-changing event. And yet, this event happens routinely every day, not only in Los Angeles, but around the country and around the world. In this strange new world, his life is now defined by his status as a special needs kid. His world becomes the world of his new status and neighborhood and family. He must cope, adapt, accommodate to the new reality while living with sometimes perplexed, bewildered, and frustrated new caretakers, and wait for resolution of his situation. He is a part of a process, a system in which he has no power, but is clearly dependent upon and terribly vulnerable.

Placement presents an unsolvable problem for the child, the resolution of which must also take place in a strange and foreign environment. For a young child the natural response is to seek proximity in order to feel safe again. However, since the child has been separated from the supposed "customary" source of soothing, the child exists in a perpetual state of fear-- placed in limbo, helpless and unable to locate any source of safety. It is ironic, though all children customarily have little to say about their welfare, it is even truer of children who have been placed. They are dependent on adults who are supposed to have their welfare in mind, yet they have no say at all in what happens to them.

The dangers of placement are often not recognized because the underlying assumptions, expectation and common wisdom are that, since the child has been removed from a dangerous situation, that child should now be "safe." Because he is with people who care, the problem is solved, so the child should now respond by feeling safe. However, this is not the case, because this assumption ignores the powerful effects primary relational trauma and then interruption of the attachment bond regardless of its defective nature. The nature of the original attachment bond with the primary caretaker must also be taken into consideration. If it was an insecure attachment or disorganized attachment to begin with, adaption and transition may be all the more problematic. All of these things have a powerful effect on the child's development because what is most needed in every child's life during the critical period of the early years is safety, security, consistency and stability. In addition to a tenuous placement, however, there is a new danger looming on the horizon, adding to the escalating trauma sequence: birth family contact.

## Intermittent Trauma

Another variable introduced into the process created by parental abuse and subsequent placement, which often becomes secondary trauma, is the court-ordered reunification plan stipulating a requirement for multiple visits between child and offending parent. These visits result in exposure to the parent who allegedly abused the child, and are often very distressing. After each exposure the child typically exhibits regressive behaviors and is unstable for a period of time after the visit. Like children of divorce, these children often need several days to regain their equilibrium after each visit. These conditions result in chronic over-arousal of the stress response system leading to predictable psychological and somatic consequences. In normal cases, the usual means of resolution is through regaining contact with the primary attachment figure. Since this is not possible, the child remains in a very difficult and strange situation. If this phenomenon is not given the recognition it needs and appropriate strategies are not in place to facilitate recovery and establishment of new attachments, the child will continue to suffer.

As the system works today, the situation can be compounded by multiple placements or numerous birth family contacts set up to attemp family reunification. This process may go on for several months, or in some cases, several years before some sort of resolution occurs. In effect, the child is removed, placed in a strange situation, taken out of it, exposed to the traumatizing parent, sent back to the strange situation, and the cycle continues. The child is left in a limbo of unresolved terror.

Placement of children in the foster/adopt programs run by the Department of Children and Family Services, involves removal from a situation "deemed to be either unsafe or harmful to a child." This is the platform for launching the whole process of primary and secondary trauma, which has serious effects on the developmental trajectory of the child. To compound the problems, the department engages in lengthy legal procedures in order to prove probable cause in a detention hearing and while all of this is going on, a child or sibling group may be removed by a Social Worker and placed with a "foster/adopt family." It is this removal which sets in motion the trauma sequence. There is an abrupt interruption of the relationship with a primary attachment figure. This breach sets into play a state of separation anxiety and panic which compounds whatever previous relational trauma may be associated with the primary parental behavior.

As presented in future chapters, relinquishing ties to attachment figures is particularly difficult for the child with attachment issues. Nevertheless, it is still necessary for the healing process that seems an almost insurmountable task. Because of placement, the child is simultaneously engaged in coping with the anxiety of placement, dealing with the uncertainties of birth family visits, the legal system, Social Worker visits, and a strange new family situation, all the while engaged in the process of relinquishing and possibly attaching to the new attachment figures.

The relationship between attachment, loss and mourning may be seen when placement disrupts attachment and, if the child already has attachment issues, the basic safety, security and trust necessary for healing is placed in danger. An already traumatized, frightened child will have a great deal of difficulty healing as well as having the necessary security and freedom to accomplish all the necessary developmental tasks of each subsequent life stage. The risk as Bowlby noted is "despair and an unalterable state of misery." Loss, especially early in childhood, can have a deep impact on the growing mind. The child's developmental state at the time of the loss will also influence the grieving process.

In this regard, I had an interesting conversation with Robert Hafetz, a consultant and frequent contributor to adoption discussions, on the internet. He made the following observations regarding the power of attachment and loss of the maternal figure:

> I have done an extensive review of the literature on this issue and it's important to keep fetal and infant mental capacity in context. There is no cognition, therefore a fetus or an infant doesn't have

the capacity to "know" or understand anything before birth and we aren't sure when the fetal brain will have a functioning amygdala and hippocampus. The former processes emotion and the latter records memory. Common sense indicates memory is essential for learning and must be active at birth since all infants do is learn. However there is no explicit memory, and no way for an infant or fetus to know or understand what attachment is in this context. Since they do process emotions we can assume an affective language is at work that we can compare to a verbal language. Emotions such as joy, fear, disgust, sadness, security, rage, etc. are the words, and mother's nonverbal communications, familiar touch, heartbeat, after 8 weeks eye contact, will serve as the voice. All of these form what we call attachment, and add to that the hormonal bond and the psychological bond since an infant and mother are literally one person, not 2 individuals. Through this nonverbal language the infant's right brain is mapped or created by interactions with the familiar mother. When there is a premature maternal separation (PMMS) the infant will record this event and make a long term memory. This is where the problems in adoptions begin. The brain will hardwire this experience into an anxiety response when love is expressed by the adopting mother who is the strange mother. There will be a sense of mistrust and fear of attachment that is non-cognitive, not known, but experienced as an emotion. The child has a compromised ability to attach that I don't refer to as an attachment disorder or part of a disease process. It's a normal reaction to an abnormal event. Sadly the memory of ambiguous grief can manifest as severe behavior or dissociation in older children and they get wrongly diagnosed and medicated.

Now that we have explored the important role of attachment in the developing child and how caregiver affect regulation shapes brain development, the sense of self-organization, and socialization of the child, it is time to add to our understanding by looking at how *loss* affects attachment by creating conditions of complicated mourning and how attachment is essential to recovery from unresolved grief.

# Chapter 4

## UNHEALED WOUNDS
### *LOSS AND COMPLICATED GRIEF*

There are many consequences of placement. One is disrupted attachment, as discussed in the previous chapter, and others are trauma and loss, which are the natural and inescapable effects of removal. There is a great deal of attention paid to trauma in the literature, but there is not as much attention paid to loss, particularly loss as experienced by children under the care of Child Welfare. Treatment models often do not give enough attention to dealing with loss as a separate issue. The lack of attention to this issue is illustrated by the fact that when I attended a workshop at the First Annual Grief Symposium in Los Angeles in 2005, there was no mention of Grief and Loss as an issue for children in the foster care system. One presenter whom I queried about this responded with, "That was not our focus in our research."

In my experience, grief and loss are not seen as significant psychological events in this disenfranchised population. Stop and think for a moment about what removal from home and family represents. What is lost for the child? First, as was previously discussed, the child's place in the family, as well as the personal and family narrative is disrupted. Because of such an inborn need to belong, when a child is removed from any family, the whole context of that child's life is lost. This is a major connection. Because we all feel a need to be connected to the people of our past, being unable to draw on this connection, this narrative, makes it very difficult to have a base for a safe and secure future. Moreover, it is difficult to grow up as a psychologically healthy adult if we are denied access to our own history. It is like a tree being cut off at the roots. Family, neighborhood, toys, friends, pets, extended family, routines, favorite foods, bed time rituals, and the familiarity of your own room; these attachments are all major components of a sense of identity, and this loss happens with shocking suddenness. Imagine yourself sitting at home on your couch in your sweats, watching your favorite TV program, when someone comes in, a stranger, and packs up all your things, puts them in three plastic Hefty bags and moves you across town leaving you with a strange family. That is what happens to hundreds of children in Los Angeles every day.

This act of removal is another trauma which compounds the trauma history of the child who is removed. Already having experienced attachment trauma of various kinds and degrees, this new trauma further accentuates what has been described in the literature as the *child's dilemma*. The original dilemma of being subjected to "fright without solution" is the same, only the child is entering a new world of fear and threat. The dynamics are the same, with the child being in a helpless and strange situation without recourse to seek proximity to a caregiver (albeit a dangerous and inconsistent, or neglectful caregiver), but are compounded by having to endure the shock of being placed with caregivers with whom the child has no previous experience. This is the dilemma with a twist. Now he/she has to deal with overwhelming loss while suffering from previous experiences of neglect, abuse or sexual trauma and being forced to adapt to a new placement. Is it any wonder they have such complicated emotional, psychological, social and behavior problems?

Because trauma and loss are all seen as part of the traumatic sequelae, it is difficult to parse out the effects of trauma and loss. However, in working with many individuals who have experienced traumatic losses, I have found that long after the initial effects of trauma have passed, these individuals have many lingering signs indicating a lack of progression past the point of trauma. In effect, they have unhealed wounds. Therese Rando in her book *The Treatment of Complicated Mourning* defines the condition by saying, "Complicated mourning is a generic term implying that given the amount of time since the loss, there is some compromise, distortion, of failure of one or more stages of mourning." (Pg. 12)

This condition has many clinical features. These are children who remain stuck and are unable to complete the natural progression of their development. The acute ambivalence and the re-experiencing of grief, as well as dealing with images, memories and intrusive recollection are all symptoms of post-traumatic stress as well as complicated mourning.

The root of the word *bereave* implies "an unwilling deprivation by force, having something withheld unjustly and injuriously, a stealing away of something valuable—all of which leave the individual victimized" (Rando, Pg. 20). This certainly fits the picture of what happens to these children in placement who, because of their situations have been confronted with too much loss occurring too soon in their lives, without adequate support and ongoing help. They have been victimized by parents, victimized by the system, and placed in situations which, by their very nature and structure, will create conditions of secondary trauma. The salient point that Rando makes is that major losses tend to compound previous losses. In the case of children, their early experiences of anxiety and helplessness, old conflicts about separation, dependency, and ambivalent or insecure attachment create a baseline experience of continual threat. "In other words, the destabilization occasioned by major loss often puts one in touch with past pain and previous times of chaos, stress and transition, and can summon unfinished business from the past—all of which can add to current distress" (Pg. 29). In sum, the *child's dilemma* is dealing with overwhelming loss in addition to suffering from a previous history of neglect, abuse or sexual trauma, while trying at the same time to adapt to a new placement.

These children grow up living with the residual traumas and loss deeply embedded in their psyches, perpetuating their wounds in their daily lives and infecting the next generation. This is because within each of us there is a processing system that protects us, helping us to defend against threat and the resultant anxiety and the depression it entails. The system responsible for this is the attachment system. This is thoroughly documented by the lives of the individuals featured in chapter 11.

By now the reader will have noticed a recurring theme: Trauma and development, trauma and attachment, and now, trauma and complicated grief. Attachment is the cornerstone, the foundation of everything which makes us human. Disruption of attachment disrupts and threatens the entire structure of the self and of human identity. Again, in reviewing the research, solid evidence that chronic mourning is also a disorder of attachment is found. This is due to the fact that chronic mourning develops following the loss of a relationship in which the mourner, in this case a child, is highly anxious and dependent upon the caregiver. It is a relationship in which the child's reliance on the parent's presence, emotional support or daily assistance in order to function is now lost. Anxious dependence, or insecure attachment, is the main feature of abused children. Many prime factors are involved in the failure to resolve traumatic loss:

- The very context of placement leaves the child in a precarious position, which adds to anxiety, depression, confusion and helplessness.

- The court has control.

- The child has intermittent contact with the birth parent.

- The child receives mixed messages regarding his or her status.

- The child feels increased ambivalence regarding his or her parents, by having to split placement family and birth family into "good parents and bad parents."

- There is placement impermanence, which adds to the impact of feeling disenfranchised, worthless, hopeless and devalued.

- The child has no fate control, which increases feelings and perceptions of a chaotic, unpredictable world where bad things happen and nothing can be done about it.

- The very act of removal and placement shatters the child's view of the world's meaning, order and predictability, reinforcing earlier experiences of family chaos and instability.

These risk factors compound the likelihood that the child will experience delayed or complicated grief, because these factors are based on our understanding of the very nature of the original attachment relationship and the characteristics of caregiving. As previously noted, attunement, regulatory, and subsequent attachment failures, through inconsistent or non-existent parenting, lead to a series of breaches. These breaches, if left unhealed, become chronic, which leads to mistrust and withdrawal. Mistrust eventually results in emotional defensiveness and distancing, which lead to lack of support, which become a self-perpetuating cycle.

One of the more pronounced reactions to abuse is heightened autonomic nervous system arousal, leading to a continuous state of hyper-arousal and changes in right brain functioning. It has been found that behaviors acquired in this state are more difficult to resolve. In other words, children of abusers have a more difficult time relinquishing the attachment in ambivalent and oscillating attachment relationships. Inherent in this cycle is a basic truism: The more difficult the relationship with the caregiver, the more difficult it is to grieve. As a consequence, it also takes longer to heal. As previously discussed, chronic elevated threat levels and negative affect lead to the alteration of critical brain function in areas like the hippocampus, limbic system, and amygdala. These brain areas are involved in regulating affect, memory, organization of the self, and the stress response.

Another risk factor that adds to complicated mourning is the child's psychological defenses, which are the residue of insecure or disrupted attachment. Dissociation becomes the child's involuntary defense against vulnerability and helplessness. Dissociation and denial prevent the child from being overwhelmed by stress and are two of the most common features of traumatic loss. In this regard, the dissociative disorder is associated with complicated mourning in children who also have been victimized and or abused. Frequently accompanying dissociation are panic attacks, which occur when the child is unable to defend against anxiety. Whether in adults or children, panic attacks are the result of uncontrolled terror breaking through the defenses. This reaction is based in the storm and shock of overwhelming feelings associated with traumatic loss.

It is common for most adults to experience some amount of shock, numbing, and dissociation due to acute grief. It is even more common, as well as necessary, in children. The main issue here is the degree of dissociation, which can range from mild to severe. This, again, is a function of the degree of trauma, the frequency and kind of trauma, the age at which the trauma occurs and the identity of the perpetrator. If a perpetrator is known and trusted by the victim, the sense of shock and betrayal will be proportionally greater.

Since a prime characteristic of trauma is the abnormal level of anxiety to which the victim is subjected, complicated mourning is associated with the risk factors of suddenness and helplessness. These are the underlying dynamics of depression and anxiety disorders. Essentially, it has been found that anxiety is not the chief cause but rather, the chief result of trauma. The unanticipated shock of the loss stuns the child and emphasizes/reinforces feelings of powerlessness and vulnerability already present in the dependent state of childhood, the exposure to unreliable parents and the lack of security and safety present in the family context. This insecurity is of major consequence, underscoring regulatory failures to successfully cope with major traumatic losses. Dissociation and numbing, as a defense against anxiety, compose the core dynamic which leads to emotional dead zones (unhealed wounds). In research related to surviving major trauma, it has been found that recovery is related to stress resilience. Stress resilience is directly related to secure attachment. Therese Rando concludes:

> The important fact must be kept in mind that sudden, random, traumatic losses experienced in highly dependent, conflicted morbid relationships function to increase 1) anxiety, 2) threat, 3) vulnerability, 4) helplessness and violations of the child's view of the world (Pg. 47).

Again, these features are all common to disordered attachment. They are foundational to understanding complicated grief reactions and the probable subsequent difficulty the child will have in recovering. Rando summarized the seven risk factors involved in complicated mourning:

- Trauma variables: Sudden, unexpected loss.

- Relationship variables: A premorbid relationship with the caregiver that was markedly ambivalent or angry. This also includes pre-existing unresolved mental health problems and or substance abuse in the parent.

- Social variables: such as the individual's perceived lack of support as in the case of disenfranchised loss: the status of children makes them more at risk because their losses are not seen as significant.

- Family variables: such as a broken family, single parent, or domestic violence. Homelessness and intergenerational transmission of family problems such as divorce, long term family destabilization, and multiple care takers all contribute to the poor quality of family structure and relationship climate.

- Abuse Variables: The amount, type of abuse, frequency, severity, neglect, and chaos in the family.

- Placement Variables: The number of disruptions to attachment through disrupted placements.

- Compromised resources: The amount of social support available through extended family, social agencies and the community.

The child in placement has all of the above risk factors. With those risk factors in mind, let us look at approaches to the resolution of complicated mourning and traumatic reactions to loss. The solutions are implicit in a thorough understanding of the problem. As noted previously, it is the unrecognized and overlooked problems of trauma and loss in children that are primarily responsible for the appalling failure to provide the necessary and sufficient remedies for helping children survive these life-transforming experiences. In fact, caregiver ignorance, misunderstanding and indifference to these unrecognized problems contribute significantly to increasing the loss experience through secondary trauma. I might also add ignorance and poor training on the part of professionals contributes to secondary trauma as well.

We also see that some of the failures to provide solutions are a result of certain prevailing ideas and misinformation within the system. The risks which often prevent recovery are based on the assumptions that placement has little effect on children. Assumptions like, "they are young and resilient," "removal from harm prevents future harm," "if one placement is not working, then move them to another," and "children just need time to get over it" are common. All of these ideas are based on false assumptions, ignorance, and an inadequate system which leads to a failure to understand the nature and complexity of relational trauma and loss.

The goal in this work is to present a comprehensive picture of the reasons for the struggles that children are undergoing in the Children's Services System. Compromised resources, lack of social support, disenfranchisement, invalidation of loss by placement, Social Workers removing and moving children while not understanding trauma/attachment/loss issues, the child's lost relationship with an abusive parent and the child's status in a broken system are significant barriers to recovery.

Furthermore, the most important and critical factor yet to be addressed is the quality of the home into which the child is placed. Mere removal is only a precursor to addressing and ameliorating the problem. We need an entirely new model which takes into consideration all of these factors. It has been found over and over again that one of the major factors related to recovery is the quality of the recovery environment.

To illustrate the impact of these compounding factors, I would like to introduce the perspective of one who knows the system well: An adolescent who recently aged out of the foster care system. It was written at my request while he was still in the system:

Try living in homes of people that you don't know: people are just "assigned" to be your guardian. I have, up to this day, been in 6 different foster homes, lived with an abusive sibling, and was taken care of by a single parent who suffers from several permanent but controllable mental illnesses. Despite these hardships, I have successfully been able to excel in many courses and activities.

I was born into a family consisting of a Korean mother, a Dutch father, and a brother: A "normal" family in my book. Soon after my birth, my father left us. My mother, at the time and to this day, suffers from Bipolar, Manic Depression, and a few other irreversible mental illnesses. These were brought upon by the loss of her son and daughter before my brother and I were born (these two children suffered accidental drowning-author's note when left with a baby sitter). My sick mother was left to care for two children on her own. We lived on welfare, which was no more than 15 hundred dollars for the three of us per month.

When I was ten years old, I could notice changes in our mother's actions. Her mental state was starting to affect her. We knew of her illness but this was the first time we experienced the relapse state of a mental patient. Complaints were filed by neighbors, which led to the arrest of my mother. We lived with our grandmother for about 2 weeks, until a Social Worker assigned our case removed us from her custody. We were then placed in our first foster home.

My brother has always been the angry type and had trouble controlling it. We would fight several times a day and it would get pretty physical. The foster parents noticed this immediately and removed him from the home. After a year and a half in the home, I returned to live with my mom along with my brother. Within a few months, we returned to a foster home for the same old reasons, but after only 3 months were all back together again.

When my brother and I were young, we were similar in size, so I could fight back whenever we fought but as we got older he grew dramatically and was much bigger than me. This allowed him to physically force me to do things that favored him. I did nothing about it because I didn't want to take the chance of being removed from my home again.

In July of 2007, sure enough, our mother relapsed again. Together, we returned to a foster home. Up until then, the abuse was going on. After a while, I realized that I had nothing to lose by telling someone about my problems with my brother. I have only to gain from moving. I could not get a hold of my Social Worker so early one morning I ran away to the police station to get help. Since that day, I have been living in a new foster home without my brother.

Sometimes I look at teens that have "problems" in their lives and I just laugh.

This tale is told by a very bright and clearly articulate adolescent boy who has endured much in his life. I would like to add that this new foster home turned out to be another disaster for him. He was placed with two other adolescent boys in a home that was very unstable. The foster parents turned out to be addicted to drugs and had a very unstable relationship which became emotionally and verbally abusive. Alex had to be moved into another placement. He has since then been able to get a college scholarship to UCLA, and because of their program designed to specifically help foster kids, is doing well. This is just one story of a child in the system: A boy who has done remarkably well in spite of and without a lot of help from that system. He, like many survivors, feels a strong sense of obligation to help others in similar circumstances. He gives of his time to speak and advocate for them. He concludes by saying, "I look forward to helping them and giving them a chance at something they might not have been able to do alone." His story is featured in chapter 11.

When I encounter these remarkable stories of survival and resiliency, I am amazed to see survivors doing much better than would be predicted, based on their histories and what we know about the effects of trauma. In Alex's case, one factor that accounts for his resiliency is the stage at which his trauma occurred; most of it occurred later in his childhood. Had all of this disruption happened at an earlier time in the critical period from birth to three years of age, the outcome might have been quite different. It is so important that children have stability and secure attachment when their core personality is developing. When it does, it serves them well when they encounter adversity later in life.

To return to the theme of this chapter, complicated mourning, the first and most obvious sign of loss is sadness. As noted in chapter 3, traumatic disruption to the primary attachment relationship creates an enormous initial loss with a subsequent series of losses. These losses are difficult to grieve under the best of conditions, and, as previously stated, placement is a unique set of complex and difficult circumstances. When a child loses a parent, the experienced sadness is a profound and natural response. Rando notes that grief under traumatic circumstances is a normal reaction to abnormal circumstances. However, this natural response becomes complicated when the child is unable to experience the feelings surrounding the loss. He is unable to experience the feelings because when he does, they serve as trauma triggers which engender reminders and old feelings of terror and abandonment.

When it persists, acute mourning that fails to come to a natural completion and does not abate over time can be defined as *fixated grief*. For children of placement, when fixated grief occurs, a collection of symptoms are present in which these children appear sad and withdrawn, are avoidant of contact and exhibit a kind of malaise or emotional deadness and emptiness. Additionally, they may appear dazed and confused, overwhelmed and helpless. Secondary to the depression is a natural correlate, anxiety, with many free-floating fears, phobias, panic attacks and frequently recurring nightmares.

Rando states that this grief is typified by persistent crying, angry protest, yearning and searching, preoccupation with loss, depression, disorganization, anxiety and helplessness, which are all typical of the first stage of a loss reaction. Children in this case appear to caregivers as if the precipitating event has just recently occurred. What it represents is continued clinging to the previous attachment and the unconscious belief that the loss is reversible. This, of course, is denial, a first line of defense to prevent shock. Clinging is what children do. They seek proximity when under threat. Placement disrupts this attachment and if the child already has attachment issues, the basic safety, security and trust necessary for healing is compromised. A traumatized, frightened child will have more difficulty healing, as well as experiencing the freedom to accomplish future developmental tasks. Relinquishing ties to attachment figures is particularly difficult for the child with attachment issues, but is necessary in the healing process.

In essence, this is a reenactment of a *child's dilemma*. The child is simultaneously engaged in the process of relinquishing and if lucky, reattaching to the new attachment figures. This is asking a lot of a young child. Rando comments on this: "When it becomes apparent that holding on is useless and even harmful, the child must let go of old attachments and ultimately develop new ones." (Pg. 49)

Again, it should be noted that the whole environment of placement with required birth family visits presents an exceedingly difficult challenge for the child--it is difficult under optimal conditions. It requires a sense of safety, security and trust, which is in short supply as the child lives under constant threat and struggles with others for control.

The child's dilemma is expressed symptomatically. Usually accompanying depression and anxiety, particularly in children, are diffuse somatic complaints. All parents are familiar with children who have headaches, stomach aches, losses of appetite and sleep disturbances when they are emotionally upset. These are exaggerated in children who have experienced major blows to their security and safety. As previously mentioned, the child becomes *dysregulated*.

In addition to depression and anxiety, there may be many exhibitions of emotional turmoil without apparent provocation, such as temper tantrums, rages, outbursts, wild mood swings, and tearfulness. Because of their age and emotional immaturity, distress is almost always manifested by overt behavioral problems as well. They may suddenly be aggressive in play, defiant and oppositional, and seemingly willing to pay any price to be in control. This aggression may then be supplanted by a kind of whiny, clingy, and very dependent behavior. These behaviors may be regarded as *affect regulation problems*.

One foster parent reported that her child, recently placed with her, would oscillate from being fearful and dependent to full of rage and eventually to a totally deflated, worthless, helpless, victim state. The foster parent, like most others, found this emotional whirlwind confusing and exhausting. If this were not enough, the child idealized and clung obstinately to the absent parents and refused to engage and accept the love of the new parent. As part of their insecurity, placed children may also cling to worn-out and bedraggled dolls, stuffed animals and broken toys. These *transitional objects* are all that children have left from their previous lives. This reveals the reality that grief and stress exacerbate underlying personality and behavior issues.

As children continue to transition in placement, different signs of delayed grief can be seen. They may continue to exhibit symptoms of irritability, restlessness, and hyper-arousal of their nervous systems. There may be continued signs of separation anxiety, particularly after birth family visits, as well as difficulty in transitioning from the visits. One little girl, severely abused by her mother and father, made a card with red hearts on it and proudly presented it to her mother at a supervised family visit saying, "I love you, you are the best mother in the world." These defenses of idealization and denial are a very pronounced feature of the failure to mourn.

The severity of these reactions is dependent upon several factors: The number of losses and placements, availability of support, disenfranchisement, overwhelming emotions, shock, age at the time of the traumatic event, and, as mentioned, the security of the attachment bond. As one can see, recovery from trauma and loss is often very prolonged, very complicated and full of many obstacles. Therefore the children present varied, complex, and difficult problems to their foster parents and the professionals who work with them.

Once the original shock of placement appears to have receded due to length of time in placement, the battle is still not won. Just because the child appears to have adjusted to the transition does not mean the problems are solved. There are many theoretical reasons for this. For the sake of brevity, I will say that in order for children to fully recover, they must also mourn what was lost. This means that in order to heal, children must re-experience the emotions of the loss and then integrate them into a coherent narrative (make sense of the experience). Because trauma is so painful, when children attempt to deal with the loss, that attempt may re-trigger the trauma, flooding the children again with overwhelming terror. As a defense they avoid the trigger and therefore cannot grieve. These feelings are often *dissociated* and may not even be experienced at the conscious level. Hence they become unhealed wounds. Further complicating this picture is the fact that children must also be securely attached and in a safe environment in order to grieve. Obviously children in placement initially have neither safety nor security. Their attachment base and safe environment have been taken away (if in fact they had it in the first place).

Trauma must be resolved by lessening the terror, empowering the child, and integrating the fragmented experiences before the work of bereavement can be successfully navigated. Being stuck in a revolving cycle of trauma and loss often exacerbated by multiple placements, leads to complicated grief. A failure or distortion of the grief process results in a subsequent failure to develop new and functional coping skills. In this case, mourning under normal circumstances is the psychological response to loss, a response which seeks to come to grips, adapt, and accommodate to the new post-placement reality. This mourning should lead to successful adaptation or a relinquishment of the ties to the original attachment figure and the final step of the eventual development of new attachments. However, since the child, who has experienced *attachment trauma,* is predictably fearful and exhibits a great deal of mistrust and avoidance of new attachments, it may take a long time to gain trust. One can see how complicated this can be, given the circumstances of a young child's life. The necessary recovery is dependent upon the fragile attachment process, which has been affected by placement and is yet to be re-established in the new context.

In summation, I will make several distinctions between special needs children and the regular (normal) population of children who experience traumatic family losses:

- These children have suffered serial, complex trauma before their loss of family.

- They do not have the presence of an ongoing, safe-secure adult attachment figure with whom they have had a relationship.

- Recovery often does not take place in a stable, safe, secure and trustworthy environment.

- Their working model of the world is based on a view of the world proven to be unsafe, untrustworthy and unreliable.

- The children are continually re-exposed to the original perpetrator of the original trauma.

- They are coping with major loss and grief issues prior to the traumatic placement.

These are the factors which may, to a great degree, impede successful mourning. This mourning involves not only relinquishment of what was lost through re-experiencing the emotions of loss, but the rebuilding of the world view, the finding of new beliefs, expectations, and roles, and the forging of a new sense of identity. This new sense of self must be formed and based on new attachments. This can only be done by learning to trust and overcoming detrimental effects of previous attachments. This is achieved by developing a new personal history narrative. For the child, it is not only who he was, but also who he is now, and who he will become. To a child, this is clearly a daunting task: Moving adaptively into a new post-placement world without the attachment figures and the whole familial context. As a reminder, it is also affected by the *Reunification Plan.* That is to say, the entire process of grief is continuously interrupted by the number and frequency of birth family visits and how disruptive those visits are. This takes us to the next step in the recovery process: Mourning. This active process of dealing with loss will be discussed in the next chapter.

# Chapter 5

## MOURNING-HEALING

### Establishing a Safe Haven

With a high degree of certainty, we know that the primary determining factor in recovery from trauma is the quality of the recovery environment. Because of the severity of the impact that trauma has on attachment, a great amount of energy must be devoted to establishing an environment in which re-attachment may grow and thrive. Creating this safe environment is the challenge facing all participants of this system that works with displaced children. On a daily basis we ask ourselves, what is needed to make the foster care environment suitable to the complex needs, vulnerabilities, and problems of each foster child? In essence, we work to set the stage for healing once the child has been removed from the dysfunctional environment of the original family.

At a more basic level, we realize that the first step is to find and create a stable placement. The question is, based on our current understanding of trauma and loss in placement, what must be present to help ameliorate these well-documented problems? First and most obvious is safety. Above all else, children need to feel safe and live in a secure and stable environment. In Alex's situation (Chapter 4), coupled with the lack of security and safety in the parental home and the well-documented mental health issues of his mother, we also see the lack of security, stability, and safety brought about by multiple failed placements.

The second important factor required for restoration is attachment. Losing safety, security, stability, and attachment is devastating, and restoration of these feelings is crucial to recovery from loss and bereavement. In fact, they are the very foundation of a successful transition from a traumatizing, unstable and abusive birth home to a new environment, which will hopefully become a healing environment. The purpose of the placement process is to create and facilitate the necessary and sufficient conditions for healing and to facilitate the growth of new, secure attachments. As a caveat, I do not think it is actually true that the stated goal of placement is to facilitate growth and new attachments; it is far more limited to merely removing the child from harm. If the rest happens, it is a happy accident. As has been noted, placement is often a disjointed, fragile and uneven process. It is not enough to just find a placement for the child, it is imperative that the placement present the possibility of being a home where new and healing attachments may be formed. I make this distinction because not all placements meet these criteria.

The approach to the process must be based on a crisis management model, because in the early stages of placement there is a series of problems which must be managed. The first is the transition period. This is an extremely critical period for the child as well as the prospective foster parent. It is like transplanting a tree; the work must be done to prepare the soil. In order to help prepare the way for placement, it is imperative for the foster parents to understand what they are undertaking. Many new foster parents have unrealistic expectations based on an idealized view of "helping a child in need." They are frequently shocked and disappointed when they find the challenge to be "far harder than (they) thought it would be." Some also told me that the parenting skills they learned through their own parents frequently did not work with the children placed in their care. They were not emotionally prepared to cope with the behaviors of the child who came to their home. During my career in this field, part of my job was to help these parents understand what has happened to their prospective child, and understand the basis of the child's "emotionally-driven behavior." This is where I think more pre-placement training could be helpful in order to focus more specifically on the development of attachment based parenting skills.

Beverly James outlines her treatment philosophy by noting that treatment of attachment trauma- related problems is an exacting, laborious, and often lengthy process, reflecting the severity and complexity of these disturbances. (Pg. 63) In order to carry out this kind of treatment successfully, five areas must be addressed. The first is educational. The second is developing self-identity. The third is learning to tolerate emotions and being able to modulate them. The fourth is relationship building, and the fifth is learning behaviors related to competence and mastery. James adds that only after the child has developed sufficient security in the relationship with the present caregivers can the work of exploring trauma and mourning losses can begun. She believes it is a clinical error to rush the process and move too quickly; this is an error which could re-traumatize the child and cause the child to confirm the belief that adults cannot be trusted. A further danger is to trigger trauma reactions, thus reawakening the original trauma experience.

In terms of education, in order to understand a child's behavior and effectively intervene, it is our role to educate the parent about the reasons for the behavior (i.e., decode the message in the behavior). As in the first stages of infancy and attachment, the parent must be adept at decoding the messages of distress. In the case of older children, the messages are often more complex. Decoding these messages can only be done if the parent is emotionally *attuned* to the child. In order to be tuned into the child the parent must be able to empathize, to feel what the child is feeling, and understand not only what is happening, but why. This means that the parents must be comfortable with their own feelings and be able to communicate empathetically. It is important to note that the process of establishing attachment in a foster child is the same, but possibly harder, than the original task of establishing attachment with a newborn. It is harder because the surrogate parent has to overcome previous attachment-relational trauma and whatever residual attachment and behavioral problems the child brings to the placement. It requires great skill to be able to facilitate repair of attunement failures and relationship breaches, and certainly there will be many opportunities to practice this skill.

The older the child, the more complex the maladaptive behavioral is likely to be. But this is where the work of learning to modulate and tolerate feelings must be done. The task remains to decipher the message the child is sending. The child may not understand the feelings being expressed in his behavior, and it is the parent's job to decode the message and effectively intervene. Once the interventions start working, eventually the task is to help the child by reflecting the meaning of the behavior back to him/her in understandable language. This process helps the child develop the capacity for understanding her own feelings, while developing the language to express feelings and understand the feelings of others. Again, it is the process of co-regulating emotion through emotional attunement and thereby helping to create synchrony and the end result: Self-regulation of emotions.

In the previous chapters I have cited many examples of emotionally-driven behavior frequently encountered by the foster parent. Remember, this is all referenced back to failed regulatory attachment. Their behaviors are the result of their inability to contain, delay, regulate, and express emotions in a constructive fashion and to communicate needs or distress directly. The often perplexing and distressing dysfunctional behavior is the result of learned maladaptive behavior modeled by the way the birth parents treated the child. When you add the result of overwhelming trauma and loss to this mix, it is easy to see why the child has an inability to adequately cope. This is where the task of mastery behavior comes into play. These defensive or ineffective coping strategies lead to many of the problems the new foster parents encounter with their newly-placed child.

As previously stated, the foster parents are often bewildered by these strange behaviors. "It makes no sense that a child would deliberately cause others to reject him when they so clearly and desperately need to be loved." This comment, often stated by my foster parents, is correct – the behavior is paradoxical and self-defeating. Unconsciously, it is what the child has come to expect and it is what the child feels he deserves. When attempting an intervention, parents must keep two things in mind: 1) The child is afraid, vulnerable and dependent and, because of abuse by trusted caregivers, does not easily trust and 2) the child is still dealing with the major effects of trauma and loss. Because of fear and mistrust, these two factors lead the child to seek control of the new environment and, in relation, the new parent. Feeling in control is absolutely essential for anyone undergoing a traumatic crisis. The battle for control becomes the first test to which the unwitting parent is subjected. A struggle ensues because the child unconsciously expects to be disappointed and hurt again through parental ineffectiveness, neglect or abuse, and perceives the new situation as a potential threat. In other words, the child continues to react to the new parent the same way he reacted to the old parent. In therapeutic parlance, this unconscious behavior is called *Transference.* This is where relationship building takes place in the dynamic of interacting with the child around the issues of trust and control.

Mystified by the child's fear and rejection, the new parent tries harder to control the situation. This vicious cycle leads to more resistance and controlling behavior by the child. This, of course, creates frustration for both parties as the child reacts with rage (which is fear of abandonment and the ever-present ambivalence about proximity), which leads to feelings of worthlessness and shame. As a result, the parents feel rejected as their well-intentioned attempts to love the child are not reciprocated. Feeling that this child is ungrateful and rejecting of the proffered love, the parents often react with anger and withdraw and become distant or emotionally unavailable. This is called *Counter-Transference.* This occurs because both parent and child are responding unconsciously to the powerful feelings related to struggles with unresolved attachment issues. The child then reacts to this self-fulfilling prophecy by saying to himself "See, I knew it all along. Adults can't be trusted and I am going to have the same old results (abandoned, rejected and alone again) -- unloved because I am undeserving of love." This is as if to say, "My original parents didn't love me, so I must be unlovable."

All of these expectations have been built up through a history of neglect and abuse and will take some time to be resolved. This is a major issue for children placed in a new and different world. They react to parenting based on previous experience (their working model of the world) and attachment paradigm, and some children respond with a classic role reversal. They respond by trying to meet their needs by first meeting the needs of the parent. We call these children *parentified*. These children are easily mistaken for the "good child, who is so easy to like and is so helpful and nice." Other children signal their distress by being overly needy, dependent and clingy—they engage in annoying whining and attention-seeking behavior (classic signs of insecure-ambivalent attachment).

Fundamental to these dysfunctional behaviors is the triad of dependency, shame and helplessness. And this is where the work of self-identity is involved. When children have been made to feel small and embarrassed by their size, they equate smallness with humiliation and helplessness. Shame is the most common and critical experience of children in placement. These attachment-based problems are compounded when children are removed from their parents. In the words of one child, "I was un-chosen." They tend to feel even more ashamed that they were not worth the devoted care of parents whom they may have over-idealized; parents who, themselves, may have had drug and alcohol problems and possible mental health issues. These children feel that their parents valued the drugs and alcohol more than them. They feel unworthy of a parent's time, devotion and energy. Shame then becomes the template. Feeling shameful, they believe there is something about them that deserves rejection and loss. The goal here is to help the child come to terms with who she is, be validated in this process and taught to value herself instead of feeling shame and devalued. All of this falls under the umbrella of creating a therapeutic alliance between the parent, child and professionals working with the placement.

Another frequently encountered transition problem is that children with attachment difficulties, coupled with grief/loss/trauma issues, have major differences in their understanding of family functioning and their place in family life. Many of these difficulties revolve around the attachment-based dynamics of permanence, power, sharing, emotional intimacy, communication, and control. After missing opportunities for love and attention, children who enter new families have overdriven (excessive) needs. These needs are fueled by fear. They may engage in hoarding behavior and may respond by wanting everything, even after having their needs met. These children have a "scarcity world view." One of my families reported that the two young girls placed with them would get up in the middle of the night and raid the refrigerator. The foster parent found a cache of food hidden under the bed.

Clearly, placement presents a huge challenge (crisis) to the possibility of achieving stability and success. It is a clash of parenting style on the one hand and the child's attachment problems on the other. As a general rule, parents who are aware of their own needs and parenting style have a better chance of responding well to the challenges of forming trusting relationships with their children. The better they are at empathy and healing relationship breaches, the better they will be at handling the demands of forming a trusting relationship, developing strategies for regulation of emotionally-driven behavior, and implementing the necessary interventions for creating healthy new attachments. The parents who are least successful have unrealistic expectations and unmet emotional needs themselves and are often attempting to find emotional security through the love of their children rather than the reverse.

These parents have their own unresolved attachment issues. It has been found that they are parenting the way they were parented, and often have residual issues and unmet needs from their own childhoods. Hence it is not possible to undo their poor histories of attachment through parenting children with similar troubling attachment problems. Siegel in his book *Parenting from the Inside Out* makes a strong case for how parenting, based on our own parenting paradigm learned in childhood, is a major factor in parenting failures. Again, educating the parents and helping them to understand their own conflicts and the origin of their parenting style will help them be more aware and therefore more effective in their interactions with their child.

In essence, the paramount task of any parent is to provide a safe, consistent, stable, and warm context in which the child may develop without fear, abuse, neglect, or violence to his or her core self. This is particularly true of foster parenting. This environment must be free of punishment, guilt, shame, humiliation, and fear of abandonment. Setting the stage for recovery will be most successful when new parents remember that the child's behavior is functional-- it is directed toward satisfying basic psychological needs:

- Safety
- Security
- Attachment
- To be in control
- To have a sense of competence
- To have a sense of self-esteem (to feel important, worthwhile, valued)

Goals 1 and 2 can only be met through number 3. That is the purpose of attachment. Until a child feels safe and secure, nothing else can happen. Furthermore, a base of understanding will be established when new parents keep in mind that emotionally-driven behavior is fueled by powerful core emotions:

- Anger
- Fear/ the experience of threat (abandonment, safety, harm)
- Longing for contact and attachment
- Need for approval
- Need for recognition
- Need to belong

Keep in mind that emotionally-driven behavioral expressions have been learned in a context in which it was not safe to directly express feelings, be vulnerable, small, needy, or make mistakes. Emotionally-driven behavior is defensive, and typically a complex, intense, conflicted, amalgam of the core emotions. Emotionally-driven behavior often arises when the child feels caught in a bind between trusting and fearing the caregiver. As mentioned, it is a paradox (a problem with no solution) in which the caretaker is both the source of dependency and the source of danger. The child's behavior is often the result of failed attempts to preserve his/her safety and meet other needs at the same time. In order for the child to attach, the child must trust. In order for the child to heal, the child must be able to trust and feel safe. It is difficult to function when the child is not able to organize a coherent solution to the dilemma.

The first goal is to create a context, a healing environment, in which the traumatized child may recover from trauma, loss, pre-placement family dysfunction, and the after-effects of placement. Richard Rose describes the ingredients of a successful recovery environment:

> Creating an environment that is dependable, boundaries that are strong, explained and visible creates an opportunity for the child to begin to relate to the external world. Especially for multi-placed children, the need they have is not for love alone, but for replication of events missed out on at the beginning of life (Rose, *Life Story Therapy with Traumatized Children*, Pg. 58).

In order for the child to relate, there must be conditions of safety and security which will lead to the development of basic trust. Again it is a process of co-regulation. The child must be given help to develop a secure base of attachment. Attachment-based parenting becomes the vehicle for the child's healing and future and, since grief and mourning are basic attachment issues, it follows that they will find healing through attuned, attachment-based parenting. First and foremost, foster parents need to learn how to be present for the child. They must convey that they are strong, capable and competent by sending clear messages to the child:

- I will protect you.
- I will care about you.
- I will not let you hurt yourself or me.
- I am not overwhelmed by your experience or feelings.
- I know it is not your fault.
- I know we can face these issues together.
- I know you are going to be OK.
- I will help you be OK. (Rose pg. 62)

## Attachment-Based Parenting

*Attachment-based parenting* is founded on research related to attachment theory and practice, as well as my clinical experience. It is designed to create a healing environment in which attachment may either be repaired or acquired, so that disturbed attachment may be replaced with secure attachment. It is only then that mourning/healing can progress. Attachment-based parenting is parenting designed to focus on the relationship between parent and child, and has the following characteristics:

- *Understanding:* The parent understands the underlying causes behind the disturbed behavior of the child and is able to help the child become aware of feelings and express them more directly and in a manner which leads to healing.

- *Presence:* The parents have resolved their own attachment history issues and can relate to the child in a free, non-conflicted, non-ambivalent, non-punitive, accepting manner.

- *Communication:* The parent engages in collaborative communication and actively listens without criticism.

- *Boundaries:* The parent has clear, firm boundaries; consistent rules created in a democratic, rational fashion, is non-punitive, and does not engage in shame or humiliating behaviors as forms of discipline.

- *Emotions:* The parent models (demonstrates) effective, expression of a range of emotions and can deal with emotionally-driven behavior, outbursts, unregulated tantrums, and emotions related to sadness, loss and fear.

- *Conflict Resolution:* The parent presents models for conflict resolution, opportunities to heal breaches in relationships and threats to attachment; offers opportunities for healing and repair of old wounds as well as current hurt feelings.

- *Attunement:* The parent embodies emotional attunement: empathy and acceptance.

Frequently after I present this list to prospective foster parents they add, "And can leap tall buildings in a single bound." To that I say, "Yes, it does require a super-human effort to be an effective parent and foster parenting is even harder than parenting a birth-child." Rose sums up the requirements for recovery in multi-placed children:

> Good care requires therapeutic parents to be available for children to explore and make sense of the things that have happened to them, and the feelings, emotions and behaviors that they communicate. Often there is lack of information, or explanation, but the opportunity to think with a therapeutic parent supports the child to think out (externalize) her preoccupations and resolve some of her chaos. Traumatized children require routine, predictability, stability and consistency rather than an excess of material provision, freedom and love. All of this is part of good care. (Pg.67)

## The Mourning Process

Clearly, the entire process of transitioning a child from the birth parent home to a foster home is fraught with many perils and mini-crises. Some of the difficulties come from the way the system operates, others are embedded in the psyche of the child involved, and still others result from the quality of the placement home. The transition can have difficulty getting traction because of the reunification plan that may prescribe several birth family contacts. In today's climate, we see the court ordering as many contacts as three visits per week of up to three hours per visit. One can see how disruptive and distressing these visits may be to a child with conflicted feelings related to trauma inflicted by the birth parent. It is also burdensome to the foster family who must find a way to accommodate the court order. It is also a burden to the foster care Social Workers. One worker in our agency had, at one time, 18 hours per week of birth family visits. This was just one case.

Transition is also complicated by the child's own trauma and grief reactions that make it difficult to form the necessary therapeutic alliance with the foster parents and any natural children they may have. It often takes several months to get the child settled in a new home. As I have emphasized, creating a safe and secure atmosphere is the first priority. This is not as easy as it sounds, because it is a working assumption that by definition, the foster parent home is a safe and secure home. It has to be in order to be certified as a foster home. However, being certified as safe does not mean the foster child will automatically feel safe. In order for a child to feel safe, the child must trust, and trust is often a long-term development. Again, it is important to remember this process cannot be rushed. It requires time and patience to acquire trust and develop a new and secure attachment. In an ideal world, the process of mourning is a succession of stages:

- Recognition of the problem
- Recollection: Remembering the memories and trauma reminders
- Reconciliation: The process of working through the feelings of grief and loss
- Rebuilding: The process of gaining new attachments.

Beverly James emphasizes that "treatment will deal with mourning the loss of relationships with its accompanying loss of security and safety in the world, and, when needed, will focus on supporting the formation of new attachments." (Beverly James, *Handbook for Treatment of Attachment-Trauma Problems in Children*. Pg. 57)

Working toward the establishment of new attachments is met with a great deal of resistance, largely unconscious, because of a recognized and frustrating reality that is not clearly recognized: The child's attachment to the abusive parent. The unsophisticated observer would look at this statement and be very puzzled. Why would a child cling to an abusive parent? It makes no sense. You are entirely correct. It makes no sense, except when we understand a concept called the *Trauma Bond*. One major reason why trauma bonds are hard to break is because there are two powerful sources of reinforcement in an abusive relationship: The arousal of excitement before the violence and the calm of surrender afterwards. Both of these responses, placed at appropriate intervals, reinforce the traumatic bond between victim and abuser. It is well established that high arousal levels and intermittent reinforcement establish behaviors which are quite hard to extinguish. Beverly James describes the Trauma Bond in the following manner:

> The child trapped in an abusive environment is faced with a formidable task of adaptation. She must find a way to preserve a sense of trust in people who are untrustworthy, safety in a situation that is unsafe, control in a situation that is terrifyingly unpredictable and power in a situation of helplessness. Unable to care for or protect herself, she must compensate for the failure of adult care and protection with the only means at her disposal, an immature system of defenses. (Pg. 34)

As most experienced therapists realize, overcoming resistance is the very essence of psychotherapy. Because resistance is fear-based and also a function of deeply learned defensive behavior, it is no small task to help abused children relinquish old defenses and old attachments and acquire new ones. This requires ongoing assessment as the process unfolds. The therapist must discover and distinguish between trauma-bond related behaviors and attachment behavior. This can be very difficult because so many of the behaviors characteristic of the trauma bond are inherent in disturbed attachment behavior. James cautions that: "The distinction becomes even more important when one is deciding whether the child should remain in foster placement or be returned to the care of a previously abusive adult." (Pg. 34)

She gives us some important guidelines in distinguishing between trauma-bond behavior and the attachment bond. The first to consider is who regulates the emotions, a second is whether or not the adult helps the child to be more independent, and the quality of her boundaries is an important consideration. Another important factor is the extent of the child's exploratory behavior. Other considerations are: How anxious the child is in the presence of the abusive parent and whether she seeks proximity to the parent. As with a case I discussed in a previous chapter, the little boy would go into a major panic attack when he found he was to be taken to visit his mother. Some of these signals are not too hard to read. Another important distinction to note is whether or not the child regresses in the presence of the parent. All of these factors must be taken into consideration when working with a child parent dyad. This relationship must not be evaluated on the strength of the connection alone, because the connection between the abuser and the abused may be due to the trauma bond; it is not a secure attachment, though it may be intensified in the face of danger. (James, Pg. 25) James likens the relationship as one of the parent taking the child hostage.

When working with the child regarding her ambivalence toward the abusive parent and the adoptive parent, the major complicating factor in dealing with the trauma bond is the child's experienced need for the person with whom he or she has the relationship. As mentioned before, separation from that person can, in and of itself be traumatizing and thus intensify the trauma bond, or may increase idealization of the parental relationship. Because of this ambivalence, it results in an inability to form another primary relationship for a period of time. Decisions and interventions in such complex relationships must be made with exquisite sensitivity to the child's wellbeing. With all of these complexities, it is easy to see why the transition from abusive parental attachment to a new foster parent is a journey fraught with many pitfalls, conflicts, regressions, and periods of chaos as the child struggles with much internal conflict. Feeling unsafe, deeply ambivalent and untrusting is the child's basic condition. It requires patience and a great deal of understanding to help her navigate to a place of safety, stability and trust; so many of the keys to understanding lie in knowing the child's attachment history.

Having said all this, in reality this recovery process is seldom a smooth one. It is much more difficult, for children than for adults who have had a single loss or trauma, usually associated with a death. It is crucial to remember that a child who has been placed is dealing simultaneously with trauma reminders, fear of recurrence, secondary losses, and previous trauma and loss of attachment figures, all while attempting to cope with living in a new and unfamiliar home environment. This is a daunting task under the best of circumstances.

In order for recovery to be successful, three tasks must be accomplished: First, we must help the child cope with the effects of trauma and loss. Secondly, we must help the child master the trauma symptoms, and lastly, we must help the child successfully accommodate the loss. These are all a part of healthy mourning and are necessary for it to proceed. In view of the normal process of mourning, the preferred order of grieving is inverted for children in that the third step of rebuilding must actually be the first step. Transitioning, trauma recovery and mourning are happening simultaneously, and usually not in the order we would prefer. By focusing on the creation of a safe and secure environment, the foster parent is already in the process of helping the child to rebuild a shattered world by demonstrating trustworthiness and facilitating attachment. Each time foster parents weather an emotional storm by dealing with outlandish acting-out or self-destructive behavior, they are showing that they are in control, that the child is loved, and that they are not going to allow the child to be hurt or hurt them.

Each intervention communicates a message of acceptance, understanding, and emotional validation by saying in effect "You are safe, I see you, I hear you, I am here for you, and I cherish you." At a very rudimentary level, this is the original attachment paradigm in action. The child is communicating distress through voice, behavior or both, and it is incumbent on the parent to decode the message and marshal an effective response, thereby eventually creating a return to a level of calm (the attachment cycle). Whether it is in changing a diaper, providing a bottle, dealing with a raging temper tantrum, or communicating clear rules and boundaries, parenting requires the same patience, emotional calm, and steady response.

This is the beginning of establishing trust, safety and security, and it may be the first time for the child. This is made difficult because the child fundamentally believes that he is in danger, the parent cannot be trusted and the situation is going to have the same outcome as every other time. Secretly the child believes this new world is fundamentally the same (a set of learned expectations); it is dangerous, and can only be survived by trusting no one and relying only on himself. It is no wonder that so many of the conflicts early in transition are about fear and control; they are the poison fruits of broken trust. This is an example of the learned working model of the world. It also clearly illustrates one main feature of trauma: The victim compulsively recapitulates or reenacts the original trauma over and over again in a self-destructive cycle.

Again, it must be said that Special Needs children are different from other children who have experienced losses. They are different in the following ways:

- They have experienced complex trauma which has often been occurring over a long period of time.
- They have been denied access to a safe-secure-stable environment with a reliable, trustworthy adult.
- Their recovery may not take place in a predictable, reliable, consistent, familiar, environment.
- Their attributional system (working model of the world) is based on one which has proven to be unsafe, untrustworthy, and unreliable, as well as even hostile, abusive or neglectful.
- It is also an environment in which they may be continually re-exposed to the original perpetrator through birth family visits. (secondary trauma).
- They are coping with major trauma as well as grief and loss issues.

All of this being said, what are the known tasks of mourning? The basic process of grieving is well known. However, as I detail this process, it is clear that there is nothing normal about the children who have experienced profound losses, nor is there anything normal about their situation or the circumstances in which they must grieve. These children are reacting normally to very abnormal circumstances. Again, mourning is not the same for children as it is for adults, and the process we might use in normal circumstances for adults must be modified for children, particularly children of placement.

The intriguing and difficult aspects of the mourning stages lie in the implementation of any interventions employed to help a child work through the losses and the trauma. It does not happen all at once and the stages do not happen in a predictable and steady fashion. Each stage is revisited more than once and regression is the norm. Children as well as adults regress under stress. They also experience acute grief reactions (AGR) when they experience triggers like anniversaries, holidays, and other reminders.

To review, the traumatic aspects of the loss must be addressed before any mourning can take place. The reason for this, as I have stated, is that trauma triggers anxiety and remembrances of the events surrounding the loss. In order to access the memories associated with the traumatic loss, the anxiety must first be dealt with. It is most important that the child experiencing the traumatic losses has access to a professional therapist. The foster parents are simply not equipped to help navigate this difficult terrain without professional guidance and support. The reasons for this are readily apparent. Healing takes place within the confines of a therapeutic relationship. It is the centrality of this relationship, brought to the child through the medium of the therapist's warmth, empathy, concern for the child and parent, as well as the therapist's insightfulness, knowledge and skillfulness that become the agent for change. Beverly James outlines her treatment philosophy of therapeutic parenting:

> Individual child therapy by itself is inadequate for treating attachment problems. We must recognize the child's attachment needs—not to do so is irresponsible and may be dangerous. Treatment must pervade the child's total environment because the child's disturbed behaviors, emotional distress and fear that adults will not protect and care for her may not emerge during weekly therapy sessions.

> These problems cannot be sufficiently addressed within that limited period of time of the treatment session. The therapeutic milieu, be it home group facility, or hospital—provides daily ongoing care for the child and can thus be referred to as therapeutic parenting. (Pg. 58)

The therapist will help the parent establish this milieu and mode of therapeutic parenting as child and parent deal with common therapeutic themes which include: Betrayal of trust by the perpetrator of interpersonal violence in the world the child had perfect reason to believe to be safe; Constant fear of trusting others;

Self-blame for the traumatic event and resultant negative impact on self-esteem and feelings of competence; Anger resulting from helplessness directed at trauma perpetrators and possibly other adults entrusted with the child's safety (this may be expressed through oppositional or aggressive behaviors); Difficulty modulating emotions and hyper arousal or other PTSD symptoms and; Loss of hope for a better future.

Professional therapists use many therapeutic modalities. One of them is *play therapy,* in which the therapist introduces various themes, situations, and events through the medium of structured play with toys and other familiar objects. The task is to symbolically act out the drama of a particular traumatic experience. Another effective therapy is the medium of *storytelling* and *story building.* The goal is to help the child work through and understand his personal story and the events which have led to placement. By creating a coherent narrative, the gaps and questions may be addressed through expressive story telling. This defuses the powerful feelings of trauma and loss and helps the child mourn what has happened. Storytelling can also afford the parents powerful insights into the inner world of their child and help them with reconstructing the child's story through scrapbooks, pictures and other activities. This is essentially the process of helping restore the child's *Narrative* by making sense of the life history. Through these activities, the child can also learn coping skills such as relaxation, meditation, and the expression and management of powerful feelings. A discussion topic in the Adoptions Network on LinkedIn went as follows:

> Narrative therapy in adoption can be very difficult. Adoptees are often disconnected from their emotions so a narrative is going to be based on cognition. The problems in adoption are limbic or right brain centered. Therefore a narrative must access the right brain emotional memories of loss, ambiguous grief, shame, anger, isolation, etc. It must also be stated that the goal of a narrative on adoption is to bring thoughts and emotions into congruency. Attachment healing can only be accomplished through the experience of the attachment in the adoptive family not by a therapeutic intervention by a therapist. An adoptee that completes a narrative about what is known about being adopted is worthless unless he can verbalize how he feels about being adopted. Ask an adoptee what he knows and you'll get a lot of responses, but ask

him what he feels and watch the lack of a response as he struggles to identify his emotions. The difference is in one word, what do you think and what do you feel: two very different questions for an adoptee.( Robert Haefz.)

This illustrates the issues of the function of *Narrative.* As one can see, all of the above themes and issues are the most common results or features of traumatic experiences. It is well documented. The research is very clear that the establishment and continuance of a therapeutic relationship with both the child and parent or other caretakers is essential for success in addressing and resolving the above issues. As this happens, the child is more able to complete the transition into the home and move in the direction of a more coherent life narrative. One of the most concrete and supportive things the foster/adoptive parent can do is to keep accurate records, pictures, family history and basic data concerning the child's pre-placement history. This is in order to help the child know his history, understand the why of placement, and finally to make sense of his early history and reason for being with his new family. This is fundamental to a more coherent, cohesive sense of personal identity. This is commonly done by keeping a "life book." Another important factor which has been found to be effective is the establishment and provision of rituals. These establish and validate the child's history and important life events and convey the message that these events have meaning and need to be celebrated. Examples are birthdays, dates of adoption and placement, and other events such as success and achievement in school.

It is expected that in the face of traumatic life events as experienced in the ongoing ordeal of placement, most children and adolescents will develop persistent and often multiple difficulties in several important areas, including regulating emotions, attachment, self-esteem, academic functioning and the ability to maintain personal safety. As previously mentioned, such children and adolescents typically exhibit severe mood instability, irritability, difficulty maintaining important relationships (or the tendency to be drawn to other troubled individuals), poor grades and classroom decorum, truancy and difficulty following rules and destructive behavior such as substance abuse. All are part of the profile of children subjected to trauma. This large constellation of problematic issues falls under the umbrella of Complex PTSD.

It is important to understand that the greatest need, when treating these problems, is a safe, nurturing, affirming and consistent relationship that has therapeutic value. It is consistently reported that the most important factor in recovery from complex trauma and resultant losses is the quality of the recovery environment. As I have stated repeatedly, healing begins as attachment progresses, so the first steps in healing begin with the first contact with the child or adolescent and continue with every subsequent effort made to create a healing home environment. Healing occurs during transition, continues through the period following and deepens as the child and parent struggle to create a trusting relationship.

This is why, in some ways, traditional mourning models must be highly modified to fit the circumstances of children in placement. Because the primary attachment figure is the source of trauma, the replacement figure must be the source of healing in the new primary attachment relationship. This is done by creating the conditions that facilitate attachment. These conditions become the primary vehicle by which the special needs child will or will not thrive in placement. Hence, the key factors influencing success as noted by Siegel are:

> The quality of parenting after placement: parents who are emotionally and intellectually prepared and receive the necessary support and resources are more likely to be successful in their parenting of a challenging child. Carefully conducted scientific studies have shown us that it is not what happened to you that matters most in determining how you raise your children; it is how you have come to make sense of your early life experiences that is the most robust predictor of how your children will become attached to you (*Parenting from the Inside Out*. Siegel, Pg 26).

I believe that a new and comprehensive approach to mourning is needed that (1) incorporates, supports and views the foster parents as essential components of treatment; (2) builds on the child's natural capacity for healing; (3) coordinates the divergent and often fragmented services offered each child. In other words, it is a multi-disciplinary approach using a variety of therapeutic modalities that seeks to engage the child at every step of the journey. This approach must be based on understanding the issues affecting attachment in children and the dynamics of their recovery environment. This is the reason that placement should and must be attachment-based.

As transition continues and the child and parent are groping their way toward a new and trusting relationship, the child is, at the same time, accomplishing stages in mourning; relinquishing old attachments while acquiring a new and more hopeful world picture. The old world view based on its destructive and abusive behaviors must be reconstructed into new maps. The child constructs maps through a corrective emotional experience, by testing everything learned about himself and the adults around him, as well as the rules for navigating relationships. Revising the internalized thoughts and feelings of the previous world is crucial to more adaptive functioning because these assumptions are responsible for needs, emotions, and behavior as well as hopes, fantasies and wishes. This new model must be confirmed through interactions with others. After all, it is the means by which we organize and make sense of the world. The shock, numbness, stress, anger, anxiety, bewilderment, sadness, confusion, disorganization and despair- the result of a shattered world- must be systematically rebuilt. This is a gradual process which comes about by continually testing the new environment. Will it confirm my victim's perspective of a hostile and unsafe world, or will I gradually come to trust and believe that it is safe to care and engage again? Much of this can be accomplished by the surrogate parents being willing to listen, being open to questions, and being able to discuss frankly and non-judgmentally the child's questions and desire to know about his history.

As the child's view of the world is continually tested and hopefully corrected through effective parenting, the child's feelings, or lack thereof, continue to present ongoing issues. This is an opportunity to facilitate the healing process (reconciliation) through helping the child to recognize, feel, and express difficult emotions. Feelings which may have been dissociated, repressed or numb may begin to surface. They may also be masked by very strong feelings such as rage, anxiety or depression. It is the therapeutic task through either formal therapy or daily interaction with the foster parent to uncover these feelings and help the child make sense of them. Secret longings, unfelt pain, and repressed memories are often expressed in play and dreams.

It is in these play situations where old wounds often are symbolically expressed in a safe place. Confronting feelings about an abusive parent is very difficult for a child who may feel guilt for resentment and anger over abusive or neglect issues. This can be confusing and overwhelming for a child. The child may feel intense loyalty to the parent, who may have sexualized her and may come to associate sexual touch with love. Or, the child may feel that pain and abuse are the price of love and that the abuse occurred because of some imagined flaw. Much of the difficulty is posed by feelings of shame and anger (due to being humiliated and victimized) which are masked by acting-out behavior.

Children blame themselves for not being lovable. The task of the parent, which is quite difficult to navigate, is to help the child through validating the child's feelings while helping the child to feel and accept feelings, understand and verbalize the feelings and learn how to express difficult emotions appropriately. How is this accomplished?

As parents, we must be sensitive and alert to opportunities to help our children work through their feelings by noticing when they are struggling with a particular situation or are emotionally stuck. Getting to know your child's particular areas of difficulty is very important. Patterns of response give us clues. For example, does your child become sad and depressed every time you attempt to correct him? Does your child fly into a rage at the least frustration or at hearing the word "No"? Does your child easily give up and become depressed over failure? Does your child become clingy every time she is left at day care? Does your child, at times, appear to be staring or lost in a moment for long periods? Does your child fall apart with even the slightest change in routine? All of these are clues that give us information about underlying issues related to abandonment, rejection, trauma, low self-esteem and loss. Much of this behavior is due to *dysregulation* caused by sudden or abrupt changes in routine, stress or fatigue.

Reading and understanding these clues as well as finding key opportunities to sit with your child and have a conversation about feelings is a potential healing moment. It is a chance to show you care, are paying attention and are present. Even sharing your feelings is an opportunity for expressing empathy and compassion which are key components of building trust and understanding. If the emotions are directly expressed at you for something you inadvertently did, then it is important to show that you are not threatened by the display, can listen and reflect non-defensively, and most importantly, that the relationship is not in danger. These are opportunities for *regulatory repair*, to teach the child how to heal breaches in the relationship as well as how to soothe and take care of painful feelings--all things not learned in the primary home.

Remember how difficult it is, even for adults, to confront another adult when their feelings have been hurt or there is conflict. At these times it seems they are dealing with these feelings as if they were 4 years old again. When adults are having difficulty with each other it is usually because an old wound has been triggered.

With children, mourning in some ways is always incomplete. There will be many acute relapses and recurrences of sadness, anger and feeling desolate as the child develops. It is in these situations that well-meaning adults often make the mistake of encouraging the child "to just put it behind you." This is based on the mistaken belief that a child must break all ties to the past and this belief subtly denies the importance of what was lost. The child's history, story, memories and identifications can be kept alive through ritual, transitional objects, pictures and stories. This becomes the means of preserving identity through a coherent, cohesive narrative. Though birthdays, anniversaries, and other things may trigger grief, these can be opportunities; ways of memorializing and emphasizing the importance of the child's history. Just because the child's past experiences may have been harmful and separation from the primary family has occurred, this does not end the relationship for the child. The child still carries around images and memories of the previous life (implicit, unconscious memory). These images and memories are what need to be worked with and they can only be worked with if the child feels safe. Change can only take place in a safe, trustworthy, and consistently caring environment.

As the child grows older, the continual process of making sense of her world and her place in it will evolve and require the revisiting of questions about origin and why she was "adopted." In his book *Acts of Meaning*, Jerome Bruner describes "...the central process of making sense of our world as the very foundation of being human—creating and sustaining meaning." For him, this always occurs in a very human and all too fragile culturally-given context. For Bruner, what organizes and holds experience together is *narrative*. The child in foster care is taken out of one context and placed in another. This disruption of an already fragile and vulnerable life creates enormous pain. Pain, according to Bruner:

> ...obliterates our connection with the persons making up the unique cultural world and wipes out the meaning giving context that provides direction to our hopes and strivings. It narrows human consciousness to the point...man literally becomes abeast. (Bruner, Pg. 22)

As discussed, through the process of learning language in a specific attachment bond, the child constructs his world. Placement disrupts and distorts the child's story. I have worked with many adults who were adopted and many continue to have "a hole in their heart where their parents should have been." Their stories have gaps and they need a new language, a new perspective and support in creating a new story that helps to make sense of the placement trauma which changed the plot or story line of their Narrative.

Finally, integrating feelings, making sense of experience, facing our histories, forgiving those who have injured us, and understanding the meaning of our personal histories through empathy and compassion is a lifetime journey. We can assist the child in making sense of his life story by starting a *life book* from the moment they come into your home. Pictures, memorabilia, and other things related to his personal history help with feelings of uncertainty about the family of origin.

I recently had a conversation with a foster parent with whom we placed a 5-year-old boy. His mother was a drug-addicted prostitute and his father was in prison for molesting the boy's older sister. We talked about the issue of how much to tell him about his birth family and reasons for his adoption. We decided to keep the story simple and just say, "Your mother had problems and was unable to care for you and had to give you up so you could be in a happy home." As for the father, he had written the little boy letters from prison and the foster father did not want to give them to him until he was older and could be helped to deal with that issue. Both parents had major problems and learning about them as part of a child's history took a lot of careful work. In this situation, many of the issues had to do with timing and sensing when the child was ready to deal with the information.

Being able to care, experience intimacy, and commit to being a whole person is a lifelong, inward journey of discovery. Through this journey we learn to understand and love who we are and those around us. To help a child gain emotional maturity, heal her wounds, and face her history is an enormous task. It is often continually being tested by the various crises of life we all encounter. In order to live, we must learn to mourn because there are many losses along the way. Each stage of life presents us with the need to adjust, face losses, and reframe the meaning of our lives and find new purposes for living. We are very fortunate if there is a caring person and a set of arms to surround us when we meet those dark times and rough waters which threaten and challenge our very notion of who we are. Without this caring, we risk having children who, as Erik Erikson wrote: "[do] not feel valued in the first stage of their lives [and] may live out their lives in a state of perpetual mourning." I close with a favorite quote from Beverly James:

> The problem of children's severe attachment disturbances and trauma related disorders are too big and too important to be relegated to the care of the mental health community alone. We

need help from everyone. The children need to belong, and they do—to all of us. (Pg. XIII)

# It takes a village!

# Chapter 6

## KATHY

### When the Systems Work Together

I first met Kathy when she was two years old. She had been hospitalized by her father under an assumed name. She was terribly underweight and had several contusions on over her body. Her mouth was disfigured by what the doctor felt was contact with a caustic substance and her hair had been cut off. The hospital Social Worker felt the circumstances surrounding this case were suspicious, so she notified children's services. As a result of this phone call, the case was investigated and Kathy was detained. After the case was heard and a disposition was made, our agency was contacted by the Department of Children and Family Services (DCFS). One of our available foster families was contacted and arrangements were made to place Kathy with them. As is often the case, the circumstances preceding placement were somewhat complicated.

In this case, the birth mother was seeking custody. She and the father were estranged because, during her pregnancy, the mother had to be hospitalized for a major mental disorder. This particular type of disorder was treated with powerful psychotropic medications which can be harmful to the fetus. Consequently, the mother had to be taken off all of her medication until Kathy was born. Often when this occurs there is a recurrence of major symptoms. In this case the mother heard voices, had paranoid delusions and impulses to harm her child. While the mother was hospitalized, the husband sought custody of Kathy and it was during his custody that the alleged abuse and neglect began.

From the case history, it was learned that when the father brought Kathy to the hospital, he was seeking treatment for her with an assumed name based on a number of complaints. He sought treatment because she had been pulling out her hair. He reported what he thought was autistic behavior, and that she was possibly bi-polar like her mother. Because of what he described as "bizarre behavior," the father cut off her hair (ostensibly to keep her from pulling it out). Kathy was later evaluated and none of these symptoms was corroborated. Additionally, there was a record of nine contacts with children's services before the final event leading to placement.

When I made the initial home visit and saw Kathy, I was saddened by how she looked. My initial observation at that time was as follows:

> Kathy was dressed in a night dress and she was walking about with a somewhat unsteady gait. Her speech was limited to the use of two or three-word sentences. She was approached by the foster mother to give her some medication and was cooperative. The foster mother then brought her into the living room and gave her some crayons, paper and a box of Legos to play with. Kathy exhibited good motor skills in assembling the Legos. She also made scribble marks with the crayons. After she disassembled the Legos she threw them about the room. Her emotions seemed very flat and when she interacted with me, she was subdued and withdrawn. Kathy's mouth and lips were badly disfigured and discolored. Her hair was cut very short and her abdomen appeared somewhat distended. Kathy had multiple contusions, scratches, and discolorations on her face, heels, arms and abdomen (*Home visit dated 6/18/02*).

After her first visit, the County Social Worker (CSW) described Kathy as "having dead eyes, no interest in her environment, was listless and possibly suffering from medical neglect resulting in severe developmental regression. She appeared to be an emotional wreck."

It was strikingly clear what the impact of trauma, abuse, and neglect on this child had been. As mentioned in previous chapters, this is an extremely critical period in the child's development: The younger the child, the greater the vulnerability. As can be expected, when Kathy was removed, she was initially anxious and fearful in her new surroundings. She was hyper-vigilant and easily startled. As discussed in Chapter 3, when a child is in a dangerous environment the stress arousal mechanisms in the nervous system work over time. This has not only short term implications, but also will affect the nervous system's development and functioning over the long term. In Kathy's case, still other prominent features presented themselves that had to do with her ability to regulate her emotions, and deal with frustration and impulse control. Again, these are all classic features of early trauma, and needed to be addressed with a professional trauma specialist. Once the assessment was concluded, a referral was arranged as quickly as possible. Because this was, in all probability, going to be a legal case. a forensic examination was done by a court-appointed psychiatrist. The psychiatrist concluded:

> The injuries for which [Kathy] was admitted to Children's Hospital were not the result of an infectious process but rather they represented findings consistent with child physical abuse: This case involves not simply physical abuse, however, but what is referred to as Munchhausen Syndrome by proxy, or fictitious illness induced by another. There is a pattern of complaints on the part of [Kathy's] father that would support this conclusion. Emotionally, [Kathy] was somewhat fearful, though warmed up during the session. She is very bright and articulate with an excellent vocabulary and interpersonal skills. She had no evidence of abnormal movements, nor any signs or symptoms consistent with autism. (The psychiatrist's name was withheld because of confidentiality)

The psychiatrist further concluded that the father had ample time and opportunity to inflict these injuries on Kathy. As is the process, once a child is detained, a hearing is held to determine a reunification plan, if the family desires reunification. In this case, the reunification plan called for weekly monitored visits with the birth mother. The father was to have visits monitored by a CSW at the DCFS office on a once-weekly basis (this was due to the fact that he was under suspicion and being investigated for perpetrating the abuse).

My initial first-visit impression of the birth mother was that she appeared quite depressed, fearful and suspicious. Her grooming was poor and she expressed feelings of hopelessness and fear that she would never get Kathy back. For our monitored visits, the foster mother would bring Kathy to a local park where the birth mother would meet us. During these visits, I monitored the contact. The mother would interact with Kathy by taking her to the swings in the park and walking around with her. Kathy did not appear fearful or avoidant with her mother. However, after the visits the foster mother reported that Kathy was difficult to soothe, remained agitated and often took a long time to go to sleep -- typical post-visit stress responses.

There were several problems in the initial visitation with the birth father. He was manipulative and tried to get around having the visits in the DCFS office. He also tried to discover the foster parent's home address. He was also suspected of trying to follow the foster mother after the visit. The foster parents were quite worried about this and the visits were often tense. Kathy responded by being agitated and difficult to manage after these visits (it is very difficult for a child to be in the presence of her abuser because it triggers secondary trauma responses).

When we had the visits at the agency, Kathy played with a frenetic energy; she would walk about the playroom, pick a toy, play with it, become distracted, and pick another toy. By the time the visit was over, the room was in shambles and toys were strewn everywhere. The interaction between the birth mother and foster mother became a critical factor in the successful outcome of this case. The foster mother would frequently sit in on the visits and talk with the birth mother, giving her critical information on Kathy's condition and adaptation to the placement. This is quite unusual. Often the birth parent views the foster parent as a rival and threat and blames her for the removal of the child.

During my visits to the foster home, Kathy was initially quite impulsive, had frequent temper tantrums, and exhibited a very low frustration threshold. Breaking a pencil lead could trigger hysteria. She could go from engaged to enraged in one second. She was also quite demanding of attention and was emotionally volatile. As with this case, managing this kind of emotionally-driven behavior is critical to the stability of the placement.

In working with the foster parents, I concentrated on behavioral management strategies. We worked on being firm, consistent, and non-reactive to these emotional extremes. We also worked with Kathy, teaching her to relax, and soothe herself. As one can imagine, managing emotionally-driven behavior 24/7 is wearing and often one of the chief reasons placements fail. I have had all-too many conversations with emotionally drained foster parents about how hard it is to deal with a child adept at pushing all of the parents' emotional buttons. The frequent lament is "this is so much harder than I thought it would be." My response is typically that foster parenting is like regular parenting, only much harder.

In the beginning stages of placement there are many significant treatment and placement tasks to be performed which are:

- Assessment: Discovery of the initial trauma and neglect a child has experienced and the probable effects of that trauma.

- Creation of a reunification plan.

- Management of the child's behavior.

- Helping the foster parents deal with the impact of the child's issues on their family life (Kathy's foster family had two other children in the home).

- Facilitation of the child's transition from foster care through to reunification.

- Helping foster parents deal with their own grief and loss issues subsequent to placement and the possibility of replacement.

- Creation of a therapeutic environment in which a child can heal from resultant trauma and losses.

As can been seen, the tasks are complex. The process is made more daunting as the difficulty of the problem is not acknowledged and /or is exacerbated by the System's complexities. Quite often it is difficult to obtain good information about child's history, and communication is often poor between CSW and FCSW. This is the theme threaded throughout this book: The impact of a large bureaucracy, archaic procedures, overtaxed workers, inadequate resources and conflicting policies, procedures, and mandates on vulnerable traumatized children and their caretakers. Added to the mix are the complexities of the birth parents, their visits, and the resultant effects on the child which the foster parents are responsible for managing.

My role as case manager was to coordinate treatment, supervise the placement, consult with the foster family and provide a supportive relationship, monitor weekly visits, develop a relationship with the child and serve as an advocate for the child to the children's court. After placement, the first step is to develop a treatment plan. In Kathy's case, the court mandated birth family visits. Additionally, there was the necessity to address the significant issues related to Kathy's physical problems, her trauma, and transition to foster placement. After the initial forensic psychiatric evaluation, Kathy was also seen at Children's Hospital and a series of surgeries were planned to correct the disfigurement to her mouth. A referral was also made to Regional Center. This evaluation found that in a number of domains Kathy was found to be above age level: Adaptive, Gross Motor, Fine Motor and Language. The assessor concluded Kathy was "doing very well developmentally and presented with age appropriate development. She was socially engaging, gave great eye contact, answered questions put to her and engaged in creative, dramatic play. She seemed to be thriving in her present placement and had an excellent relationship with her foster mother." It was clear from the outset that the major placement issues would be related to trauma.

After the assessment and development of a reunification plan, the next step was to search for a therapist competent to treat a young child with issues of trauma and neglect. The particular therapist we found was helpful, cooperative and willing to collaborate. She formulated a treatment plan which not only included Kathy, but the foster and birth mothers as well. She saw Kathy weekly for therapy. The collaborations with the foster mother were particularly helpful because she was able to give accurate, insightful and helpful information to the therapist. For example, she observed that Kathy had difficulty bathing alone and was often frightened of the bathtub. By observing and listening carefully, she reported to the therapist that there appeared to be some connection between the trauma, the father and the bathroom. This pertinent information led to play therapy that resulted in a discovery of trauma triggers related to the father and the bathroom. By also working closely with the birth mother, the therapist was able to work toward a favorable reunification with Kathy and her mother.

Compressing a case history into a few short pages in no way does it justice. There were frequent difficulties caused by litigation between the birth parents, legal procedures filed against the birth father, the severity of Kathy's abuse, and the slowness of treatment for such extensive trauma. Through it all, the foster parents provided a consistently caring and stable environment and went out of their way to bring Kathy to the numerous family visits. Through the course of treatment she made progress and her symptoms lessened. The birth mother was also in treatment and her therapist felt she was making significant progress. The birth mother was also living with a friend, a nurse who helped provide structure and support.

After two years of visits, therapy, and continual monitoring, the case was reviewed by the Children's Court and the decision was made to reunify Kathy with her mother. A series of transitional visits were set up and Kathy began spending whole days with her mother. These visits were unmonitored, and finally Kathy had several overnight unmonitored visits. These proved successful and Kathy was returned to her mother. Even after reunification, Kathy and her mother remained in contact with the foster parents. There were birthdays celebrated, holiday contact, and occasional visits. This is very unusual and significant to the rest of the story, because after two years with her mother, things began to unravel. (We are now 4 years into this case). The foster mother kept getting reports from the nurse friend that the mother was not doing well, she was moving around a lot, was becoming less stable and having frequent relapses. The mother finally moved out from her friend's house and left the county.

Finally, after more months past, one day the foster mother got a phone call from the birth mother. She told her that she could not do this anymore; caring for Kathy was too much for her, and she could not keep her life together. "Would you be willing to take her back?" she asked. The foster mother consulted with her husband and they agreed to take her back. .It should be noted that this was very significant development, because the family had two other foster children, and the father was stretching his tolerance levels because his wife (his second wife) was the one who wanted to have children. He already had two children from a previous marriage and was finding foster parenting a little more than he had bargained for.

The end result of these events was that a phone call was made to me and I contacted DCFS. Initially there were some bureaucratic hurdles overcome, so we had a team decision meeting (TDM) to discuss this evolving story. In this meeting, all parties involved met to discuss the case and to see if we could formulate a plan that would serve the best interests of the child. The mother was present and she stated that she could no longer care for Kathy and that she was willing to relinquish custody so that Kathy could be adopted. This, of course, was a very difficult decision for the mother, but in this case she put the best interests of her child ahead of her own.

As you can imagine, leaving her mother and returning to foster care was not an easy transition for Kathy. To her, this was another failed placement symbolizing "abandonment and rejection." Kathy reacted predictably by regressing to her former level of distress. Her temper tantrums returned. She was extremely jealous of the two other children in the home, demanded a great deal of attention, and was extremely volatile emotionally. This was very taxing and stressful on the foster family. Both parents were working and had stressful jobs. It was not an easy task to work all day, and then come home to family chaos. Managing this transition again involved a team of therapists, family, and Social Workers all working together to help support both Kathy and the family. To complicate matters, the birth mother fell apart after her brave decision and tried to change her mind. At one point, she even called the child abuse hot line and reported that her child was being abused by the foster family.

When an allegation is made, there has to be an investigation. Police cars arrived on the scene, along with a county investigator. Their task was to investigate the allegations of child abuse. This caused considerable embarrassment for the foster family. The neighbors, of course, saw the police activity and gathered to watch the drama. The family thought "no good deed goes unpunished." After all they had been through they were accused of abusing Kathy! Fortunately, the charges were not substantiated. But it left its emotional scars and it resulted in the foster family breaking off all contact with the mother. After several months, adoption papers were signed and an adoption party was held. Kathy was now a permanent, legal member of this family. Fast forward two years later and the family brought Kathy to an agency picnic. She ran up to me and gave me a big hug. Today, she is doing well and has finally found some stability and security in her life.

There are many things to be learned from this case. The first is the importance of teamwork and communication. CSWs, psychiatrists, psychologists, lawyers, Children's Court, physicians, hospitals, law enforcement, and the foster family all worked together with the foster care agency. Information was shared, team meetings were held, and the foster family was diligent in taking the child to numerous family and doctor visits, supported the reunification plan and participated in the psychological treatment plan. This is noteworthy because it is not the norm. In fact, as will be seen in the following cases discussed, some or none of the above occurs, always to the detriment of the child.

Because of this high level of cooperation and teamwork, it was possible to create an environment in which Kathy could heal. The foster family was the key to providing a safe, stable, consistent and nurturing context for Kathy. They were very gracious in permitting many intrusions and demands made upon them by all of the involved professionals. In spite of very busy work schedules, the additional family demands of two other active children (one a teen age girl, also a foster child with issues) and the time required to stop everything and transport Kathy to family visits, this family persisted. I developed a very warm and long term relationship with this family through our mutual collaboration on Kathy's behalf. For their efforts, our agency awarded them the Foster Family of the year Award which they richly deserved.

As an off shoot of the foster family's cooperation and participation in the reunification plan, a supportive and friendly relationship was developed with the birth mother. Again, this is quite unusual for a variety of reasons. First is that the birth parent is often unwilling or unable to participate in the visits in a consistent manner. Because of drug abuse, mental illness, transportation problems, homelessness, lack of family support, or too many other competing needs, the birth parents frequently do not follow through with their reunification plan. Missed visits, lack of follow through, and resistance to the reunification plan create an adversarial relationship. The birth parents often see the foster parents as the enemy, as the ones who have "stolen my child." Because the foster parents often are in better financial circumstances and are able to provide clothing and other necessities, the birth parents feel threatened, angry, and guilty and are often jealous.

In one of my cases the birth parents were schizophrenic, unemployed, and inappropriate during their visits. They resented that the foster parents were affluent, employed, and provided their children with a place to live, took them on outings to Disneyland and gave them new bicycles. The birth parents deeply resented the loss of their children, hated the system, and felt helpless to prevent the removal of their children. They were losing their children and knew there was nothing they could do to prevent it. One can empathize with how devastating it is to be homeless, afflicted with a devastating mental illness and unable to maintain steady employment. The resulting loss of one's children is a painful consequence. That they resent the system and those who are caring for their children is understandable.

In other cases, the foster families see the birth parents as a threat and an unwelcome intrusion into their lives. The frequent visits, the resulting emotional impact of the visits on the children, and continual ups and downs of court rulings all play havoc on the emotional lives of foster parents. Also, it is common that the children feel divided loyalties between their foster family and family of origin. The foster parents often bear the brunt of the conflict through emotional outbursts and volatile behavior. The child's behavior often worsens after family visits.

It can be seen that the successful outcome of this case was due to everyone doing their jobs effectively by communicating and creating a climate of teamwork, a foster family willing to commit to the child persevere in spite of stress, hardship, loss of privacy, impact on their normal family life, time demands, and the creation of a relationship with the birth family that benefited the child. It was also critical to this case that everyone recognized the devastating impact of trauma and subsequent losses on Kathy and worked to create an environment in which the issues could be addressed, thereby giving Kathy an opportunity to recover. As a result, a child who started her life under very unfavorable circumstances, was severely traumatized, and faced multiple placements was able to regain some semblance of normalcy and get back on track developmentally. She now lives in a stable and loving home and will have a second chance at life. As a final note, the birth father was charged with child abuse, found guilty and was sentenced to a term in prison for his crime against Kathy.

I think there are many lessons to be learned from this case. The first is that the whole system functioned as a team and was focused on the goal of doing what was deemed best for the child. Secondly, all members of the team representing the diverse professions of social work, psychology, psychiatry, medicine, and law were included in the process. A third remarkable factor was the stalwart commitment of the foster family to deal with all the intrusions and inconveniences which serve as very real burdens and stressors on family life. The Children's Law Center listened to input from the professionals and, in my view, made the appropriate ruling not to reunite Kathy with her birth mother, which in itself is often not the case. In other words, they placed the mental health considerations of the child ahead of the "rights of the birth parents." This case illustrates how cooperation, shared information, teamwork, inclusion, and devotion to the welfare of the child created an outcome which placed a child in a family permanently, and thus gave her a future which will ultimately be under her control.

# Chapter 7

## THE SMITH FAMILY

### A System in Disarray

The Smith family first came to the agency as a referral from DCFS. They wanted to place six children (between the ages of 3 and 13), all siblings, with our agency. We were able to place three children in one home and three in another. I was the case manager on the four youngest children- a boy, age 3, a girl, age 6, another boy, age 8 and their 9-year-old sister who was placed in another of our foster homes. The other two older siblings were placed in the same home but were seen by another Social Worker from our agency. The placement was required due to 37 allegations of abuse, ranging from physical abuse with the 3-year-old boy to sexual abuse of two of the older girls. Domestic violence was included in this complaint as well.

This story is memorable because it started on my first day on the job, and it was so overwhelmingly stressful that after it was over I wondered what I had gotten myself into and thought seriously about quitting. The adventure began after I located the two foster homes in South Los Angeles and picked up the four children. After I picked them up, I had to take them back to the Agency for a monitored visit with their parents. The route took me right through the middle of town at rush hour down the Harbor Freeway in Los Angeles at 6:00 p.m.

The freeway was its usual mess of commuters struggling to get home at a snail's pace of two miles per hour. Suddenly, an apple whizzed by my ear and splattered against the windshield. It was accompanied by a piercing scream. Pandemonium broke out. There was chaos in the back seat, and the children were totally out of control. Michael, age 3, was trying to get out of his car seat, his

6-year-old sister was hitting him, his 7-year-old brother was yelling at him to stop, and his 9-year-old sister was sitting mutely in the front seat. I was trying to drive, pay attention to traffic, restrain Michael and restore order, while dealing with my own jumbled emotional reactions.

This whole trip was required because in the initial phase of the case, a reunification plan was ordered in which the court required monitored visits. The visits were to be monitored by the CSW or by the Agency Social Worker (FCSW). Each week my responsibility was to pick up and transport the four children from the foster homes to the agency for a two hour monitored visit with their parents. Getting them to the agency was a major ordeal because the children exhibited all of the typical symptoms of abuse: poor impulse control, emotional volatility, rage, anxiety, depression, and physical aggression. These symptoms were exacerbated by the anticipation of seeing their parents. They were experiencing a complex mixture of fear, confusion, shame, hurt and anger, all boiling to the surface due to the impending visit.

When we arrived, the children greeted their parents with a mixture of glee, fear, guilt, and apprehension. The visits took place in the playroom of our agency. During the visit the father mutely sat like a statue, allowing the children to climb on him. The children all frenetically vied for their mother's attention, but when she could not give each one the attention they craved, she would lose patience and shriek at them to calm down and stop fighting. Thus the visit went. It was a reenactment and perpetuation of all the problems which led to their removal; intense, emotionally-charged, loud, frenzied, and chaotic attention-seeking behavior from busy, active, emotionally-needy children wanting attention from their parents. As the parents were unable to deal with their children's many needs or cooperate and support each other, they functioned independently, unable to respond with appropriate parenting skills. As I became more experienced, I realized that this dysfunctional visit was indicative of the typical parenting style in a household symptomatic of both domestic violence and generally inadequate parenting skills.

This situation is by no means unusual. It is replicated every day across the nation as parents struggle with their own issues while trying to parent. Most parents do an adequate job while others fail. These failures often come to the attention of a variety of social service agencies.

This case happened to be my first one with the agency. Interestingly enough, it has stood out as one of the most frustrating, difficult and complex cases in my ten years of working with abused children. It serves as an enduring example of what happens when traumatized children enter a system that often breaks down. This system dysfunction is due to a number of reasons. As previously mentioned, there is little communication between DCFS and other agencies. Good case histories on the children being placed are not easily obtained and, in addition, information sharing between all agencies has historically been problematic. In addition, because of the size and geography of the territories, and with so many agencies involved, it is difficult to figure out where things go wrong; it is even harder to figure out solutions and get agreements between the various agencies (What was needed with my first case was a unified and coordinated treatment plan). Furthermore, there are competing agendas among the agencies. The County is vested in family preservation, foster family agencies serve as advocates for the child, and the courts lean toward preserving the rights of the families, often to the detriment of the children.

Finally, it all comes down to the competence of the department personnel and the DCFS Social Worker's management of the case. In the Smith case, there were several workers involved over the life of the case. This also made cooperation and communication difficult. As with this case, it is also common for new Social Workers to be appointed to the case, the FCSW is not notified, but finds out about it weeks later. This is one of many reasons for cases getting off track.

Many times, it is because the CSW does not follow through with paper work. Other times it appears that the CSW is young and inexperienced. Most commonly, the CSW is totally overwhelmed by the sheer number of cases that require attention, resulting in the child getting lost in the system. In this case it was evident that the CSW was implementing department policy (family reunification), an agenda that often does not serve the children well, leading to catastrophic results. This will be examined in due course. Finally, there are CSWs with varying degrees of competence, motivation and interest in the children.

With the Smith family, all of the above reasons presented a daunting problem. The sheer number of agencies working with various pieces of the puzzle was a huge issue: DCFS, Family Preservation, FFAs, the Children's Law Center, and the Children's Institute (a mental health facility which provides therapists to children). There was also an agency serving as an advocate for preserving African-American Families.

In discussing this case, the following points will illustrate the problem that displaced children have when entering the system. The *first* is the effect of pre-placement abuse. Each child is removed for cause. The nature of the abuse, the identity of the perpetrator, the severity of abuse, and the duration and complexity of the abuse are all determining factors in assessing the possible long term effects on the children, their response to removal and eventual recovery. The *second* factor is the removal and placement process which in itself is traumatizing. As previously mentioned, removal from one's home and neighborhood, and placement in the home of strangers would be difficult for any adult and is even more problematic for a child, particularly one who is suffering from the relational trauma of abuse by caretakers.

A *third* major complicating factor is the birth parent visit. Keep in mind that when a child is traumatized, to continually re-expose that child to the abuser is to create an ongoing state of secondary trauma. Secondary trauma occurs when traumatizing circumstances continue after the original traumatizing event (This is the 'benefit reward' question regarding birth family visits). This is a very difficult issue for the children and those who work with them, because the court has an obligation to "protect the children" and, at the same time, "work toward family preservation" if at all possible. I have had to write many reports carefully documenting how the visits were going and offer the opinion that "it appears in my judgment that the visits are 'detrimental' to the child and therefore they should be stopped." In this Smith case, the reports were apparently ignored. As discovered later, the CSW did not give the information to CLC.

A *fourth* factor in case management is the children's behavior while in the foster home. The transition into foster care is always difficult, and, as mentioned, the pre-placement factors are central to the success/failure of the transition. The final major factor with displaced children is the number of previous placements. Obviously, the greater the number of placements, the greater the degree of traumatic impact on the child; each placement increases the difficulty in procuring a stable placement. It is not unusual for children to be in several placements in their career as foster children.

As can be seen, there are many reasons for placements to go awry. The critical variable is how well all of the parts of the system work together. It is most effective when the system works as a collaborative team with the best interests of the child at heart. In the case of the Smith children, this did not happen.

Another critical variable of successful placement is the experience and parenting skills of the foster parents with whom the children are placed. The first step to be taken in a new placement is helping the children and foster parents through the transition period. This is the most critical phase because it sets the tone for the well being of the children. Remember, these children have been terribly abused and their behavior reflects the level of abuse to which they have been subjected. Most foster parents have no idea what they are in for. They are naïve and well-intentioned, and most "just want to give a child a good home." In the first few weeks a great deal of time is spent talking about the adjustment problems they are having. In this case, the youngest child, Mikey, had no impulse control. He had to be monitored closely for fear that he would run away, dart into the street, pick up a rock and throw it, or drop onto the ground with a screaming fit of rage (He was the one who whizzed the apple core by my ear). My first lesson learned was, while in a car, do not give objects to children that can be thrown. (This was not taught in graduate school).

In one memorable visit with his parents, Mikey walked into the play room, started picking up chairs, toys and anything else at hand and began throwing them. I had to restrain him until he calmed down. His older sister had other problems. She would destroy anything that was given to her, and the oldest sibling in the home, a boy, would stand in the hallway at night and scream, "I want to go home!" This behavior eventuated in his emergency removal by request of the foster mother, because he was totally out of control. On New Year's Day, he was placed in another home where he was the only child and the foster parents could give him more attention.

Imagine how disruptive all of these behavior problems can be to your nice, cozy routines. In addition to these problems, the children would complain to the CSW that the foster parents were abusing them. Of course, each complaint needed to be investigated, to the embarrassment and stress of the foster parents.

As with this placement, other troubling behavior issues may surface. It is also not uncommon for children to soil themselves or play with and smear their feces. Eating disorders and compulsive sexual behaviors are typical for children who have been severely abused as well. In this case, the foster mother observed the youngest girl, Angie, rubbing her genital area frequently. The foster mother took her to a pediatrician who found evidence of old sexual abuse. The doctor informed the foster mother that the child did not have an infection, but rather was compulsively masturbating. This required a whole new course of interventions, including reporting the abuse to the CSW and requiring court ordered therapy for Angie to deal with issues related to sexual abuse. The foster mother was quite embarrassed when we discussed how to handle a young girl who had been sexualized at an early age.

In this case, I worked constantly with the foster parents to address all of these issues. They were amazingly caring and worked tirelessly to be consistent in dealing with the multiple problems presented by these deeply wounded children. They found a special school for Mikey because, as a 3-year-old, he was functioning at a developmental level of one year. Angie was put in a special treatment program for girls who have been victims of incest.

This case unfolded over a period of four years, where the normal time for disposition is approximately 18 months. The case went through many stages and crises. It was because of these various crises that it took four years to achieve resolution. In this particular case, the children were adopted or placed in long-term foster care. Also during this 4-year period, the birth mother became pregnant three more times and gave birth to infants immediately placed with the system. It is customary that, when a birth mother already has children in the system, any new children are immediately placed. Some birth mothers have as many as 13 children in the system. These statistics raise a multitude of issues, of course. The most obvious is the issue of dysfunctional, often mentally ill and drug-addicted women continuing to bring children into the world when they have already demonstrated an incapacity for caring for them. There is an old adage bandied about in the profession: in order to operate a motor vehicle we require a license, but none is needed to have a child. A license is taken away if the operator is deemed irresponsible or dangerous to society. No penalties are invoked for having children and overburdening a social system, not to mention scarring children for life.

It would take too long to adequately document every stage in this case. Suffice it to say that the monitored visits were not without mishap. In one memorable moment, chaos reigned as the birth mother lost emotional control and threatened to abandon the children if they didn't start "listening and behaving." When the children failed to comply, she got up and walked out of the room. The children panicked and ran down the halls of the agency to try and stop her from leaving. It took several Social Workers to intercede and calm everyone down. At other times the visits were characterized by the birth father not showing up, or the parents scheduling a visit and not showing up. In spite of all this chaos and lack of consistency, the court ordered the visits to move to unmonitored status (over my strongly-worded letters of objection).

After the unmonitored visits began, I wrote the department to notify them of several factors which were becoming problematic. In writing the report, I commented on the status of the unmonitored visits and how they were affecting the children. I concluded by stating that the visits with their parents would serve as potential threats to their emotional and physical well-being. This conclusion was based on information gathered from personal observation, reports from foster parents, the children's therapists and interviews with the children themselves. After reviewing our notes and compiling information from consultations with the foster parents, therapists, and children, we all concluded that the granting of *unmonitored visit* status was premature and would have serious negative effects on the children. With regard to Angie, the following factors not present during monitored visits began appearing immediately following the granting of unmonitored visits:

- Angie complained to her foster mother and her therapist of auditory hallucinations instructing her to kill her siblings

- She also began experiencing nightmares which had not been in evidence for some months.

- Once the unmonitored visits began, Angie started tearing up her clothes, became assaultive with her foster sister, and also began destroying toys.

- She appeared more subdued and withdrawn in her moods.

- Her school work was also affected by inattention and wandering about the classroom.

- Her classroom teacher sent home a memo to the foster parent indicating that Angie had been defiant, saying "I told her to sit on a bench for not paying attention in the class and she refused."

- Angie's therapist indicated that her regressive behavior had become so pronounced that she wanted to return to a twice-weekly schedule of therapy. In discussing this with Angie, she acknowledged that she had been in trouble at school, saying "My teacher is mad at me because I have been bad all the time at school."

In a phone conversation with Angie's therapist, she reported that she had been seeing her once per week, and in these sessions found evidence of more troublesome behavior. There is an "exacerbation of old symptoms. She is destroying property, delaying going to school, having trouble focusing in the class room, and being aggressive with her foster siblings." The therapist also reported that Angie appeared to be troubled by the visits with mother in which she was "accompanied by a male friend. Angie is having trouble accepting the divorce and feels threatened by the appearance of this new man in her mother's life."

Furthermore, the therapist stated that she had to file a report of suspected child abuse on 9/18/02 when, after a session with Angie, she divulged that her parents "would put on gloves and examine her 'privates,' and were attempting to put bread in her 'privates.'" These incidents allegedly happened when Angie was four years old. The therapist stated that Angie had been divulging more information since they had been going through the book, "Secrets." This is a book which teaches children about "good touch and bad touch." Angie divulged in therapy that her parents had to check her privates for needles because she might have gotten one by lying on the floor without panties. Clearly, there is a direct connection between the unmonitored contact with her parents and the precipitous regressive behavior by the children.

Another example was when Michael became more difficult to manage at home and in therapy. One incident in particular reflected this regressive trend. On the way home from school, the foster parent had to stop the car three different times to prevent Michael from climbing out of his car seat. She said, "He was screaming and uncontrollable." This behavior largely had been improving until the unmonitored visits began. The therapist reported that Michael had been having tantrums during his sessions and was impossible to soothe. She had to interrupt the sessions and return him to the foster mother.

Reports from the foster mother also corroborated this trend of regressive behavior. The foster mother stated that the birth mother arrived very poorly dressed and unkempt. According to the foster mother, the birth mother said she was doing very well and that she was looking for a multi-bedroom apartment to house the children in anticipation of reunification.

It was evident to me after reviewing all of the information gathered from foster parents, therapists, children, and my own observations, that the unmonitored visits had clearly become problematic and were causing the children to exhibit serious regressive behaviors.

When I submitted my reports, I later found out that the CSW had not passed them on to the court. We also discovered that several other supplementary reports had not been provided to the court. One report in particular specifically detailed inappropriate behavior on the part of the birth parents and the effect it had on their children. A sample of the kind of information contained in the report, along with the concerns of myself, therapists, and others who were working with the children is as follows: As a foster care Social Worker for the Smith children, I was asked to provide supplementary information regarding the status of the children since the father was granted unmonitored visit status on August 22, 2002. The nature of the request stemmed from concerns that unmonitored contact with the parent was a potential threat to their emotional and physical well-being. After reviewing my notes and compiling information from consultations with the foster parents, therapists, and children, I offered this information with the hope that it would be taken into account when reunification plans were being considered.

In my report I documented a specific unmonitored visit with the father. In this visit, the birth mother appeared at the father's residence. The father became upset and told her to leave. A loud argument ensued in which the father reputedly told the children that their mother didn't love them anymore. Apparently the mother wanted to take the children to the store and the father refused. Angie came back to the foster residence and appeared to have been crying. Michael was returned to the foster residence looking "like he had been rolling in dirt with the dogs." The children were seemingly afraid of: 1) the father's anger, 2) the recurrence of the domestic anger and violence between mom and dad, and 3) the father's lack of control over the situation. The birth father called me to tell me that "whatever I had heard was not true." He denied that anything had happened by saying, "The mother came and left and that's all." I encouraged him to call the CSW to inform her of the incident.

In a conversation with the children's therapist I learned that the children were expressing concern and fear regarding reunification. In fact, two of the children expressed a desire to remain in their foster placements. A letter received from the therapists for Michael and Angie stated "We do not support reunification at this time and recommend that both Angie and Michael reside in their current placement."

All of these incidents seemed clear to us. They represented a pattern of continued parental behavior which reflected gross negligence and an inability to consistently and effectively parent their children. Mr. Smith was erratic in the conduct of his personal life, neglectful of their personal hygiene, safety, and nutrition, and had not acknowledged his responsibility for the children being in placement and was not consistent in setting boundaries and providing structure. There were also questions of appropriate judgment and implementation of safety needs. Over the previous several months our concerns regarding the plans for reunification seemed to be ignored.

Again, it seemed clear to us that the overall pattern of this parental behavior was having serious detrimental effects on the children: clear patterns of regression, exacerbation of their presenting symptoms and general emotional distress. Foster parents, therapists, and foster care Social Workers all had come forward to say that the unmonitored visits were seriously affecting the well-being of these children and we all expressed grave concerns about the forthcoming reunification plan. We collectively registered a dissenting opinion about the suitability of the reunification plans.

This case clearly illustrates the numerous problems that frequently occur in managing the care of children placed in the social services system. The problems largely stem from failure to communicate important information between agencies. In this case, I did a thorough job of reporting my concerns. However, the reports were not heeded, lack of cooperation between agencies was present, critical information regarding the safety, physical and emotional wellbeing of the children was ignored and the consequence of the family reunification philosophy being pursued was detrimental to the children.

One further incident occurred, which further illustrates another critical factor. It appears that there is a wide variance in the level of training and knowledge related to the psychological status of children in the system. The incident occurred at a team decision meeting (TDM). In attendance were Social Workers, therapists, members of Family Preservation, supervisors and myself. The goal was to share information and review the progress and goals of the case. The issue of parental visits came up and the CSW in charge of the case was making a strong appeal for reunification. Finally, emotionally upset and frustrated, I blurted out. "I can't believe you are continuing to push for reunification. It is well documented by the children's therapists that the father has sexually molested them. The mother physically abused them, has endangered their safety and health by hanging out with known felons, has been arrested for prostitution, has brought more children into the system, and the children continue to regress after the visits." The Social Worker replied. "I just feel that the father has such a passion for his children, he should be given another chance." I said, "Of course he has a passion for them. He has been molesting them."

As a consequence of this meeting, the therapists and I asked for a meeting with the Minor's Lawyer representing the children. She informed us that she had no idea that all of this was going on and immediately informed the court that parental visits should be terminated because they were detrimental to the welfare of the children. Apparently the CSW had not forwarded our reports to the Children's Court. Once this information had been shared, the case progressed. The children were left in their foster families and were eventually adopted and the father was charged for sexually abusing his daughters. Unfortunately, this particular case is not an isolated one. It clearly illustrates ongoing problems in the system, a system in which countless children suffer because the policy of reunification takes precedence over their welfare.

The problems are numerous and well documented. Poor communication, lack of inter-agency cooperation, strategies and policies which do not have the child's best interest at heart, indifferent and poorly-trained professionals, system overload and lack of resources for supporting and training foster parents all lead to children being abused by the system assigned to protect them. In the Smith family case, due to Social Worker malfeasance, the original parental abuse was allowed to continue via unmonitored visits. These problems lead to multiple placements, continued uncertainty and anxiety for the children, and a protracted period of being in limbo. It goes without saying that they also contributed to the considerable distress experienced by the foster parents and the professionals who went through the ordeal with them.

It cannot be stated strongly enough that every time the system malfunctions, children suffer. It is trauma compounded by further trauma. The suffering is not confined to a short duration until the case achieves permanency. Rather, it continues for a person's whole life and in all probability will be passed on down to another generation.

As a final footnote to this case, at the age of 13, Mikey was still in foster care and had been removed from his original foster home because of allegations of abuse. The last I heard he was pleading to return to that original home. Ten years in the system, multiple placements, severe trauma and instability and he still had no permanent home. Though technically resolved, the effects of this case will continue to linger on in the lives of the children who endured years of abuse by their family and the system mandated to protect them from such abuse.

# Chapter 8

## MARIA AND LAURA

### Limbo

Children enter the system for a variety of reasons: neglect, abuse, domestic violence, and sexual abuse. Most of these children are involuntarily detained by court order. Occasionally, however, a parent will make contact with a Social Worker and request a voluntary placement, often because she is already receiving services. In the case of Maria and Laura, it was because their mother realized she was unable to provide adequate care. It qualified as a voluntary placement because, at that time, the mother was seriously considering placing them for adoption, feeling that this was in their best interest. This case illustrates the full range of preexisting problems children bring with them when entering the system. At the time of placement, they came with problems caused by their birth mother and then suffered the effects of family disruption and placement. If this was not enough, they were then subjected to the after-effects of ongoing placement. We have seen how all of these factors significantly and adversely affect the lives of young, very vulnerable children.

Examining this case will allow readers to understand how the above-mentioned factors can be exacerbated when one member of the team fails to do her job, a failure with major consequences for the rest of the team, and one which had significant consequences for the wellbeing of the children and those who became involved with them as caretakers. This is the cascading effect of dysfunction within the system.

The case began in 2008 when two Hispanic girls were removed from the custody of their mother who, at the time, was an unmarried 16-year old girl pregnant with her third child (since this placement, she has given birth to that child and is pregnant with her fourth. This phenomenon of serial children from underage mothers is not uncommon). It was later discovered that she also had a 7-year history of drug abuse.

Initially, the children were placed in foster care under a *Voluntary Reunification Agreement,* and since then have not returned to the care of their mother. Our agency was approached and found a suitable home for them, certified for both foster care and adoption and known as concurrent placement. When placed, Maria was 3 years old, while her sister Laura was 2 years of age. Also at the time of placement, they were both malnourished, had few clothes, and appeared subdued and withdrawn. It was later determined that they were suffering from Reactive Attachment Disorder, neglect, and had significant speech delays. After mandatory physical exams, it was also discovered that Maria had hearing loss in one ear due to an untreated infection.

During my first visit, one of the foster parents described the girls as "quiet and withdrawn. They appeared frightened and did not communicate well," and it was reported that "they stayed by the front door for hours, frightened, and looking as if they were expecting to leave." Gradually they began to transition into the home. It was found that Maria suffered from severe dental problems, an abscess in her two front teeth and sinus and ear infections that compromised hearing in her left ear. She needed almost an entire dental reconstruction due to damage incurred by leaving her alone with a bottle of milk in her mouth, ( this caused her teeth to rot).

I chose to discuss this case because, first of all, I was the Social Worker assigned to it, and secondly, it illustrates the myriad of problems children encounter when entering the system. Lastly, it demonstrates how system malfunction can exacerbate health, developmental and learning problems of the children involved. Though this case was a voluntary placement, it soon became complicated by several factors primarily related to the mother's erratic behavior.

The first was that, during the first few months of placement, the birth mother began missing visits. She explained that her behavior was due to having to be on bed rest. She later admitted that she was never put on bed rest by her doctor. Following this, she blamed her missed visits on the foster parents not returning her calls. The birth mother would often schedule a visit at a local park and not show up or, when she did show up, would be late or have someone with her who was not cleared to visit. She would also call at the last minute to request a spontaneous visit. She appeared to have little regard for the schedules of the foster parents, or she did not understand that they could not rearrange their time to run to a visit. During the visits, she would talk to the foster parents about adopting her girls and expressed a desire to give them a good home. At times, she also appeared to be under the influence of an unknown substance. This behavior was distressing to the girls as well as the foster parents and presented many challenges to maintaining a stable placement.

To add to the numerous complications in this story, the mother delivered a baby boy in 2009. This baby was detained and also placed in foster care due to the mother's lack of compliance with court orders and unstable home situation. Other family members were evaluated for possible placement, but none were found to be suitable.

To further complicate matters, an unexpected development took place that necessitated the girls placement in another home. After eight months in placement, and after having the girls assessed for developmental problems, the foster parents notified the agency that they were considering changing their minds about adoption. Their stated reason was that it appeared that Maria's learning and language problems might possibly require "several years of special programs and services," and they did not feel prepared to deal with these issues or make the necessary commitment to see the placement through to completion. Additionally, one of the foster parent's fathers had died. As a result, they were emotionally drained and caring for the two children's needs was too overwhelming. They requested removal and both girls were placed in their second foster home in February of 2009.

All factors that affect placement and the necessity to move the children to a new home require preparation, planning and cooperation between agencies and Social Workers. When the County Social Worker does not communicate or help in the planning and placement or is not performing her duties, it has a deleterious effect on the well being of the children, as will be seen in the following discussion.

The first process of note is the County Social Worker's requirement to authorize and arrange for services rendered to the children. Referrals must be made to the Regional Center responsible for assessing and determining the need for services and then providing remedial services based upon the determination of the problems. Children in the system have a wide range of special needs running the gamut from learning disorders to psychological and physical health problems. The sooner the determination of need, the quicker the services can be delivered. Communication and cooperation between agencies is essential.

The second crucial element is the children's transition into the placement home. There are many factors affecting this process. As I have noted in previous chapters, pre-existing problems have a significant bearing on the type and degree of adjustment problems the child will have in successfully adapting to a new home.

A major factor that affects the stability of placement is the birth family visitation plan. In most cases, the County Social Worker regularly works with the birth family and often has frequent contact with them. It is incumbent upon the CSW to communicate with both the birth parent and the Foster Care Social Worker to facilitate a regular visitation schedule. When the birth mother behaves in an inconsistent and bizarre manner, it needs to be dealt with by the CSW and coordinated with the FFA Worker in order to support and assist the foster family. When this does not happen, things quickly become complicated. Because needed services were not arranged for Maria and Laura, the caregivers had, with the assistance of the FFA worker, to find and arrange for speech therapy and dental care for Maria.

The problems in this case were compounded after the children were moved to the second foster home. While in this home, the caregivers found services for Maria by themselves and worked diligently with her. Unfortunately, as she was beginning to make progress, she and her sister were abruptly moved to another home (their third placement). The circumstances of the decision to move them again are not clear. What is clear is that after five months of not visiting the children in the new home, the CSW called one afternoon and announced that she would be picking the girls up the next morning and moving them to another foster home. This was a clear violation of accepted protocol, which set in motion a chain of events with serious consequences for the well-being of the girls who were thriving in the home. We were aware of nothing that would make the CSW act in this manner.

The CSW gave various reasons for her actions, none of which appeared to be well-founded. For example, one reason given was that the birth mom had requested the removal. However when we talked with her, she professed to have not made the request and in fact felt she had a very good relationship with the current caregivers.

The caregivers were punctual when they brought the children to every visit. They talked with the birth mother and gave her information on their progress and well-being and supported her during the visits when she asked for help. Additionally, the therapist assigned to the case worked with both the children as well as the mother in attempting to assist the mother in understanding her children and being more effective as a mother. Our Adoptions supervisor was very supportive and spent many hours talking with the mother, encouraging her to go back to school, to increase her reading skills, and to talk to her attorney to get the assistance she needed from her CSW.

When the CSW called our agency to say she was moving the girls, our Adoptions supervisor requested a formal meeting. The TDM is a team meeting which includes members from the County as well as representatives from our agency. The purpose of these meetings is to get everyone on board with the treatment plan, share information and make decisions that will benefit the children. This is done in order to preserve the placement and create a needs and services plan that serves the best interest of the children. The CSW refused to have a meeting of any sort to try and work things out. We contacted her supervisor and she stated she would abide by her CSW's decision. We explained that the decision was inappropriate and was based on inaccurate information. Several explanations for the decision to move the children were based on false accusations. One was that the birth mother was not allowed to attend doctor visits with her children. This was false. She was invited on several occasions and attended several visits. As an addendum to the whole fiasco, the foster parents informed me that the CSW called the day before at 4:00 pm to inform them that the girls were to be picked up. (removed) She did not give any reason for this. Additionally, the children's attorney refused to work on a request to Children's Law Center: in order to stop the proceedings before the children were taken. She refused to hear their side of the story and sided with the CSW, even though what the CSW was doing was unethical. It was discovered later that the CSW had falsified the documents and the CLC (Children's Law Center): deferred to what the CSW had written. The foster family felt that it was significant that these details be made known in order to illustrate the dysfunctional nature of the system and the unacceptable treatment they received..

Another reason given for the move was that the CSW wanted the children to be in a home more convenient to the birth mother. In contrast to the given reason, the caregivers were providing the transportation, and the move to a new foster home was actually farther away. Finally, the CSW stated that the attorneys were sending her e mails about the case and that the mother needed services and needed our agency to back her up and that we had not been doing that. The opposite of this was true. Our agency had arranged for all the services and had been highly supportive of the mother. The children were also moved into another foster home not certified for concurrent care. This was against the policy that states that all children under three years of age must be in a home capable of providing adoption planning.

Finally, it should be noted that the CSW interfered with and prevented the children's therapist from continuing her relationship with the girls. This had been one of the most important and stable relationships the girls had during all of the instability. So, in one week, the children lost their foster parents with whom they had an excellent, warm, stable relationship, their foster care Social Worker, their school, and their therapist's precipitous action taken by the CSW to serve some unknown agenda.

The saddest thing about all of this is that none of this had to happen because the decision was made by someone who had minimal contact with the children and the family. It appeared to happen because one individual felt threatened and needed to exercise control over a case she had so clearly mismanaged. The final example of her incompetence was that on the day she came to take the children to the new home, she arrived with no car seats. This is a California State law. When she took them down to her car she had to wait for someone from her office to bring her car seats. This was indicative of how she handled the whole case.

As a final note, we tried going up the chain of command in the regional office by leaving numerous messages with the ARA, as well as leaving him a fax. but he never responded to any of our attempts to reach him. This is a clear example of how one individual charged with protecting children in her care risked their emotional health and ended up hurting the two girls even more in order to exercise control over a case she mishandled: all of this, of course, seriously affecting the mental and emotional well being of the girls.

When the relationship between agencies becomes dysfunctional and the dispute has to be litigated, charges are made and counter-charges are offered. Allegations of abuse are made, the police are called, investigations are conducted, lawyers go to court, reports are written, time is wasted, and rulings are made. All the while, the children languish-- out of control in their lives with no say in what happens to them. They suffer, get moved about, and each time a placement is disrupted, this adds to the accumulation of trauma. The necessary, normal attachment process is disrupted, with the children not knowing who to trust and growing increasingly anxious. If unresolved, the situation becomes chronically insecure with no one providing a secure base. With Maria and Laura, this condition continued for 18 months and then took a surprising turn. The birth mother called the former foster parents with whom she had remained in contact and asked them if they would like to adopt her children. "Of course," the foster parents replied. Arrangements were made and the two girls were returned to the foster parents, but not before an acrimonious TDM in which the Adoptions Social Worker and the County Social Worker had a dispute over returning the children to the previous foster home. This was totally unexpected.

All of the above problems were accelerated exponentially by the County Social Worker's mismanagement of the case. After five months in their new home, a series of events occurred, including sudden removal from this home. As a result, a litany of problems led to the agency filing a complaint charging:

- The CSW was totally unavailable.

- Did not visit the children.

- Did not return phone calls.

- Her voicemail was always full, making it impossible to leave messages.

- She did not respond to faxes advising her of problems with the birth mother visits.

- She did not make home visits as required by law.

- During the 5 months that the girls were in the third home, she did not visit the new home once.

- She did not assist in getting speech therapy services for Maria. When Maria came into placement she made very few sounds which were understandable. It was found that Maria was not hearing impaired as originally thought. It was the new foster parents who found a speech therapy program and worked with her tirelessly at home.

- The CSW was so unresponsive that her supervisor had to be called and frequently asked to relay messages, which were apparently either ignored or not delivered.

- The CSW moved the children to another home without adequate notification and preparation of the children for the transition.

- She promised the children they would continue to see their therapist after they moved and then did not allow the therapist to continue with treatment, even though there was a court order for mental health services.

- She told the children they would have a visit with their former foster parents and she never arranged that.

- She told the children's attorney false information about the need to change therapists.

- She failed to obtain a Regional Center referral for 15 months.

- She failed to address Maria's severe speech problems.

- Later, as the case progressed several other charges were added:

- The CSW used the birth mother to relay messages to FCSW and Caretakers.

- The CSW failed to limit the birth mother's visits and allowed unmonitored visits in spite of court orders to the contrary.

- She continued to allow the birth mother to have unmonitored visits despite the fact that she was using drugs and had no stable place to live.

- The boyfriend of the birth mother was allowed to provide transportation to visits despite not using car seats and not having been cleared by live scan or background check.

- The CSW granted unmonitored visits to the birth mother without verifying she was in a drug program, failed drug tests and failed to show up at other scheduled tests.

- In spite of the birth mother's relapses in drug treatment and the court order that the mother's reunifications services be terminated, the CSW liberalized the mother's visitations up to and including overnight visits.

When they were returned, the foster mother reported that the children were very thin, dirty and unkempt. They told her that the other foster mother did not feed them regularly and would not allow them to bathe. When examined by a physician, he found them to be 25% below normal weight.

According to the foster mother, the children were very happy to be back in this home that they had to come to think of as their own. The children ran to greet them and called them mom and dad. The situation was far from resolved, however. They continued to have a weekly two-hour visit with their mother, who continued to be erratic in her behavior and sporadic in attendance while the family court monitored the situation. There was an attachment assessment and it was found that they had more of an attachment to the foster parents than to their mother. There was supposed to be a hearing to terminate parental rights, but it had to be rescheduled because the proper paper work was not filed. In order for the case to be resolved, parental rights would have to be terminated. All of these factors continued to generate a climate of uncertainty which affected both caretakers and children alike. What should have taken 12-18 months under "normal" circumstances has taken four years.

In the mean time, while the clock was still running on this placement, the Department continued to push family services and continued to insist on birth mother visits. Additionally, at the last scheduled hearing, it was learned that the birth mother was filing an appeal requesting custody, stating that she had not been offered her family reunification services. The foster family had been expecting that at the next hearing, the parental rights would be terminated along with reunification services. Each time they were disappointed and the process was prolonged.

A month after the last scheduled meeting, another unexpected development occurred when the foster parents found out that the department had granted a request to allow the birth mother unmonitored visit status for 4-hour blocks. In one month, visit status went from one monitored visit to two monitored visits and eventually the new ruling of four unmonitored hours. The decision was made in spite of reports from psychologists, physicians, and a therapist attesting to the visits being traumatizing to the girls, and, in spite of the children stating that they are afraid of their mother and did not want to see her. In fact, one girl developed enuresis (an uncontrolled discharge of urine) after each visit.

The birth mother visits have been problematic for several years. As mentioned, she has been inconsistent and erratic in her visits. On several visits the crying girls had to be forcefully removed from the foster parents and told they must visit their mother. Participation in the visits was very disruptive and distressing to the girls.

Following are some excerpts from a birth mother visit that illustrate how difficult and complicated the process can be for all parties concerned: the birth mother, the county Social Worker, the foster parents, the FFA worker, and the children.

Having been delivered per the request of the county, the children arrived at the visitation site in Pasadena. They were asked if they wanted to see their mother and they both declined. Under duress, but encouraged by the foster mother, Laura agreed to a few minutes of visitation. She was taken to the visitation room and met her mother. The whole process was fraught with confused messages. Though there was a court stipulation that the girls had a right to refuse, they were strongly encouraged to visit their mother because she wanted to see them. This places the children in a terrible dependency bind, feeling guilty and conflicted, caught between attachment to their foster parents, pressure from the court, and the knowledge that their mother is waiting and wants to see them. At the time of this visit, the birth mother was upstairs in the office demanding her rights to see her girls.

One can see how difficult interactions can be between the monitoring Social Worker, the birth mother, the girls and the foster parents. All participants have different agendas and it is awkward for all parties concerned. From the birth mother's point of view, she is dealing with an entire bureaucracy that has taken her children away from her and is intruding into her relationship with them by imposing all kinds of conditions on the visit. From the FFA worker's position, he is attempting to fulfill the mandates of the court while fulfilling his job description to protect the well being of the children. He also has to deal with the foster parents and try to preserve the tenuous relationship between them and the children. From the children's perspectives, they are caught in a bewildering montage of relationships between them, their mother and their foster parents. This again had tremendous implications for their present as well as future mental health.

During a visit I monitored, the mother greeted her child and tried to engage her in conversation and play with toys at hand. Per policy, the mother was not allowed to discuss the case, nor pressure the child in any way about her feelings about the birth mother or foster parents. During the visits, observations were made about the quality of the relationships, the child's distress level, and the mother's effectiveness at being attuned to the child and her skill at establishing rapport. Generally, the more anxious the child, the greater the distance she places between her and the mother. When a child engages in solitary play while the mother is in the room, this usually indicates lack of attachment. When a mother is busy with cell phones and other objects and does not engage the child, this is evidence of lack of attunement, nurturance and attention and failure to engage with her child. All of these behaviors were noted on multiple occasions.

As with this case, even after a visit is concluded, the effects of the visit linger for several days. This is what makes birth family visits so problematic for the well-being of the children and those who care for them. The task for the foster parents is to deal with the lingering emotional consequences of the visit. It begins with welcoming them back after the visit and then transitioning into their regular routines. Transitioning is an important part of learning to cope with emotional experiences because it teaches them how to contain and regulate distressing emotions.

To summarize, a two hour birth family visit is difficult, but it seems clear that when these visits occur and are against the child's stated refusal of the visit, they are troubling to all involved. The level of distress has both long and short-term effects for all concerned. The visit clearly raises the stress level and is a potential threat. What matters is how the threat level is managed and how the children are aided in their management of potentially dysregulating emotions. The children are caught up in a vortex of emotions while embedded in the legal machinations of a system, which is designed to preserve the law, but does not necessarily protect and serve the children's emotional well being.

The children are in a difficult bind. In their status as children they are dependent on adults to protect them. The bind creates an attachment conflict. In the need to feel safe, they seek comfort, but because of the situation they experience a high level of emotional arousal. They become flooded with anxiety, need, loyalty, anger, and the fear of punishment or abandonment. These conflicts wage war within the emotionally-vulnerable child's mind. It is a conflict without resolution. Nevertheless, they employ a number of strategies to reduce their distress: compliance, dissociation, and withdrawal. They may disconnect from the mother in the session and engage in solitary play, or they may dutifully comply with mother's questions. Laura was once placed in a severe bind when the mother asked her if she loved her. What was she to say? Maria, on the other hand, chose a different route: She was given the choice of not participating in the visit and chose not to see her mother. This, of course has another set of troubling emotional consequences.

Obviously the mother is also in a very awkward situation. She is visiting her children in a situation that is very unnatural. She is being observed and has had her children removed from her because of neglect. She wants to regain her children and has to try to prove that she is capable of mothering them. To further compound the problem, this situation has gone on for several years and she has not had the opportunity to form a real attachment bond because she is only interacting with her children for a few hours per week.

In sum, the visits become a charade in which the actors were carrying out roles prescribed by the legal system that mandates visits long after there is a possibility of reunification. It places everyone in legal limbo and the children suffer as a result. They and all others involved cannot get on with their lives or try to heal because of the constant disruption and distress caused by the weekly visit. Stalling tactics by the DCFS did not serve the children well. The case had gone well beyond the legally set time limits of 6 -12 months, and the foster parents had been caught up in this Catch 22 drama as well. They love the girls and want to adopt them, but have become victims of a laboriously ineffective system that is prolonging their agony and leaving them to twist in the wind.

What should they do? If they give up, they risk further damage to the girls, and if they persist, they are seen as having an agenda or not supportive of reunification. Their lives are disrupted on a daily, weekly and monthly basis. They have also incurred a financial burden of hiring legal counsel to help them achieve the desired result of adoption. The emotional distress is considerable. They have been granted de facto parental status and, at the time of this writing, were considering pursuing legal action to stop the department from further attempts to reunify, as well as terminate parental rights so that they may pursue adoption and end a 4-year legal nightmare, a nightmare from which the girls will take years to recover. This is what happens when the legal rights of a parent take precedence over the mental health and well being of the children. As long as they are in limbo, their suffering is compounded and the possibility of having a safe, stable, and caring recovery environment is delayed.

On Friday September 7, 2012, I received a very distressing note from the foster mother. In it she informed me that at 4:45 she had received a call from the Foster Family Agency saying they received a court order stating that the girls would not be returning home-- that this was permanent. They were being reunited with their mother who was living in a shelter at the time. The 5-year ordeal was over. The foster mother noted that they did not have an opportunity to say goodbye to them. She and her husband were completely shocked and numbed by this abrupt removal. They had fought an uphill battle for five years. There was no opportunity to prepare them or the girls for this change. Usually the move is carefully planned and, for several weeks, transition visits, including overnight stays are made. The foster mother stated that she believes what the courts have done is in total disregard for the wellbeing of the girls, and "it is criminal what they have done and it is extremely damaging to the girls who also did not have a chance to say goodbye."

I was extremely disappointed to hear the outcome of this case in which I had been involved and have followed closely even after my responsibility ended. I believe that this case is *iconic* in that it exemplifies all that I have written within these pages. From the beginning it is typical: Two small girls placed after it was decided that their 16 year old single mother could no longer care for them. They were judged to be victims of severe neglect. They were malnourished and suffering from multiple developmental problems, and then they were deprived of necessary services. The next step in their journey through *Wonderland* was that they suffered multiple placements and several disruptions of the attachment bond. They were victimized by an incompetent Social Worker who failed to do her job in multiple ways. They were further victimized by the legal system, which continued to impose court ordered Reunification Services, even though the mother had been in and out of drug rehabilitation programs, had been erratic in her visits, and had given birth to more children.

These reunification visits were traumatizing to the girls, as they repeatedly stated they were frightened of their mother and did not want to see her. They were forced to continue with the visits even though they were very distressing to them and finally, the ultimate betrayal occurred: after five years of being with a stable, committed, caring, competent family and developing a strong emotional attachment to them, they were removed. This family devoted considerable time and resources to find and provide necessary services for their developmental problems and were exhibiting every effort to see that their physical and emotional needs were met. After mental health experts filed numerous reports stating that the girls had a firm attachment to them, and that it would be detrimental to their mental health to be reunified, they were removed. Add to that the repeated statements from the girls that they were afraid of their mother and did not want to see her.

Despite all of these factors, the girls were suddenly and, without any preparation, removed from a safe, stable, secure, and caring home, and were reunited with an illiterate single mother with a documented history of substance abuse who has given birth to two other children, has failed several rehabilitation efforts, has been demonstrably unstable and inconsistent in her parenting efforts, and has demonstrated poor parenting skills during the visits. Over these objections the girls were reunited with their birth mother. This is why I wrote this book. This case is clearly the most egregious example of a failed system in which these two girls with a traumatic beginning to their lives had a brief respite and glimmer of normalcy, but now have a tenuous future. Broken systems shatter lives. Parental rights trump the well being of the children they purport to serve. It is ironic that the courts, quick to remove a child in "imminent physical danger," seem to have no problem returning them to the parent who neglected them, thereby placing them in imminent danger of psychological harm. On a final note, the girls begin a new school, and their foster parents try to grieve their loss and overcome the wounds caused by their well-intentioned wish to give them a loving home. It will be some time before they heal from this devastating event and return to normal. What is so distressing is that this was not the only case where a miscarriage of justice took place. It continues to happen with tragic consequences.

# Chapter 9

*THE FAMILIES WHO CARE*
*FOR SPECIAL NEEDS CHILDREN*

As I have discussed, the process of placement is traumatizing to children. What is often overlooked, however, is that the families with whom the children are placed also experience varying degrees of trauma due to the circumstances surrounding the placement. These families experience trauma, shock, numbing, anxiety, depression, grief, vulnerability, loss of control, anger, hopelessness, and hyper-vigilance. They exist in a veritable state of suspended animation. Why? Because the minute they agree to a placement, they hand over control of their emotional lives to a large, impersonal, malfunctioning system in which their needs have no consideration, and they have little legal recourse to events that have the power to profoundly affect the stability and well-being of their lives. Their hopes, dreams, wishes, and imagined future with a child who enters their home place them in a psychological state of limbo for however long it takes for the placement to run its course. It is a case of voluntary helplessness. The perpetrator, in this case, is the system that places the children in the homes and governs the terms of the placement. Resolution can, under the best of circumstances, take as little as six months. At worst worst case, it can take several years.

Imagine sitting and waiting for a phone call telling you your wish has been granted and that a child has been found for you. Then imagine getting the child and thinking that, at last, the long search is over. Further imagine, then, being told that, per a court's order, there is a reunification plan requiring three-three hour visits per week with the birth family. From then on the nightmare continues with missed and cancelled visits, subjecting your child to the emotional trauma of being forced to have contact with the abusers resulting in a three day reaction of hyper-emotional, unstable, and out of control behavior. Compounding the situation, no one answers your phone calls, the lawyers give you little or no information, and court proceedings are delayed, postponed, and cancelled because a Social Worker did not file the appropriate paperwork. Families who have experienced this kind of treatment are extremely aware of how frustrating, confusing, disillusioning, disheartening, and disturbing it can be to their family life.

Families who bring children into their homes with the best of intentions are part of a vast system of Children's Services. It is an overburdened system tasked with the mandate to protect the most vulnerable of children. Unfortunately, as previously stated, it is frequently unable to adequately achieve its goal. Foster/adopt families are part of a broken system and, as such, unwittingly participate in the disenfranchisement of children placed in their homes; disenfranchised because the children are from broken families, are treated as second-class citizens products of mentally ill, homeless, substance abusing, impoverished parents. They are all served by a program that is underfunded. They are also disenfranchised because the role of caring for these children is not highly valued by the rest of society.

Children who have been removed from their families because of neglect, abuse, domestic violence, or abandonment need the best care that can be provided. As discussed in previous chapters, these children end up in a kind of limbo, and are often moved from foster home to foster home while the system slowly works out a permanency plan. Thus the system, whose mandate is to protect, frequently compounds the problem. In short, foster/adopt families do not play on a level playing field to begin with, and their situations are made even more difficult by the problems the children bring with them into their homes. Given this level of behavior/emotional problems, the parents are then not given adequate support or access to needed services.

Up to this point, the system and the effects of placement has on children have been reviewed. It is time to take a look at the families who provide homes for them at considerable cost to themselves. Who are these families and why on earth would they take on such a difficult task? There is a heterogeneous population of people who sign up to be caretakers to the children of the system. They have a variety of motives which compel them to open their homes and lives to children needing new homes. They come from a wide variety of backgrounds. They are young and old, single, married, gay and lesbian, and from a disparate background of education, occupation and ethnicity. The main reasons they give for wanting to be foster parents, is that they feel a burden of concern which leads them to want to help a child in need and give him/her a better life. Those who want to adopt usually do so because they are unable to have a child or because they are gay, lesbian, or single and still want to have a family. Currently the balance seems to be shifting from foster placement to adoption. Of the 81 children placed in the agency last year, 44 % were adopted. 20 % returned to their families, and 5% were emancipated from the system. The number of children returned to their homes or placed for adoption is a shift which appears due to a change in agency philosophy, a philosophy striving for greater permanence for children: Hence the number of children lingering in long term foster placement is smaller than it has been historically.

The children who come into the system are products of another failed system: the American family. The types of families they come from contribute to the disenfranchisement factor mentioned in the introduction. "The effects of poverty, HIV infection, substance abuse, single parenthood, violent and emotionally damaged parents, and homelessness, combine to produce a population of children who have often survived severe neglect and dangerous environments where drug-dealing, prostitution and violence are the norm." (Levy, pg. 153) The confluence of all of these circumstances creates a very hazardous gauntlet of detrimental experiences: domestic violence, emotional, physical, and sexual abuse and neglect, developmental and emotional delays; behavior difficulties; and disrupted attachment. Childhood is challenging enough without these additional dangers. There are numerous contributing factors to family failure in this country. Drug and alcohol use are two of the major factors. The relationship between alcohol and drug abuse and child abuse and neglect is consistent and supported by numerous studies. Approximately 70-80% of detained children come from substance-abusing families. Parental substance abuse is closely associated with various levels of child neglect, ranging from inadequate supervision, to complete failure to provide for basic needs, and abandonment.

Certainly when a newborn infant tests positive for drug exposure it is grounds detaining the infant, but the damage begins *in-utero*, as prenatal drug and alcohol exposure leads to fetal alcohol syndrome and fetal distress. It is a tremendous hazard for the developing fetus to be exposed to drugs during the first trimester of pregnancy. This leads to a variety of birth defects as well as faulty development of the central nervous system and brain. Childhood poverty, single parenthood, and homelessness also combine to produce children who are physically, socially, and psychologically impoverished. The back story, of course is, that many of their parents are mentally ill and are second and third generation citizens of the intergenerational abuse cycle.

Another startling statistic is that the children in the system are approximately 70-80% "children of color." This is because they are also most often of a lower socioeconomic background. As one speaker at a symposium I attended quipped—she was an African-American lawyer from Washington D.C.—"The children of Woody Allen do not go into the system when their parents get divorced." Needless to say, all of the above factors result in producing children who have tremendous needs and present major challenges to the parents who volunteer to take them into their homes. They must singlehandedly fill a number of critical gaps in parenting the child. It is a challenge that involves multi-tasking. While simultaneously trying to understand the discrepancy between the child's chronological age and his or her developmental abilities and emotional age, they must also deal with the child's inability to learn. The parents must understand strange and erratic behavior that is far different from what they were expecting. This adds tremendous stress as they try to maintain some semblance of family normalcy. The role of foster parenting is a dauntingly complex task which results in the parents being surprised at how overwhelming the role of foster parenting actually is.

Why do they do this? Potential foster-adopt parents do it because their children are grown and they enjoy parenting, or "we are unable to have children," or "I just want to help these needy children," or finally "I was raised in a foster home myself." In recent years, more lesbian and gay partners who wish to have families are choosing adoption as a means of having a family. They must go through the somewhat arduous process of becoming eligible to receive children in their homes. This is, of course, a controversial matter in some segments of this country. There are also those individuals who become foster parents as a "cottage industry." This trend is on the decline because of the move toward permanence. Motivation for being a surrogate parent to special needs children is very complex. Often the stated reasons are not the same as the unconscious psychological motivation. As I mentioned in a previous chapter, one individual, a gay man, actually ended his long term relationship with his partner (who did not want children) so he could adopt a child. The reasons eventually surfaced. His mother, an alcoholic, died in a car crash, and he was unconsciously trying to undo this childhood trauma by becoming a parent to traumatized children.

As is often the case, these unresolved attachment issues become activated by the interaction with attachment disordered children, and both the parent and child suffer as a result. If the expectation is that "I will make myself happy by having a child to love," then the project is doomed to failure. This motivation is also seen in single teenage moms seeking to find love. These parents soon become disappointed and very angry when the child does not appear to return their love and "fails to appreciate all the sacrifice and hardship of parenting." This illustrates the maxim that all of our old wounds are activated when we parent a child. It is even truer when parenting a foster child because they make more psychological demands on individuals and their relationships.

There are numerous and unexpected problems which surface after placement. The demands on families are severe and the problems encountered are many: psychological, as well as, legal and social. In *Handbook of Attachment Interventions*, Terry Levy has succinctly enumerated some of these difficulties:

- Prolonged delays in permanency plans.

- Unspecific requirements for parents to retain parental rights.

- Poor or no matching of the child and families.

- Faulty screening of adoptive or foster parents.

- Failure to adequately evaluate the child's needs for specific services.

- Failure to provide specialized services for children.

- Failure to discuss important information with surrogate parents.

- Failure to demand that mental health service providers have experience and training in the areas of adoption/foster care/abuse/neglect/attachment issues.

- Failure to adequately support foster and adoptive parents experiencing difficulty with the children placed with them.

I would add three more areas which in my experience have proven to be very problematic.

- Lack of legal standing of foster and adoptive families. They stand at the bottom of the totem pole when it comes to having power and legal rights.

- Birth family visitation as mandated by the courts.

- The extreme financial crises in local, state and national government. Budgets have resulted in major funding cuts to mental health services for children and other special programs. (Pg. 266)

This chapter will outline case examples that demonstrate how these factors affect the lives of the foster and adoptive families I have worked with over the past 10 years. I will do this first by looking at the ways in which the foster/adopt families are impacted psychologically by the placement of a child in their homes, and secondly by examining the effects of the legal system on the placements.

The process begins when children with well-documented problems end up in foster and adoptive homes. These homes, so necessary for the care of children whose life circumstances make it impossible for them to live with their birth parents, are inextricably linked to this traumatizing cycle. Levy put it this way: "Foster and adoptive homes who take these children in are emotionally and intellectually unprepared to deal with the extent of the child's problems. It is as if they have unwittingly imported a virus into their very own family system."

Over time, chronic and severe emotional demands associated with the numerous issues that arise in parenting children with traumatic injuries begin to take their toll on the emotional life of the parents and the family system. Remember, it is the unrecognized and untreated issues of traumatic loss which pose the greatest danger to a stable placement. When untreated problems are allowed to fester, a climate of disillusionment, frustration, tension, and hopelessness gradually begins to permeate the family atmosphere.

After a time, the families I have worked with began to reveal to me that "this is much harder than I dreamed it would be." They were commonly disillusioned, angry, demoralized, and often experienced caregiver burnout, or as one author put it, "the exhaustion of compassion." This is a condition which leaves the couple at odds with each other as they question the wisdom of their decision to take this child into their homes, "What on earth have we done?" They frequently experience a form of projected ambivalence. In other words, they begin to participate in the child's attachment ambivalence. They are severely conflicted. They want to love and parent this child, but the child's persistent refusal to be loved and the rejection of their best efforts leaves them wounded and bewildered. They rightly think, "It makes no sense that a child so desperately in need of love would be so difficult to love!"

Levy notes that it is common for parents and other family members to experience:

> Secondary traumatic stress disorder, the result of the chronic tension and stress associated with the demands of living with and caring for the child with an attachment disorder. This leads

to emotional exhaustion, the breakdown of the family system and family burnout. The psychosocial environment of the traumatized family is characterized by anger, frustration, hopelessness and despair. (Pg. 247)

It is unfortunate that the family home becomes the stage in which the tragic drama unfolds. Children with attachment difficulties spend much of their time locked in constant power struggles with a primary caregiver because the thing they desire most (emotional closeness) is also the thing they most fear. It reflects almost perfectly a reenactment of the original Traumatic Bonding Cycle--an exhausting cycle of struggle without relief. It often begins with the child becominb distressed. Angry, sad, or afraid and lacking healthy ways of soothing and expressing these emotions, delaying impulses, and asking for attention, the child attempts to connect with the parent through negative attention-seeking behaviors. These, of course, are very annoying and the parent becomes irritated and resentful, does not feel disposed toward expressing empathy or understanding and does not express warmth or affection, often responding by criticizing, which threatens the child. The child reacts by tuning the parent out or accelerating the attention-seeking behavior. This becomes a recapitulation, or reenactment, of the traumatic bonding cycle the child experienced with the family of origin. Now the new family and child are trapped in the same cycle, a cycle characteristic of individuals suffering from early childhood trauma: *reenactment of the early trauma over and over.*

One family I worked with serves as an excellent illustration of the reenactment problem. The family unit was an African-American single mother with whom we placed a sibling set, two African-American brothers ages 12 and 10. The older brother was placed first, followed by the younger brother who had been residing in a group home was placed later. They had the typical profile of children in the system: a single drug-addicted / homeless mother, and an unknown father. The foster mother, who had two adult sons still living in the home, chose to foster parent because her mother had been doing it for years.

The boys were in the home for six years. The older boy was an average student, but an exceptional athlete, and participated in all the high school's sports programs. He was outgoing and gregarious, seemed to get along well with others and presented few management problems to the foster mother. She described him as a good son who became easily integrated into her home. This foster mother had a very busy life. She worked, trying to improve her career by taking classes on the weekends and evenings. She had successfully raised three other natural children. Two older sons were still living at home. They were an active family and attended church regularly.

Elaine, the foster mom was continually on the edge of total exhaustion because of her busy schedule and the demands of work. What was pushing her over the edge was the behavior of the 14-year-old. He presented multiple problems, having been diagnosed with Bi-polar Disorder, Oppositional Character Disorder and Attention Deficit Disorder. In her words, this translated to:

> He is rude, obscene, uncooperative, defiant, kept getting suspended from school, ran away frequently, had very poor impulse control, stole from his brother, and broke things in the home. When I made as the foster care worker, my regular visits to the home, he related in a sullen, hostile, rude, and uncooperative manner. For example, when I as tried to engage him, he would sit and stare, refused to talk, or answered with monosyllables. In a typical adolescent way, he sat and texted. In short, he appeared to be very angry and depressed. He saw the world as unloving and dangerous. He blamed others for his problems, and lacked insight into why he was 'picked on by adults, teachers, and peers.

Dejuan was constantly on the verge of being asked to leave the home by the foster mother. His behavior was a self-fulfilling prophecy, in that he felt unloved and as a result was very difficult to even like. He was reenacting his earlier experience of abuse and neglect by his mother, and he felt and acted like a victim.

This problem was cyclical: He pushed his foster mother to the brink, she threatened him with a seven day notice, I would intervene with an emergency session to defuse the situation and get him to agree to be more cooperative. His behavior would improve for about six months and then it would happen all over again. One of the triggering events was contact with his birth mother. For some reason, she would call him he would refuse to talk with her and then his behavior deteriorated.

This case is very typical of the difficulty in parenting an adolescent who has been in the foster system for years. Even though he said he wanted to be a part of the family, he felt unloved, did not trust anyone, had difficulty managing his anger, and had uncontrollable mood swings ( a classic example of a child with an attachment disorder who never learned to self-regulate). Even though he was on several psychotropic medications, participated in weekly psychotherapy sessions and had other support programs, he was very difficult to manage. Over a period of years, this be came extremely wearing. The foster mother, coping with multiple stresses in her life as well as being a single parent, felt at times as if she was at her wit's end. To complicate matters further, another problem surfaced, adding to the burden. Someone in the neighborhood phoned in an anonymous report of child abuse. The complaint alleged that the children in the home were dirty, unsupervised, neglected and abused.

As mentioned, reports like this are not uncommon. They often result from well- meaning neighbors not understanding the situation. Sometimes, the foster child himself will lodge the complaint just to get even with the foster parent. The complaint sets in motion a whole sequence of visits by the police, an investigator from social services, an interview with the children and an audit of the managing, responsible Foster Family Agency. The foster parent is embarrassed and inconvenienced and subjected to all sorts of intrusive inspections of her home and parenting style. In this particular case, it is truly remarkable that she was able to function and keep Dejuan in the home. She did so in spite of all the provocations and legitimate reasons she had to give up on the situation. It was an ongoing struggle to preserve this placement.

There are thousands of teenage foster children and their families who live like this, always on the edge of falling apart and being sent to another home. With each failed placement, the odds of successfully making it to functioning adulthood become less. It is a familiar pattern:

- The child experiences strong negative emotions and is unable to calm down.
- Lacking relationship skills, the child seeks attention with demanding, annoying behaviors.
- Lacking empathy, the adult feels irritation and expresses it inappropriately.
- The child feels more anxious and insecure and responds by tuning out or becoming more aggressive.
- Feeling frustrated and helpless, the parent gives in, withdraws or raises the level of conflict, and tries to gain control by defeating the child.
- Ending in a stalemate, the net effect is that both parent and child feel less intimacy and satisfaction.

In sum, because of the damage from dysfunctional parenting by their birth parents, these children with histories of compromised attachment are compulsively reenacting their learned parental patterns of relating. The attachment paradigm is working: inviting rejection, withdrawing, becoming depressed, and believing they are unworthy of love, these children overtax the most well-intentioned parent's ability to remain positive. Their working model of the world is one of an untrusting victim and the world as victimizing. The situation can become very confusing if the replacement parents have their own attachment-related problems.

To further illustrate this difficult cycle, one couple with whom we placed two siblings (a boy and girl) with severe Reactive Attachment Disorder, were almost destroyed within three months by being continually emotionally and physically assaulted by the 5-year-old boy. It was devastating to the mother who stayed home with them every day to be repeatedly met with anger, rejection, physical assaults, and oppositional behavior. On one visit, I clearly remember spending an hour trying to help her deal with a situation. The little boy was locked in the bathroom, demanding that she come in and wipe his bottom for him. He had set up an impossible situation for her. He was demanding that she come in, yet had locked the door and also demanded that she do something he could do perfectly well for himself. He at the same time saying that he was a big boy, but also wanted her to baby him-- a no-win situation.

Below is a note from the foster parent log, typifying some of the feelings, reactions, and behaviors:

> **(9-1)** "B" is a wonderful, loving child 95% of the time, but little things are starting to set him off. He will pout and start a tantrum over a very small request, such as being asked to return a toy to his sister, or to drink with a certain cup. He wet his pants today. When questioned why, he stated that cartoons got him too excited and he forgot to use the toilet: Poor behavior overall. He was placed in time out and displayed uncharacteristic behavior such as attempting to scratch, kick, and hit us both.

> **(9-2)** Same behavior as yesterday, including that disturbing behavior in time out. He again wet his pants while in the bathroom. We are concerned and confused about his behavior since Thursday. In a four day span B, has received only one good behavior sticker out of eight attempts. One explanation is that he possibly heard my conversation with his mom on Friday.

> **(9-3)** I made the usual Monday call to mom at her half-way house. They said she no longer lives there.

> **(9-4)** Better behavior today, although he again urinated in his pants while in public with Susie. I spoke with him about the problem; he said he would try to do better. Also today B said to Susie, "I love you and I want to live with you, but sometimes I get upset."

Note the conflicted feelings expressed by both parent and child and the erratic, puzzling behavior. After four months, it all came to a head when B assaulted Susie and then trashed his room. Susie and her husband gave a seven-day notice. The two children had to be replaced for the third time. Their birth mother had left treatment and was never heard from again.

In sum, parenting an attachment disordered child is difficult under the best of circumstances. Typically encountered are difficulties related to trust and intimacy, control battles, triangulation, social isolation, lack of support, and increased marital stress and conflict. A phenomenon called *Triangulation* occurs when a child is hostile and oppositional with the mother during the day and very compliant, superficially charming, and cooperative with the father in the evening. Family interactions are often dominated by constant power struggles. Management of temper tantrums and impulsive behavior can also be very taxing. One mother reported that it took her an hour to drive two miles to the grocery store because the child kept trying to get out of the car seat and trying to hit her. Going into the grocery store was also problematic because the child had screaming fits and threw things in the store.

One very sophisticated and competent couple reported to me that all of the things they had learned about parenting from their own families were not working, and they realized that "normal parenting skills were not going to do it." We then began to collaborate on learning new attachment-based parenting skills. These eventually enabled them to reverse the negative behaviors and restored some order and harmony to their home. I once wrote an article describing foster parenting as being like parenting only much more difficult.

The psychological and emotional toll which stems from continual interaction with a child who has attachment difficulties is often underestimated and, if not directly addressed, has considerable long lasting consequences for both the parents and the children. It becomes even more strenuous when there is more than one child involved and when the children are teenagers. Though these kinds of emotional struggles occur in most if not all placements, not all end badly; many parents persist with support, education, and ancillary services. As a result, they finally are able to stabilize and create a caring family experience for a special needs child.

Adding to the psychological toll of interacting with a child with severe behavioral problems is the stress added by having to interact with the Department of Children's Services and the legal system, which present challenges to placement through the demands of court-ordered birth family visits. The following story is a poignant example of a family who has experienced devastating and traumatic losses due to a court decision. In addition to these losses, they were also subjected to ongoing frustration, disappointment, and exasperation with people who did not do their jobs. Their history of trying to create a family is a long and very sad story.

The family is a lesbian couple. One works as an Information Technology Consultant, the other is an Occupational Therapist who specializes in assessment of neurologically impaired children in a hospital. They have a long-standing relationship and are very competent, well educated and sophisticated. Their story began in 2004 when they were working with a private adoption agency who had arranged for them to adopt a child from a woman in North Carolina. They made two trips to visit and get to know her. When she delivered the baby they were ecstatic, but their joy quickly turned to sadness when she "changed her mind and kept her child." During this time they had put our agency on hold thinking they were soon going to have a child to adopt. Showing remarkable persistence and resilience after that disappointment, they renewed their relationship with our agency. We found an infant girl for them who was supposed to be a "safe surrender" infant. As it turned out, the little girl was placed with them for two weeks, and then they were notified that they had to return her because she was being given to her father. She should not have been removed in the first place and certainly not placed with them. In this case, DCFS failed to do their homework and did not investigate to discover that there was a father who very much wanted to keep the child. Imagine what it is like to go through the preparations emotionally, as well as logistically, to get your house set up for a newborn, have her for two weeks and then be told to give her back. "Sorry, tough luck!" Actually there was not even an apology. This disappointment took place in 2005. Unfortunately, the string of devastating losses continued after a successful two-year interlude.

I first began working with the couple when an infant boy was placed with them. This placement should have been very simple and easy. What makes a case "low risk"? (1) His mother gave him up at birth--another safe / voluntary surrender, and (2) the placement was not contested. The normal time line for this scenario should be no more than six months. Because the CSW on the case did not know what she was doing and did not take the necessary steps, the process took two years. She apparently had a problem with organization. According to the foster parents, "She did not come to the home for visits, and when she did, she was not prepared (did not even have a pen or paper to take notes), and at each visit she acted as if it was the first time she had been there." They reported that the CSW could not even find her way to the home even though the office was only two miles from the home (each visit, she would have to call and ask for directions). Time and again when there was a hearing scheduled, it had to be postponed because either the wrong paper work had been filed or none had been filed. In fact, to illustrate how bad it got, the child's birth certificate was lost. It took months to "find" it. There is also a procedure which requires the department to put a public notice in newspapers to notify any family members of a hearing so they might appear and appeal it. This notice was not filed, which is another example of how the family suffers when the case is not handled in a competent fashion. Even though it was a frustrating and stressful process, after two years he was adopted finally. The little boy has done very well in spite of the system and all the obstacles, and the parents have done an excellent job providing a stable and loving home in which he is thriving. His adoption was supposed to be a very simple process; however it was needlessly complicated simply because of the incompetence of the caseworker.

In spite of their previous disappointment and difficulties with the system, the couple decided to persevere, because they desired one more child to complete their family. It is important to note that the stress related to finding placements is not just confined to the adults. Every failed placement and disappointment affected them and their son. They noted to me that he became very anxious and upset when another child entered the home and then left. This caused him to feel anxious, confused and threatened. He worried that someone would come and take him away like they did with the other children.

After waiting several months, we found another infant boy from a woman who had four other children in the system. The fact she had other children in the system, was supposed to lower the risk of complications. The child was a 10-month old Hispanic boy who was placed with them in August of 2010 and removed in September of 2010. The circumstances were as follows.

At the time of his placement, the boy was living with his birth mother. He was removed because of severe neglect. On the occasion of my first visit I observed the following:

- Low weight

- Glazed eyes and flat affect

- Poorly groomed and dressed

- There was a flat spot on the back of his head (from sitting in an infant seat all day long)

- He made no eye contact with the caregiver and did not cry

- He was not oriented to food, only taking nourishment from a bottle

The foster mother, the child specialist, observed that he appeared to spend the first day as if in a daze or a dissociated state, exhibiting signs of severe neglect, shock and trauma. She, being highly trained in this area, was quite correct that all of the above signs were classic signs of neglect. Within just two weeks of placement, there was a remarkable change in this child. On my next visit I observed the following:

- He was alert

- His eyes were clear

- He met my gaze and was interacting well with the foster mother, who interacted with him by talking and offering him toys

- His motor skills had improved, he could reach and grasp.

- He was taking nourishment by mouth with a spoon and was also taking some finger foods.

- He began interacting with the two year old boy in the family.

I concluded after this visit that Jose "In this stable, consistent and highly skilled caring foster home had made remarkable progress in just a short period of time." It was very clear to me that his improvement was directly related to the highly competent care-giving which provided social stimulation, constant verbal interaction, consistency and caring-- the very opposite of neglect.

We all were shocked when one day the CSW called and abruptly ordered that Jose be delivered to her local DCFS office immediately. The maternal grandparents were being awarded custody. These were the grandparents who were aware of Jose's condition and of their daughter's neglectful parenting. The prospective parents and I were completely shocked at this turn of events. This is a sad and frustrating example of a sudden and apparently unfeeling decision made without warning by the Children's Court, who in spite of the CSW's recommendation to leave him in placement, acted to remove him. Apparently it was the minor's attorney, only on the case for a week, who recommended placement with the grandparents. I was so angered and dismayed that I wrote the following letter appealing this decision.

> I am writing to share information about our mutual client Jose, age eleven months. I question whether the court was made aware of several important factors. First, I do not believe that the well-being of Jose was taken into consideration. (I enumerated the observations I made during my visits) I concluded that Jose was thriving in this stable, consistent, highly skilled and caring foster home. I was very surprised when the CSW called to inform me that the court had ordered Jose to be given to the maternal grandparents, against the recommendations of the department and myself. Here are the reasons for my incredulity: (1) The grandparents are elderly, both have major health issues: both are morbidly obese. (2) The grandmother is a double amputee and is confined to a wheelchair. (3) I question their ability to successfully parent Jose because he requires feeding in the middle of the night and is not toilet trained. Who is going to do the middle of the night feedings, changing and bathing, etc? Also, they are also caring for 4 other children, 2 of whom are receiving services from Regional Center because they are developmentally delayed. I concluded: As Jose was clearly thriving in a very stable foster/adoptive home I do not believe it was in his best interests to be placed with elderly caretakers, who in my judgment lack the ability to give him the stimulation, attention, social environment and just plain physical care to which he responded so positively. The ramifications of placing Jose with his grandparents have long term consequences. For example, what

will be the home conditions and health of the grandparents in the years to come? Will they be able to provide him with the necessary emotional, intellectual and psychological environment necessary for his mental and emotional health to develop? Do they have the ability and resources to care for 5 growing and active children? I wish to go on record that I believe this move was not in the best interest of this child.

There was no response to my letter. The foster parents were devastated by the abrupt, insensitive manner in which this was handled. There was no time for transition, for emotional preparation for the move, and in my view no consideration given to what was best for the child. What was given precedence was "family preservation."

When decisions like this are made, the emotional impact on the foster family is very painful. It took them months to grieve the loss and risk becoming vulnerable again in order to receive another placement, not to mention the impact on their adoptive son.

This is an example of the Court acting consistently with the directive of family preservation as its primary goal. In this case it seemed to me that the emotional and mental health of the child would have been better served if he had remained where he was. I believe he would have had a far better chance at a normal life in a stable, caring, and high-functioning adoptive home than the one provided by his grandparents. This, of course, is a matter of considerable debate. The long term consequences are numerous, illustrating how vulnerable and powerless the foster/adoptive families are. Their happiness is dependent on the decisions made by the Courts. It is a roller coaster ride, full of ups and downs and severe disappointment, loss and grief. The most devastating factor is that these families have so little to say over what happens to the children in their care.

As if this disappointment was not enough to totally discourage this family from pursuing their dream of having a second child, after several months they decided to give the system one more chance. In December of 2010 they were contacted by our office, offering a "low risk" placement. By this time, they were extremely skittish about any risk at all. The placement was a baby girl, born in November. Her mother was incarcerated and she had three previous children placed in the system (notice a theme here). After placement, the mother got out of jail and entered a drug rehabilitation facility. The court ordered a Reunification Plan, of course. There were supposed to be two visits per week for 2-3 hours at a time. The Department promised support and transportation to the visits. Can you imagine how disruptive it would be to your family life to stop everything and go to an appointment twice a week for 3 hours and still maintain some sense of family normalcy, not to mention trying to hold down a job?

The mother began immediately contesting termination of her rights to her other children. Since the mother was technically in compliance with court orders, the court could not terminate parental rights. The foster family was once again in limbo. There had been a flurry of e-mails attempting to set up a visitation schedule, which were continually cancelled at the last minute because the mother had a job. In the month of August she only made one visit and that had to be on the weekend. The family was trying to schedule a vacation and kept having to change their plans because of last minute notifications. There was supposed to be a court hearing in September to terminate parental rights, which of course the mother appealed.

Once again, what was thought to be a low risk placement turned into another nightmare. The foster family had endured what they characterized as a "7-year Batan Death March." This process was characterized by disappointment, uncertainty, living under constant threat, having no control over their lives, frustration, and constant turmoil. For them, this was clearly a series of secondary traumas. Their lives had been continuously disrupted by broken promises, lack of communication, and continual change of direction. They lived in dread of the next phone call. They could not make any plans with the continual changes, and their lives were totally consumed by the process. It dominated the emotional life of the family and affected their relationship. They entered family therapy to help them deal with the situation. It was a dilemma. They wanted to do the right thing by the child, but every day they became more attached to the little girl. What should they do? They could not stand another placement. As I interviewed them, they told me that it was agonizing, because they were afraid it wouldn't work out and their fear was that maybe the next phone call would be "the one" and they would have to pass it up only to have this one taken away. They were extremely conflicted and under an enormous amount of stress. This had been going on for seven years with no end in sight. The clock kept ticking and the e-mails went back and forth in which the birth mother kept appealing, while remained in rehab. The latest update from this family was that the infant girl was reunited with her mother. You can imagine the devastation after another failed placement.

These difficult conditions are managed by the Children's Law Center, which has the task of deciding the fate of thousands of families and their children on a daily basis. The judges are expected to have the Wisdom of Solomon. In this next example, I will describe a case where the issue of birth family visits became the prime focus of the Court's decision.

This case came to me in 2010: The placement was a four year-old Hispanic boy who was living in a foster placement. Since the foster placement family was not in a position to adopt, a search was made for an adoptive family. A family in our agency was eligible, contacted, and agreed to take Manuel. He was placed and I began my weekly visits to the home. The family consisted of two gay men who had been partners for 20 years. Both were highly educated, had successful vocations, and lived in a spacious, historically-significant home. They had successfully parented an 8-year-old girl since her adoption at infancy.

When Juan was placed, he had been participating in court-ordered family visits twice a month with his mother at the DCFS office. These visits were ordered to continue. Manuel's birth mother has two other children in the system, one a male adolescent, and the other an older sister. The alleged father was incarcerated for sexually abusing the oldest boy. Manuel has had three placements. He apparently has lived with both his mother and his father at one time or another. He was placed because of domestic violence, abuse, and neglect. When Manuel was placed in his new home, I made my first visit. He appeared somewhat shy, but not unduly upset by the new placement. He appeared to settle in and make the transition to his new home well. He apparently had a good relationship with his previous foster parents, and they were sad to see him leave. They maintained contact with permission of his new family and expressed happiness that he was in a good home. This made his transition into the new home easier. The new fathers were very delighted to have a boy to be a brother to their daughter. It took a month for Manuel to transition and become adjusted to his new home with new routines, schedules, and living space, as well, as having a sister and two fathers. It is a huge adjustment to deal with three placements in four years.

After Manuel had been in his new home for a month, the mandated birth mother visits resumed. The first visit occurred on 1/25/11. It was for 90 minutes. As reported by the foster father who took Manuel to the visit, he was frightened, distressed and clingy. He expressed that he did not want to go to the visit. "After the visit, Manuel remained agitated for several hours. As the evening wore on he became increasingly agitated and oppositional, was more whiney, clingy, and when put to bed had nightmares and difficulty sleeping." The next day, Manuel had difficulty at the preschool where he was enrolled. The school reported that Manuel was aggressive, pushing and hitting other children. After the visit, it took Manuel several days to settle down and become more cooperative. This is not an uncommon reaction that children have after birth family visits. It is a uncommon reaction even in children whose parents go through a divorce. Whenever their routines are interrupted and spend a weekend with the non-custodial parent, they take a few days to return to normal. It is just more pronounced in foster children.

On February 3rd, I made a home visit. Foster Father John was home with Manuel. They had just arrived from preschool. When I arrived, John was attempting to get Manuel out of the car so we could have our visit. Manuel was crying and refused to leave the car. He kept saying he wanted to go back to school because he had left his candy there. He continued to cry, refused to get out of the car, and became more agitated. Finally, without giving in to bribery with a promise of candy, or coaxing John picked him up and carried him into the house. By now, Manuel was escalating and became totally out of control. He began hitting, kicking, and head butting John. He screamed and struggled and evaded John's grasp, so I held Manuel to prevent him from hurting himself or John. I held him for several minutes, all the while he continued kicking, biting, scratching, and head banging. When I became tired, John held him. We tried calming him by speaking soothingly and reassuring him that he was not going to be hurt or allowed to hurt himself. Finally, John sat in a chair and held Manuel firmly. He gradually settled down, and after half an hour he became quiet and ceased struggling. While this was happening I explained to John that what we had just witnessed was an example of a classic rage reaction: Manuel had become flooded with rage over which he had no control. So John's task, if it happened again, was to restrain Manuel so that he could not run about the house and possibly injure himself. John stated that this had never happened before and was concerned about what he and his partner could be facing. He was also worried that Manuel could possibly take this violence out on his adopted sister. I explained that this kind of volatility was not uncommon and that Manuel had undergone several major stressors in the past month: He had been re-placed, had a visit with his mother, and had to deal with an entirely new living situation, as well as adjust to a new school situation. These are too many large losses and difficult changes to handle in a short amount of time. Added to these stressors were the previous placements and whatever possible trauma Manuel had undergone with his birth parents (all factors contributing to the child becoming dysregulated). I also stated that John and his partner should arrange to have family therapy for themselves, their daughter, and Manuel in order to learn how to cope with all of these stresses and changes. After Manuel became calm, I terminated the visit. After this episode things were quiet for two weeks until the next birth mother visit.

This visit did not take place because Manuel was so distressed when they arrived at the DCFS office; he refused to participate in the visit. He would not go in and was extremely fearful and crying. The foster father took him back home and it again took

Manuel several days to settle down. The same pattern of behavior was noted after the visit. "Manuel is difficult to manage, becomes assaultive with the foster parents and was difficult to manage at school as well-- hitting other children."

It was clear to me that this behavior was directly linked to the birth mother visits in that they appeared to trigger a threat of abandonment by the present foster/adopt parents. Additionally, the visits with the mother were triggering whatever pre-placement trauma he had experienced with his parents. I wrote a report to Manuel's CSW. In which I stated my observations, conclusions, and recommendations. "It is my opinion that the visits are psychologically overwhelming and traumatic to Manuel and should not be continued and that, in the interests of his mental health and stability of the placement, it would be best to have the visits terminated."

After receiving my report, the CSW walked it into Court. The birth mother was notified. She contacted her attorney, and her attorney, who appealed the report. I was subpoenaed to testify regarding my opinion, and the next week, I appeared at the Edelman Family Court and testified. Present were the CSW, birth mother, Judge, Manuel's lawyer, and the birth mother's lawyer. The mother's lawyer asked me why I believed there was a connection between Manuel's behavior and the visits. "Could not his behavior be caused by other factors?" In my testimony I stated the basis for my conclusion. First I laid out the foundation for my conclusion by discussing that Manuel's emotional state was caused by pre-placement trauma, the trauma of placement and the ongoing stress of the visits which led to his vulnerable, and fragile condition. Then I described the a normal reaction of a child with secure attachment to seeing a parent from whom he had been separated. The normal reaction of a child who is anxious is to seek proximity. That is to say, the child sees the parent as a source of security and safety and seeks comfort by being close to that parent. The child's reaction is a strong indicator of the nature of the parent/child relationship.

Since Manuel reacted with apparent distress when he saw his mother-- screamed, protested, cried, became agitated, and wanted to run away-- I concluded that this was an indication of avoidance. When a child seeks to avoid the parent, this indicates that the parent for whatever reason poses a threat to the child. Under conditions of threat, children become distressed and their behavior becomes very regressive. Since I observed extremely distressed behavior in Manuel after the visits, I saw a direct correlation and thus recommended termination of the visits. After my testimony, the Judge apparently accepted my opinion and terminated not only the visits, but also parental rights.

Since that decision, and cessation of visits, Manuel had no more rages. The family entered therapy and they are working on family issues such as their daughter's difficulty in giving up her only-child status. The parents are also dealing with the usual sibling rivalry. Manuel continues to learn how to express his anger by not hitting, and how to get along with peers in school by being less aggressive and appropriate. In short, the destabilizing visits with the mother were a very large trigger for previous trauma and were a significant factor in the volatile behavior which threatened to destabilize the placement. I am happy to report that in August 2011, final adoption papers were signed. Everyone ate chocolate cake and celebrated the successful completion of this case.

This drama occurs many times every day as the Family Court orders family reunification plans children newly placed in foster homes. These visits, as well-meaning as they are intended, present a situation where children who have been abused and traumatized by their parents are forced to remain in contact with them. Often the visits are scheduled for several times per week for several hours at a time. This dilemma presents many obstacles and challenges to the well-being of the children and the homes in which they are placed. The visits present a condition of Secondary Trauma in which victims are continually re-exposed to the person or persons who originally traumatized them, thereby exacerbating old wounds and making it difficult for them to heal and transition into a new life. This occurs because the legal rights of the parents are given precedence over the well-being of the child.

Paradoxically, children are removed from the abuser for their safety and then forced to remain in contact with them in order to be reunited. This should only be done, in my opinion, if there is a strong likelihood of rehabilitating the family. This, of course, is a huge issue subject to great debate. While it is going on, the Court and Department of Children's Services need education on the whole issue of attachment, trauma, and loss in the lives of the children and what needs to be done to further safeguard their well-being. It is not enough to remove the children from physical harm; their emotional well-being must be vigilantly protected as well. The homes in which the children are placed also need much more in the way of support, education, and resources.

As I was finishing writing this chapter, I had the good fortune to have a conversation with a good friend who mentioned an interest in the book I was writing, she inquired about its topic and I told her. she expressed reading a chapter or two and so I gave her this chapter. She found it interesting and told me that she had been involved in raising foster children. I thought it might be interesting to have her write about her experiences from a personal point of view. I thought it might humanize the process even further. Karen is a mother of four children, she has eight grandchildren on whom she dotes and brags about continuously: always with the latest pictures to show, of course. She has been a kindergarten teacher for 30 years and is very active in her church. She enjoys sewing, knitting, gardening, and loves to spend weekends at Laguna Beach with her entire family. When you walk into her house it always has delicious aromas coming from the kitchen. Karen was a foster parent in the 60's and 70's and has a unique perspective with much to offer. Here is her story.

## A FEW WORDS ABOUT FOSTER PARENTING
### By Karen Thompson

My career as a foster parent began some forty years ago when the pastor of the church we were attending asked if my husband and I would consider temporarily caring for a child whose mother was struggling to care for him. We agreed, and even before we were licensed as a foster care home, Evan – a lively 6-year-old in first grade – came to live with us. He was not difficult to care for, to my way of thinking, and made the transition fairly well. Meanwhile, we began the application process to become foster parents.

My husband was the one who didn't fare well in terms of the placement. He was overwhelmed by the demands Evan – who had never known his father – made on him as a male caregiver. Several months into the placement, he informed me that "it was either him or Evan, one of them would have to go." We all knew who it would be!

By then, a social worker who had come to know us during the review process had another "child" waiting in the wings. Donna was a teenager who had lost her parents and had been living in Altadena with an aunt and uncle, but they felt they could no longer care for her. We took her in and she remained with us perhaps close to a year, but we finally had to have her relocated when she refused to follow curfew hours.

From those initial placements, I learned two things: first, don't take a foster child who is in the age range of your biological children, because it creates to much competition for them, and second, once a case worker knows you and your home, there will always be someone he/she wants to place with you.

Our next adventure was with Tom, an 18-year-old who came our way because of his friendship with Donna. She had already left by the time he appeared on the scene looking for her, but we wound up taking him in, even though he was technically over age. I managed to talk Pasadena High School's principal into admitting him and did my best to help him over the hurdles of academics. He stayed for quite awhile, but eventually the difficulty of trying to forge friendships and make a life for himself at PHS proved to be too much. He came from a family of twelve or thirteen children, and he often remarked that our home was the only place he had lived where "no one was crashing through plate glass windows." But he had learned early on that pulling a geographic was his best solution to problems, so he would simply pack up his meager belongings and hit the road (thumbing his way across the country to wherever he wanted to go next). I am still in contact with Tom to this day. For many years, I would receive the proverbial letter: "Dear Karen, I am in (fill in the blank) jail. Could you send me (fill in the blank) dollars to buy toothpaste and shampoo? Please write to me. Love, Tom."

He went into the Army, but received a general discharge within a year. He continued to wander from one end of the country to another, winding up in the clinker somewhere because he had been drinking and did something stupid. Finally someone in a VA hospital somewhere picked up his depressive disorder and got him started on antidepressants. He has maintained a clean and dry lifestyle ever since – he and his wife even drove out here from Texas to visit us several years ago, and he calls me every few months (and not to request money!)

We then became foster parents to Ivy, a six-month-old just released from UCLA Medical Center, where she had been treated for a skull fracture (her hair was still growing back from areas where they had drained fluid pressing on her brain. She was a beautiful little baby, a mixture of American Indian (Pueblo), Portuguese, Hawaiian, and a few other racial contributions. She had suffered a fractured femur (longest, strongest bone in the body) at the age of two months, but no one followed through on that and she was returned to her parents, eventually suffering the skull fracture. The hope was that over time her brain would begin growing, but every exam my pediatrician made on her resulted in the same pronouncement: Her skull circumference was 16 inches, and that never changed in the ten years we had her. It was quite a challenge to develop a care plan for her, and here again, I was pretty much on my own. She had completely lost her sucking reflex, so I had to spoon baby food to her, give her liquid through a tube I inserted in her throat, give her liquid calcium to supplement her practically nonexistent milk intake, give her frequent enemas because the brain damage had left her with virtually no muscle control, etc. I found a school in Pasadena that catered to developmentally disabled children, and enrolled her there, until she was old enough for the Pasadena Unified School District program at Roosevelt School. This is when I learned the third lesson of foster parenting: You are pretty much on your own.

I need to add a sidebar here: I think there have been improvements over the years (my foster parenting experience was at least thirty years ago) in the level and frequency of involvement by case workers, as well as their education and training and field experience. I personally had been educated and credentialed as a teacher, so I knew how to seek out answers and resources in my community. I began with the case worker, but if I couldn't get help there, I went on into the local community to look for help. I didn't have the internet, but I did have my telephone, and I contacted schools and school districts and physicians and medical centers and anyone or anything else I could conjure up. I pored over the telephone books and followed up on any suggestions or referrals that I was offered through my phone calls. In Ivy's case, for instance, my family pediatrician would take Medical and see her for yearly checkups or routine medical emergencies, but I looked in vain for a neurologist who would accept Medical. I finally found a local neurologist and "badgered" his office, saying that I would pay his fee in cash at the beginning of the examination – before he even saw her – just to get him to take a look at her and give me ideas on how to proceed. Eventually he agreed to see her UNDER MEDICAL and became very interested in her case and saw her for a number of visits. From what I know of the foster care system of today, I think there are a lot more resources for foster parents. I wish I could have read Gary's book! It explains so much of what I coped with, and I could have been so much more effective with a little more information and not as much flying by the seat of my pants!

We kept Ivy for over ten years, but her development was stunted. She grew very little, perhaps to the size of a three or four-year-old, but never was able to sit up or crawl or walk or feed herself. She became a very sweet baby after recovering from her trauma, and would coo back to me when I talked to her. I kept her in the kitchen with me when I was working there, sitting propped up in a beanbag, since she could not support her head otherwise. For weeks after she turned three, I drove her to Roosevelt School for the Handicapped, four miles each way, twice a day, until she received her specially-fitted wheelchair (a.k.a., "the moonwalker"), which had special rotating supports for her head and neck once she was strapped in. She then rode the bus back and forth to school.

People registered great interest and even surprise when I took Ivy out in public. Usually I was carrying her, because I couldn't get the wheelchair into the car, so I would strap her into a seatbelt for the trip and then carry her. When strangers saw us together, I heard comments such as, "Oh, my dear, did you take the pill?"

Ivy's birth parents were very regular in their visits to our home for the first 8-10 months. They had a one-hour visit every weekend, but could not remove her from our home and we needed to be present to monitor the visit. When they saw for themselves that she was not going to progress, the visits became farther and farther apart, and eventually stopped altogether. They later divorced. There was never any type of prosecution or jail time for them; they simply lost custody of the baby and then lost interest in her. No one detained them following either severe injury. The social worker told us that it was the department's policy not to go on the offensive, for fear that the parents would defend themselves through the court system and then be able to win custody. It was felt to be a better strategy to remove the child from the home and then work with the parents in an educational, non-threatening setting. After more than ten years of caring for her, we relinquished her to another local foster home, where she developed pneumonia and died within two months of leaving us.

Janice and Julie were two teenage girls whose placements overlapped by a few months in our home. They were both replaced after having lived with relatives and in other foster homes. Julie was definitely a "hippie" who liked to sunbathe topless in our backyard, much to the delight of the neighborhood boys (my own son included). She had no boundaries and had to be painstakingly educated about appropriate social behavior. She set her room on fire with a candle one evening and then disappeared into the neighborhood for several days, apparently afraid to face us. We eventually had to have her replaced when she started bringing her boyfriend home to sleep with her. Janice began to push the envelope by exerting her independence over curfews and finally, after months of working with her and her social worker to address the behaviors, she was also moved.

A fourth lesson I learned from foster parenting: The adolescent foster children were so emotionally and physically deprived when they arrived, EVERY ONE of them ate themselves sick, literally until they were vomiting, in the first few days after their arrivals. Food had been locked up where they came from, and they had to reassure themselves that we would feed them and nurture them.

A fifth lesson I learned from foster parenting: Your foster child will display behavior that will BEG you to reject him/her, over and over again. The message seems to be: I KNOW I'm going to be rejected, therefore I will be in control of that rejection. I will behave in a way that will cause you to reject me, and when you do, I will know why and I will have planned it out myself. It involves a lot of patience and walking through routines and reassurance to the child until this behavior runs its course.

I repeat, once a case worker knows your home, he/she will be after you forever! I had a call from a case worker I didn't know personally, but who said she had been given my name by a co-worker. She was most anxious to place a teenage girl in our care, and when I told her we had decided not to accept any more foster children at that time, she begged me to let her JUST COME OVER AND TALK about her teenager. I put her off further, saying that we were having company for dinner and I was busy preparing the meal. She BEGGED to come, sit in my kitchen while I was cooking, so finally I relented and she did come and she did sit and she did pour out the whole story while I sliced and diced.

She told me about Debbie, a fifteen-year-old who had lived with her mother and three siblings in the area, but had been recently placed in the Florence Crittenden Home for Unwed Mothers. Debbie was not, nor had she ever been, pregnant, but the family (egged on by a grandmother and aunt) were scapegoating her and labeling her as a troublemaker. The mother had put her in the Crittenden Home to get her out of the way, but the case worker was adamant that Debbie was NOT institutional material and needed to be with a normal family. Of course we caved and took her.

She was extremely bright and knew how to manipulate a situation to her liking, but she quickly settled into a very good routine with our family. She thrived on family life and its interactions and socialization. She remained with us for four years, with the exception of one attempt at reunification with her birth family. She was with them for fourteen days, lost exactly one pound of weight for each of those days, was reunited with us and regained those fourteen pounds in another fourteen days. She left our home at the age of nineteen, when the social worker realized that she need to be on her own – it was time and she had learned what she needed to know during those four years. I have remained in close connection with Debbie, and my own children have done the same. We consider each other REAL family ☺. She and I talk or meet many times over the course of each year. She lives in South Pasadena with her husband and two sons.

The final foster child is Mary, who was in placement with some friends of ours, and was cared for by our family when they went on trips or out for special events. At that time, foster children could be babysat only in licensed foster homes. We became acquainted with Mary as an infant and when it appeared she was going to be released for adoption, her social worker made arrangements for her to be moved to our home. He had originally hoped to reunite the family, but the father kept getting into trouble and going to jail and the mother could not manage Mary on her own. The mother already had three older children who had been placed for adoption (Mary's half siblings).

So we brought Mary into our home at age 18 months. The case worker told us to get a lawyer and initiate adoption proceedings. He himself obtained relinquishment papers from the parents. We adopted Mary one year later, with Debbie (who was still living with us), her former foster family of six, our own family of four, and a few assorted other relatives there to watch, and the judge invited us all into his chambers and made each person in attendance tell his/ her name and connection to Mary.

Mary has turned out to have definite social and emotional issues, partly a result of being removed and replaced from several homes early in her life, and partly a genetic tendency from her birth mother, which has caused mental health problems. She is currently undergoing treatment and is on medication. I see her and talk with her frequently, and we are both committed to our relationship and keeping it positive and productive for both of us. She struggles with wanting to be recognized for her growth and wanting to achieve her independence, with a pattern of moving forward for a short time and then collapsing in a heap. But the forward movement is becoming more consistent and the heaps have become valuable life lessons for her. She is the mother of an autistic teenage daughter who had to be placed in a foster home herself, and Mary is understanding so much more of her own adolescence as she parents Rachel.

My experience with the foster care system is not current, and I am certain a number of things have changed since then. But many of the difficulties and frustrations and issues are probably in play in foster placement today. The system was flawed, as a foster parent I had no idea what I was undertaking, there was little or no support, and a lot of things had to be addressed independently by me as a placement parent. Nevertheless, the experience of parenting a variety of children with a wide range of needs was a very informative and enriching experience for me. Whenever I became discouraged, wondering if I was really doing anything worthwhile, I only had to stop and say to myself, "Think of what this child's life would have turned out like if our family hadn't been part of it." Even a small effort is better than none at all!

A few years after Ivy died, I became pregnant with my fourth child – a totally unexpected pregnancy, and a difficult one in many respects, including physically. After John was born, however, I came to realize that he was God's way of blessing me with a healthy baby after all the years I devoted to a terribly damaged one. His healthy development erased the memories of how the damage Ivy's parents did to her played out in her short life. Now I can remember her cooing softly back to me with great joy...

While many children do well in their new homes, and the families manage to find a way to normalize their lives, many children in the system are reunited with their families. Unfortunately there are often disastrous results. In the past three years, according to a recent article in the Los Angeles Times written by Garret Therolf, there have been 70 deaths of children whose lives are governed by the Child Welfare Department. It is to this topic that I turn in the next chapter: Children dying while in the system.

# Chapter 10

## REQUIEM

### For All the Children who have Died in Protective Custody

This chapter is dedicated to all those children who have died in a system mandated to protect them from abuse, neglect and, most importantly, murder. In this chapter, several cases, now public knowledge, will be discussed. One of my cases was under the care of our agency: Sarah Chavez. Several other deaths will also be examined for their common elements. Obvious problems which surfaced in the post mortem review, attempts to reform, and the overall status of children under the care of the child welfare system will be discussed. First let us look at the big picture in order to provide a context for understanding individual cases.

Violence against children is shocking. When it leads to murder of a child it is incomprehensible. Death stemming from abuse or neglect is unpardonable. When violence occurs towards children under the protection of an agency whose mandate is to safeguard their welfare, it is even more disturbing. Unfortunately, an almost daily occurrence of tragedy, is all too common. In my time with a Foster Family and Adoption Agency (FFA) we had placement referrals of children with ample evidence of this sort of violence: numerous healing fractures of arms, legs, ribs, and even a skull fracture, all of which occur too frequently: when violence rises to the level of torture, it even more reprehensible. Death of a child at the hands of an adult is should never happen. We have the inclination to view these perpetrators as monsters, yet they are ordinary parents who explode with a suddenness and depth of rage and total lack of impulse control that is difficult to predict or prevent. Therefore, returning a child to a violent parent after removal is inexcusable and certainly preventable. The occurrence of violence against children is an epidemic and a national disgrace.

Children are victimized by violent parents every day in a disturbingly wide variety of means and situations. For example, I was called to pick up an 8-month-old boy from Kaiser Permanente ICU-Infant Care Center. His CSW wanted to place him with one of our families. The preliminary information we had was that he "had some minor medical problems," implying that they were not anything requiring a special medical placement. When I got to the unit and talked with the Charge Nurse about the case, she reported that the boy was a victim of *Shaken Baby Syndrome*. The parents had brought him to the hospital claiming that he "had fallen out of bed." The nurse informed me that shaken baby incidents are very common and seldom lead to successful prosecution.

After I had reviewed the neurological report on the child, I discovered that he was in a coma, and was blind, deaf, and would probably be in a permanent vegetative state. I deemed that an ordinary foster placement for the child was not appropriate. The CSW had made a serious misjudgment regarding the severity of the injury and had no business trying to place him with one of our families. Someone did not have all the facts when the decision to refer for placement was made.

This serial epidemic of violence against children is on the rise and raises disturbing questions about its causes and how we as a society can better protect our children. In addition to overt violence against children, there are other factors affecting their well being that also have profound long-term consequences. The very structure of our society and its institutions charged with protecting and educating our children are complicit in this failure.

In my view, the plight of children in the United States cries out for national attention. Dietrich Bonhoeffer, a German theologian who died in a Nazi prison camp protesting Hitler's regime wrote, "The test of the morality of a society is what it does for its children." The statistics are dismal: In America, a child is abused or neglected every 36 seconds, 556,000 children are in our foster care system and 131,000 are awaiting adoptive families. A child is born into poverty every 41 seconds and one in five is poor during the first three critical years of life, the period most critical to the development of the brain's cognitive, social, and emotional domains. Additionally, a child is born without health insurance every 59 seconds, while 90% of more than nine million uninsured live in working families. A child or teen is killed every three hours, or eight each day; 90,000 children and teens have been killed by guns since 1979. Furthermore, it is estimated that 20 percent of our children live below the poverty level, Nearly 12 million children are poor and millions are hungry, living in terrible housing conditions, or even homeless. Finally, almost three out of four poor children live in working families. These statistics reflect the grim confluence of factors contributing to abuse, neglect, and death: poverty, mental illness, drug addiction, disrupted families and lack of any social safety net. The following statistics represent a day in the life of a child. Please remember that each statistic is a child with a story.

- 3 children are killed by abuse or neglect
- 5 children or teens commit suicide
- 8 children or teens are killed by guns
- 77 babies die before their first birthday
- 183 children are arrested for violent crimes
- 381 are arrested for drug abuse
- 404 babies are born to mothers who receive no prenatal care
- 846 children are born at low birth weight
- 1,243 babies are born to teen mothers
- 1,455 babies are born without health insurance
- 2,104 are born into poverty
- 2,360 babies are born to mothers who are not high school graduates
- Children in Los Angeles foster care are abused at rates higher than anywhere else in the nation
- 2,302 are abused or neglected

- 6% of the 30,000 foster children of LA County are abused and neglected

- About 1% of the general population are abused

These statistics are the byproduct of a number of interacting variables. Clearly, no one factor is responsible for a particular number, but in analyzing all of the facts, abuse statistics can be attributed to a number of causes: poverty, mental illness, drug and substance abuse, inter-generational abuse, the decline of the American family, unemployment, homelessness and poor education. When all of these factors are found in one particular family, as they often are, the outcome is predictable, the result being violence against a child and all too frequently the death of a child. In short, the plight of these children is that their deaths are the inevitable consequence of much larger and complex social problems.

To completely understand even one child's death we have to look at the whole societal context in which it occurs. The context provides the frame and background for our understanding. In the particular cases I have become aware of, there is always the story within a story: the contribution of one particular agency functioning within a social structure and political system that funds its activities has a particular responsibility for the welfare of each child. Within that particular agency, there are individual Social Workers and their supervisors who fail to do their jobs. However, there are also a great number of individuals within that organization who provide exemplary service. The picture is complex, and it is only in looking at each individual case that we can understand what went wrong to produce such a tragic outcome.

My first encounter with the death of a child under my care was Sarah Chavez, I am not violating confidentiality because her case was chronicled in several major newspapers and is a matter of public record, who was placed in foster care with our agency on New Year's Day 2005. She was placed when her mother called 911 after delivering a stillborn baby into a toilet in her grandmother's home. It is unbelievable, but the story gets worse. At the time Sarah, who had just turned two years old, was staying with her aunt and uncle in nearby Alhambra, a working class suburb of Los Angeles. A Social Worker noticed a cut on her nose and bruising under both eyes. Records indicated that Social Workers and police were concerned about Sarah's injuries, and investigators worried that her mother and grandmother were trying to cover up the injuries to avoid giving Sarah being taken from them. Because of her overall condition, investigators felt there was sufficient cause to detain her. In this case our agency was contacted, and we matched Sarah with one of the families on our waiting list. Our families are screened, trained, and certified before a child can be placed with them. In this case we placed Sarah with a couple, both professional women in their 30's. They had a previous record of success with our agency, had a long-standing committed and stable relationship, and were very interested in adopting a baby girl. They were ecstatic when we placed Sarah with them, and they immediately did everything they could to ease Sarah's transition into their home.

After being informed of Sarah's availability, they picked her up at the Agency and greeted her with a teddy bear. They were appropriately concerned and aware that Sarah would be scared and overwhelmed after removal from her family and they did a very good job of anticipating her fears by providing a number of welcoming and reassuring activities. They demonstrated an excellent example of sensitivity and attunement to the child's emotional needs.

Over the next weeks and months, Sarah and her caregivers handled the transition well. In fact, Sarah was thriving. She was eating well, had recovered from her injuries, and was participating in weekly family reunification visits. There were times when Sarah would become upset, usually after one of the family visits, and would try to choke one of her foster parents. These concerns were reported because we felt that they were classic indicators of child abuse and potential sexual abuse as well. These kinds of regressive reactions were indicative of Sarah's sense of imminent danger. As previously mentioned, this is how children demonstrate that they are feeling threatened. The Department reported that they were aware of her condition and told the couple "not to worry."

As the months went by, the foster parents became very attached to Sarah and were delighted that she seemed to be so happy and thriving under their care. They were unaware, however, that Sara's aunt, Frances Abundis, from whom she had originally been removed because of suspicious bruises, continued to go to court to push for custody. As is often the case, these proceedings take place and neither the foster care agency nor the foster families are kept informed about the proceedings. The regulations do not require that foster parents be notified of court dates, and they are in fact discouraged from participating, because they "might show their bias" with regard to deciding the case in favor of adoption. At that time, the inclination of the county and the court was to push for family reunification.

Communication with court-appointed lawyers is often difficult. Time after time, they do not return calls or respond to requests for information. Advocates across the country say foster parents are often the last people consulted about what is best for the child. Nationwide, studies show that frustration over being ignored is a leading reason foster parents decide to stop the adoption process. I have repeatedly told foster parents that they are at the bottom of the totem pole when it comes to having legal recourse to push their cause. Having so little power and feeling at the mercy of a very complicated system is emotionally difficult for foster parents; it is like riding in the back seat of a car in which there is no driver. Or worse yet, three drivers all struggling for control.

As the court proceedings dragged on for months, the foster couple continued to try to get their concerns heard by the CSW. They pleaded with them to investigate whether Sarah had indeed been abused as they suspected. It never happened. Documents show that an examination at a clinic was cancelled and never rescheduled. The couple also tried to contact Sarah's lawyer. They were discouraged because this "might" antagonize the court. Miscommunication also occurred between the court-appointed attorney and the CSW when the attorney relied on the CSW's report stating that the Social Worker had apparently changed her mind regarding custody with the aunt. Records indicate that on the morning of April 25, the court referee ordered Sara reunited with the aunt because the Social Worker assigned to investigate the case lifted her objections to reunification.

The couple was notified abruptly, and ordered them to return Sarah. It was a difficult day for them. They told me how they had to tell Sarah and as they tried to pack her clothes, she cried and tried to put them back in the drawer. "It was heart breaking, because we knew we were sending her back to someplace unsafe."

In the months after Sarah was returned to the Abundis home, there were troubling signs of regression: She stopped talking, had trouble sleeping, and began to show erratic behavior. Examinations by physicians in May and July found that, again, Sarah had behavioral problems and abrasions on her neck, but Social Workers assigned to the case took no action to remove Sarah, according to the case file. The L.A. Times reported that when Sarah's aunt took her to Garfield Medical Center for treatment of a severely broken arm, no one on the medical staff at the hospital called to report abuse (they are mandated by law to report abuse and in this case should have detained her). Sarah was released against medical advice and returned home. The very next morning the Alhambra Fire Department found Sarah dead at the Abundis home, killed by a severe blow to the abdomen. The cause of death was officially ruled as blunt force trauma. The uncle was suspected of committing the act and was later arrested, tried, and sentenced for the crime.

At our agency, we were shocked by this news, and of course the foster couple was devastated by this event which should never have happened. I spent several weeks after Sarah's death working to help them deal with this tragic and traumatic loss. We all felt such an enormous sense of guilt, helplessness and outrage at such a tragedy, such a failure to protect an innocent, vulnerable child entrusted to us for safeguarding. What followed was predictable: A public outcry, a post mortem to assign blame, a review of the procedures and decisions which led to the death, workers reprimanded and punished with desk time. After all of this happened, more deaths continued to occur. There was even some national attention after the event was featured by local television: ABC did an unprecedented look at a range of foster care issues by airing stories on World News Tonight, Good Morning America, Night Line and 20/20. The foster parents, Corrie and Dianne, published a statement saying, "So many of you have been so supportive to us over these past few months as we struggled with the loss of Sarah. We remain tremendously grateful, for your kindness, friendship and love continues to provide us strength."

There was a great deal of attention and articles appeared in both the Pasadena Star News and Los Angeles.

> The tragedy highlighted what many say is a widespread, if sometimes overlooked, weakness in the child welfare systems nationwide: As Social Workers, attorneys and judges look to reunite children with their parents or relatives, they too often ignore voices of the foster parents who have been tucking the children into bed every night. Local child welfare officials acknowledge they must do more to reach out to foster parents like Corrie and Dianne.

David Sanders, then director of the department in 2005, had this to say: "It's really critical that we have information from them. They spend 24 hours a day with the children, while our Social Workers spend maybe two or three hours a month. Unfortunately, our system is not at that ideal." Sanders added that since Sarah's death he has begun working on ways to ensure more involvement by foster parents. Sadly, since that time everything seems to have gone back to business as usual. That means more deaths and more headlines.

Given all of these mitigating factors, it is still a shocking event when we hear of another child's death. Each time a child dies under the supervision of the Department of Children's Services there is a public outcry, articles are written in the Los Angeles Times, and the Los Angeles Board of Supervisors orders another study with a demand for accountability. Most recently, on June 6, 2011, the head line shouted: "A child's death renews concern over child welfare agency." Garrett Therolf, who covers these incidents on a regular basis, has written another article in what has been an ongoing refrain. This all too familiar story line details the death of another child, Tori Sandoval.

At the agency for which I worked, the news of the latest death angered and frustrated the staff, bringing up old wounds and highlighting the daily frustrations of case management. During a regular staff meeting/case conference, we had an hour long discussion about one of our active cases which was eerily similar to the one noted in the article. The discussion ended with a collective sense of helplessness. One staff member ended the meeting with, "Well, we know what is coming next. Whenever a child dies, the County doubles its vigilance by demanding more audits, and gets even more demanding in terms of making sure that all of the paperwork is in order." We know that the problem is usually not at the FFA level, and that increased audits and more meticulous record keeping is not the solution. We are also quite aware that all of our attempts to sound the alarm when one of our children is in danger often go unheeded.

The particular case we were concerned about in this meeting: The father, a paranoid schizophrenic who behaved erratically during monitored visits and exhibited very little awareness of the appropriate care of his two children, had just been given unmonitored 4-hour weekly visits with them. Because of our concern, we sent letters to the Children's Court and County Social Workers stating that we felt very strongly that the children were in imminent danger. It did no good.

Staff meetings like the one just mentioned are an accurate barometer of the staff's morale. As the sense of futility mounts, when our efforts meet with failure, when children remain in jeopardy, when the Children's Bureau denies mental health service requests, when DCFS drops the ball, and when the Children's Law Center makes seemingly questionable decisions, it becomes increasingly discouraging. The job of working with Special Needs children is hard enough. The emotionally-draining task of working with abused children, monitoring their contact with their parents, and managing their transition to foster care is made even harder when it is compounded by the lack of public awareness and support, along with the daily onslaught of tragedy and bureaucratic ineptitude. The toll is compounded and becomes exceedingly difficult when one of our own children dies. The continual demands of the job are exhausting. To care for so many injured children while simultaneously fighting the system drains the worker's capacity for compassion and empathy, leading to emotional depletion and loss of hope. In short, burnout is a continual risk.

When more deaths are reported, the collective sense of outrage and helplessness mounts. Once again, this story follows the predictable pattern of poor judgment, inept case management, and systemic incompetence. Therolf's article, mentioned above, covered the case of Tori Sandoval. Tori, a 17-month-old toddler, was released from foster care to her biological parents and died months later. She was found to have healing bruises on her body, and a fractured rib and blood tests suggested she died thirsty and hungry. It was observed that Tori's weight during the time she was with her parents dropped from the 50$^{th}$ percentile to below the 5$^{th}$ percentile for children her age. No charges were filed, but police and county Social Workers say the parents are "suspects" in the investigation. She had just turned two years old the month before her death. Months before Tori was released to parental custody, the director of the foster-family agency wrote a letter to the presiding judge expressing "grave concern," stating that the court system had not properly considered the risks of returning Tori to her "long-troubled" biological parents. Garrett Therolf writes:

> Her case has sent fresh shock waves through the county's child protection bureaucracy, still struggling to implement reforms after more than 70 maltreatment deaths over the last three years of children who had been under the system's supervision.

> Below is the copy of the letter written by Linda Contis to Judge Michael Nash of the Children's Court, Monterey Park:

> *Honorable Judge Nash,*

> The purpose of this letter is two-fold. First I am asking you to review the history and outcome regarding a little girl named Vyctorya Sandoval. ...Vyctorya is child number 9 of Jennifer Dalhover. She does not have custody of her eight other children. Vyctorya came into the system as a newborn and at the 18 month hearing, was released by Commissioner M. Mackel on September 1, 2010.

There has been extensive documentation of our concerns....The history of the biological parents involves domestic violence, child abuse, sexual abuse charges (against Ms. Dalhover, age 36, by the mother of Vyctorya's biological father, Joseph Sandoval, age 17 at the time of Vyctorya's birth, and a restraining order filed by Ms. Dalhover against Mr. Sandoval for physical abuse. The biological parents had separate visitation because of the restraining order before they disappeared in April 2010 for several months. They were found living together at a shelter in Pasadena with their newborn daughter. They were allowed to resume visitation together at the end of June and without completing the court ordered programs, 77 days later Vyctorya was returned to their custody

My concerns are many. There was no post reunification oversight ordered nor was Family Preservation suggested. I was told by Attorney Vasquez outside the courtroom that "the history of the family does not matter, the goal is to reunify". I know that reunification is primary and always work toward that goal, however there are cases where common sense must prevail and history is relevant.

My secondary concern regards the courtroom itself. I, as one of the Founders and Directors of Serenity, have been in many children's courtrooms over the past 20 years, and I have never seen any conducted in the manner in which I witnessed that day. Commissioner Makel dominated her courtroom with intimidation and anger, to the point that the attorneys present barely spoke above a whisper with simple answers. One substitute attorney started to speak and was chastised by Commissioner Makel "to never ever even attempt to speak when I speak". Three teenage siblings of Vyctorya were at the witness table and when she asked them about what they liked to do, one started to answer and Commissioner Makel turned away from her to berate the court attendant. No one spoke on behalf of Vyctorya. No one acknowledged the reams of concerns and pages of documentation over the last years. Vyctorya, age 17 months had no voice in Commissioner Makel's courtroom.

I ask only that you review Vyctorya Sandoval's file from beginning to end.

*Signed Linda Kontis, M.S.*
Director of Children's Placements
Serenity Co-Founder.

This letter has called into question whether the court system and the Department of Children and Family Services did all they could to safeguard Vyctorya. This letter was one of two warnings officials received about her welfare in the months before she died, according to sources familiar with the case. Apparently neighbors were reputed to have phoned in a report to the department after hearing from the girl's relatives that Tori's condition was worsening. Despite these letters and expressions of concern by neighbors, the court and county left Tori with her parents.

A critical review of this case reveals many factors which put Tori at risk. In my view, the biggest error was that the court did not fully assessing the mental health status and capability of the parents to realistically parent Tori. I strongly disagree with Commissioner Makel: History does matter! First and foremost, parents who already have nine children in the system are manifesting gross irresponsibility by having that many children for which they are unable to care. Second, there is the issue pointed out by the Kontis letter outlining domestic violence, child abuse, and sexual abuse charges as well as classes that were never completed. These are strong indicators of mental health issues, poor judgment, poor impulse control, and a lack of even the most basic parenting skills required to provide a stable, safe, secure and nurturing environment for a child. This case exemplifies the profile of a parent who is at high risk for further abuse.

History does matter, and it is probably the best predictor of future behavior. It is my judgment that failure to seriously consider the family history is based on naïve assumptions which gravely minimize the serious underlying psychopathology of repeat offenders. Their violent and neglectful behavior is a result of deeply rooted psychological problems that one class on parenting or anger management will not even begin to correct. It is unfortunate that, because of the legal categories related to parental rights, the mental health status of the parents does not fall under the matters that can be considered. I was informed that it is not illegal to be "homeless" or "mentally ill," however, when considering reunification, these factors, though technically irrelevant legally, are of tremendous import practically and in fact may be matters of life and death. This was clearly a case where Family Reunification was the controlling factor in the judge's decision.

The County has repeatedly erred in creating and throwing more and more resources at Family Reunification Programs. There are some families which should not be preserved and their children should be spared the torture of reunification. These issues notwithstanding, it is obvious that poor case management also contributed to Tori's death. The glaring signs of abuse and neglect should have been noticed by the CSW who was supposed to check on Tori's condition during monthly visits. Obvious decline in weight, poor grooming, regression in behavior, and bruising are all tell tale signs of physical abuse. What has been the response?

### Attempts At Reform

As reported in the introduction, I was shocked to see another story written by the Los Angeles Times regarding more horror stories of violence against children. This was three years after the headline which shocked me into action. Here are two more shockingly brutal stories unveiled by Garret Therolf.

One example given was of 2 year old Abigail returned to parents after Social Workers failed to look into extensive parental abuse histories and question their weekend stays in jail. A month later Abigail was found dead, covered in bruises. The parents apparently attempted to cover their crime with blue paint!

Another case was that of Viola Van Cleef, who was allegedly killed by her foster mother—Viola Barker. Before her death the county abuse hot line received seven calls regarding Barker's home. Each time the investigating worker was not aware of the previous calls, according to the Time's report. In another case torture was cited in a report about a young boy, Johnny, who was beaten and underfed by a drug addicted mother. This mother had 5 drug tests scheduled by her CSW, but she refused to take them or missed them all. She also missed her scheduled meetings as well. The report goes on, "Without interviewing key witnesses, including the person who was identified as the likely caller to the hot line, CSW's closed the case and decided the child was not at risk. Three years later police went to the home following another tip. They found Johnny in a dark closet, much of his body burned by a glue gun. He had been starved, sodomized and forced to eat his feces."

There is nothing more to be said, the examples speak louder than anything I can say. Only it should be noted these examples came three years after the attempts of reform noted below. Which puts reform in rather poor light, it seems to me.

Persistent public scrutiny has illuminated several factors which appear to have contributed to abuse, neglect, and finally the death of a child. Seventy deaths in the past three years, public outcry, and constant investigations by the Board of Supervisors have placed enormous pressure on the Child Welfare Department. Consequently there have been numerous attempts to address the problems, various changes in procedure, improved technology, and communication; but the problems persist. Reform efforts have led to 300 workers being redeployed to child abuse investigations, thereby reducing investigator caseloads from 25 to 18. An additional layer of review before reports of abuse can be declared "unfounded" has been created. Problems persist:

- Children falling through the gaps: Probation, DCFS, Group Homes
- Failure to address mental health issues
- Multiple placements in succession
- Lack of coordination between agencies: Probation, Justice, DCFS
- Poorly supervised foster families
- Family dysfunction, multiple children in placement, poverty, transiency
- Children abandoned, neglected
- Children placed with other family members/relatives
- Untreated medical conditions
- Failure to support difficult children in foster care

- Inappropriate placement of children with relatives
- Failure to track and investigate cases
- Poorly trained, inexperienced CSWs assigned to Emergency Response Units
- Poorly functioning and inadequate Supervision
- Case loads that are too large
- Policy of Family Reunification resulting in inappropriate placements

As one can see, any one of the above factors can place a child at risk. Often several factors occur at the same time. Public outrage, when it increases and is fueled by the death of children coalesces into demands for change. This has led not only to attempts at reform, but also to playing musical chairs at the top of the department. The L.A. Times reports:

> The interim chief of Los Angeles County's troubled child welfare agency is quitting, a spokesman confirmed...The resignation of Jackie Contreras, effective September 16, is the third departure by an agency director in nine months. Trish Ploehn, the embattled former chief, was forced out in December. In May, her replacement, Antonia Jimenez, quit after defying the Board of Supervisors' plan to reform the Department of Children and Family Services. (August 2)

It is not clear who the Board will appoint as the next chief. At the time of the Contreras removal, the Board was undergoing a four-month search for a permanent director that revealed one candidate, but he apparently took another job. In part the search difficulty was compounded because Contreras did not appoint a chief deputy director after she assumed the top job. Because the job is so difficult, the problems so endemic, the department so large, and the politics of the job so treacherous, it will be difficult for them to find someone willing to take on such a Herculean task. Nevertheless, the cry for change continues, children continue to die, and one thing after another is attempted. Some might view the changes as "shuffling the deck chairs on the Titanic," but the Board continues to try various things based on what have been identified as glaring problems.

## Data Reporting

Just bringing the department into the 21st century of technology seems like an obvious improvement, as there have been glitches in reporting and tracking data as well as problems in interdepartmental communication. One problem has been the lack of communication between police and L.A. County. One response to this issue by the county authorities was to announce an electronic system for information sharing on suspected child abuse among Social Workers and police agencies. The goal is to reduce the number of abused or neglected children whose cases sometimes fall through the cracks. This system, the first in the nation, is viewed as a huge leap forward by the District Attorney. Since its inception in April, 2010, about 28,000 reports have been entered.

Previously, California law required cross reporting simultaneously of incidents by child welfare and law enforcement agencies. This led to a patchwork system via fax or e mail which often resulted in lost reports or reports being sent to the wrong agency. This delayed the process, causing errors or children getting lost in the shuffle. Sara Chavez is a good example of poor interagency communication and coordination. In other cases charges were often dismissed or lesser charges were filed.

Under the old system, it was hard for Social Workers to find out if charges were filed or keep track of the court case. In the new system, investigators working on a case will be able to see a previous report of suspected abuse, including incidents that are often not on the suspect's rap sheet but can be evidence of a pattern of abusive behavior. Again, in the Sarah Chavez case, her uncle's family had a rap sheet indicating numerous incidents of gang violence and gang-related violence. Now when a report is made, this information is shared through the internet in the child's region. Police and welfare agencies will be making crucial information more readily available.

However, the reporting and tracking of data presents its own challenges in terms of being able to determine the actual numbers of abuse and death related cases, or the actual definition of what constitutes abuse. Welfare agency death data was sealed until a law was signed by California Governor Arnold Schwarzenegger in 2007. This law allowed public access to child abuse figures. This has been somewhat controversial because some believe that "tragic and personal details" of a child's death should not be raked over by the newspapers. Director Trish Ploehn felt that the department was unfairly targeted and denigrated by placing the harsh spotlight on the most tragic cases. County Counsel objected under the grounds of confidentiality and privilege of law enforcement agencies. Among the 31 deaths over the last two years that met the county's standards of abuse and neglect, then-Director Ploehn identified 18 cases in which Social Workers committed serious errors.

## Family Reunification

While blaming directors has been an ongoing pattern, the past several months have seen other attempts at reform through changes of policy and procedures. One such revision came about as the Department examined the existing policy of *Family Reunification*. Up until 2009 the policy was designed to return children to their birth families as quickly as possible. This policy was encouraged with federal inducements. According to Garrett Therolf in a February 2009 article:

> In 2007 the department wagered that it could drive the numbers down further. It entered into an experimental federal program that pays the county a limited sum for foster care services. If it exceeded that amount, the county had to pay the difference. If it spent less, the county could use the savings to reduce child abuse and neglect as it saw fit.

This policy was examined, resulting in a policy shift. In 2009 at least 17 children died of abuse or neglect even though child welfare officials were well aware of their troubled family histories. After 14 youths died in 2008, these deaths led to reexamination of the push towards family reunification. However, it continues to be a somewhat contentious issue and has led to an increase in both the frequency and length of birth family visits. Nevertheless, children continue to die in spite of policy change.

## Poor Case Management

In the Sandoval case there is considerable evidence of improper case supervision which, had it been managed properly, would have picked up on the more obvious signs of parental misconduct: Dramatic weight loss, bruising, and behavioral regression. Again, Kontis's letter pointed out that "reams of concerns and pages of documentation over the past years were apparently ignored." Add to all of this the manner in which the court hearing handled the evidence, and this is how children die in the system.

Numerous other cases illustrate the same problems. The Los Angeles Times reported two more cases, stating that Jorge Tarin and Deandre Green died because of poor use of technology and lack of experience.

In the first case, an 11-year-old boy, Jorge Tarin, hung himself with a jump rope in his mother's home. Jorge, who had previously spent 15 months in foster care, told a school counselor that he intended to kill himself because he "was tired of people hitting [him] all the time." Just hours before Jorge's death, a Social Worker was sent to investigate the claim and left without him. Interestingly enough, this particular case was not categorized as abuse or neglect and hence was not statistically reported. "County Supervisor Zev Yaroslavsky was quoted as saying: "A reasonable person would say Jorge's suicide was caused by abuse or neglect. ...I don't know what the rationale was for that case." In the case of Deandre Green, an illegible computer printout sent a Social Worker repeatedly to the wrong address, and 2-year-old Deandre Green was beaten to death at his Long Beach home.

## Poor Judgment

In still another case, toddler Angel Montiel and his siblings were reunited with their parents after the couple enrolled in parenting classes, drug testing, and other family preservation services. Angel was subsequently beaten to death. An autopsy found dozens of injuries, some fresh and some healed, including broken bones and burns. Originally charged with murder, the mother pleaded no contest to manslaughter and was sentenced to 15 years in prison. In this case, the responsibility for poor judgment was shared by the CLC the CSW and the supervisor on the case. Critics of the case concluded, "Such deaths share familiar and persistent threads: Social Workers who did not follow procedure, did not have the information critical to make proper assessment, failure to communicate, poor judgment, and poor case supervision."

## Gross Negligence

Garret Therolf (March 24, 2010) reports:

> Responding to the killing of a 2-year-old foster child this month, Los Angeles County Supervisors voted to develop an investigations unit with the power to end contracts with troubled foster family agencies such as the one responsible for the child's death.

The most recent case had to do with a child under the care of United Care Inc. Viola Van Clief was battered to death in March while under the care of the above named FFA, an agency with a history of poor supervision and financial mismanagement. United Care, which oversees approximately 88 homes with over 200 foster children, has been repeatedly cited in recent years after caregivers choked, hit, or whipped their charges with a belt. In 1997, a foster child drowned while swimming unsupervised in a pool.

As a result of these incidents, County Supervisors created the investigative unit which led to consideration of cancelling the contract with United Care. The Welfare Agency has already begun removing children from the Agency's care. The investigative unit, created on a motion by Supervisor Michael Antonovich, is similar to a unit that was disbanded in 2004 during a departmental reorganization. The unit is designed to scrutinize the county's 60 nonprofit FFAs that oversee the care of 6,000 foster children.

What has changed with this motion could make a big difference. According to Antonovich's motion, regulators routinely investigate individual cases of abuse or neglect in the homes overseen by the various FFAs, but no one routinely examines the agency's overall track record with the authority to terminate contracts when problems accumulate. Only after the death of Viola Van Clief did investigators learn that United Care improperly allowed her foster mother's boyfriend to live in the house despite a violent armed robbery on his record. Her foster mother and her boyfriend were arrested on suspicion of murder. However, according to police records they were released two days later with no charges filed. "Police are continuing to investigate."

The story does not end there, because there is also culpability on the part of the County. It may have committed its own errors. The foster parents had been the subject of five previous child abuse complaints involving their own child and other foster children, a record that the department should have known about and would have precluded Viola's placement with them. In addition, it is suspected that the county Social Workers did not perform all their required checkups at the home and did not demand to see a locked room that would have revealed that the child was living in substandard conditions.

## Summary

What are we to make of this disturbing material? Children are dying in the system, and being abused at alarming rates. It is a system in disarray, and a social safety net with gaping holes in it that fails to protect and provide safe solutions to suffering children. Moreover, there is a vicious cycle of poverty, mental illness, and substance abuse among families that produce multiple victims. Reform falters, comes to a stop, goes in another direction or changes directors. Public rancor, blaming and looking for scapegoats occur. All the while the troubles of the nation's largest child-welfare department remain, many of them substantially unchanged. Failed attempts at meaningful reform have been well documented. Since early 2000, a task force reported the county's foster care system was in disarray and cried out for reform.

Several years of attempts to alter the system, we are still seeing outrageous reports of children dying. "A Canoga Park child was allowed to stay with his mother despite six previous warnings." Supervisor Molina severely criticized then Director David Sanders, saying, "This is about people not doing their jobs...the same ill-prepared, ill trained Social Workers could have hurt other people. Don't you consider it a dangerous situation when you have something as blatant as this?" Six years later children are still dying, the Board of Supervisors continues to ramp up the pressure and continues to call for reform. Questions about oversight, policy, and management still plague the department.

The attempts have ranged from improved technology, changes in the policy of pushing family reunification, increased investigative power, and Social Workers disciplined. Still children die. In 2009, 17 children died even though officials were well aware of their troubled family histories. In 2008, 14 children suffered such deaths. There have been more than 70 maltreatment deaths over the past three years. Each death is a tragedy. The deaths point to the overall complexity of the problems and difficulty in changing a large and unwieldy, problem-riddled system with insidious roots. It is hard to know where to begin.

Currently, we are not able to prevent mentally ill people from marrying and having unwanted children. We cannot prevent unmarried, illiterate teenage girls from getting pregnant. We are not able to prevent domestic violence and its root of substance abuse. Children will continue to be abused and neglected because of poverty and parents who do not know how to parent. The same women continue to produce multiple children that enter the system, furthering the burden. Of course there are programs designed to target each of these pressing social problems, but again, they lack funding because this particular sector of social policy always receives the biggest hits during difficult economic times. We should still advocate for preventive programs. In the meantime, we must take a long and serious look at the system mandated to protect the victims of all these social problems. Our children deserve better.

In the ten years I worked in the system, I have seen what I believe to be correctable problems. I have observed county Social Workers clearly not doing their jobs-- not making their mandatory visits, sloppy case management, poorly educated in critical areas of child development, overwhelmed by the sheer number of cases, not cooperating with fellow professionals, and clearly lacking knowledge about their cases. I have encountered the Children's Law Center making decisions that favor birth parents over the mental health of their children. I have encountered difficulties in contacting the lawyers for the children. I have had to deal with birth parents clearly not suitable to parent their own children. There are mothers with as many as 13 children in the system; who continue to produce even more children. I have had to sit through court-ordered birth family visits, painfully traumatizing to the children. All of these maladies have a cumulative negative impact on the children. Each time a mistake is made, a child suffers. Some mistakes are tragically fatal.

Below are some changes I feel would make a difference. First, at the County level: I would recommend training for the Social Workers in psychological issues related to attachment and child development along with abnormal psychology. This would lead to greater awareness of the severity of the birth family dysfunction and would give the Social Workers better tools to evaluate the quality of the attachment between parent and child. There needs to be better training for supervisors and more hands- on supervision with less time spent in meetings. One recently reported case in New York came to public attention when a supervisor found herself charged with contributing to the death of a child. Why?

> There were no case notes because the caseworker was spending an incredible amount of time in family court. Everybody in New York City for the most part knows that the family court is a notoriously inefficient system. So essentially he was spending hours on a wooden bench every day waiting for cases to be called that he was involved in. He might be there 3 or 4 times a week. He could be there twice a day and the Supervisor was spending an extraordinary amount of time, perhaps most of her hours of the day in meetings; many of these meetings which she and her coworkers consider virtually useless in terms of getting their jobs done. Many of the inefficiencies are baked into the system. Both the court system, and the child welfare system in this case need to be examined closely to sort out the complicated question of how much of it is personal failings and how much of it is systemic failings. (*Interview: All Things Considered from National Public Radio News*)

These are complex systems interacting with complex problems, being dealt with by all too fallible human beings.

Secondly, if family reunification is being considered, it is imperative that the birth family be subjected to an extensive assessment of the realistic possibility of the family being able to rectify the problems that led to the removal of the child. It is not enough to recommend a short series of parenting classes, or a short class in anger management, or a drug rehabilitation program. These measures are largely ineffective, and the programs are often not even completed.

Thirdly, there needs to be a change in the legal definitions related to birth family rights so that *history does matter* and multiple charges of incompetence, violence, and legal charges are considered when reunification is in question. This includes better background checks for families. This would, of course, necessitate cooperation and communication between court investigators, attorneys, County Social Workers, police, and feedback from Foster Family Social Workers.

Finally, regarding birth family visits, the traumatizing effects on the children must be given more weight. If the child is exhibiting severe reactions to contact with the parent, the visits must be stopped. If they are clearly detrimental to the child's wellbeing, the child should not be subjected to further abuse. Just because it is a mandated visit under supervision does not mean that the visit is not traumatizing.

In this regard, there also needs to be an appeal mechanism for review of cases when they develop problems, there is apparent dispute between agencies and the birth family, or there are apparent risks to the wellbeing of the child. The mechanism called a team decision meeting (TDM) is often a charade and does not produce meaningful outcomes. I have been in several where, as an example, there was a flawed reunification plan for a child to be being returned to live with his mother along with ten other family members in a 2-bedroom apartment. In another, well-discussed case, the CSW had an agenda which ran counter to all common sense and severely imperiled the children because the father was a sexual predator. In the Laura-Maria case, a CSW was allowed to run amok for four years while the children were shuttled about like suitcases from one placement to another. This case had it all: Incompetence, poor case management, poor supervision, bad judgment, injurious legal decisions regarding reunification, and no cooperation between team members.

Change will not be easy. It will not come quickly, and will be resisted by the sheer inertia of a large system composed of several interlocking agencies. Flawed systems, flawed people, and technological failures make for a lethal recipe in which children die. The thread of hope which runs through all of this is that there are caring, committed, aware individuals in these systems working for change. I hope that with continued pressure, informed citizenry outraged by continued deaths, scrutiny, and intelligent assessment change will come. The children cannot wait.

# Chapter 11

## THE ELUSIVE SEARCH FOR IMPLICIT IDENTITY
## SURVIVOR STORIES

*"Trouble?" echoed my sister; "trouble?" and then entered on a fearful catalogue of all the illnesses I had been guilty of, and all the acts of sleeplessness I had committed, and all the high places I had tumbled from, and all the low places I had tumbled into, and all the injuries I had done myself, and all the times she had wished me in my grave, and I had contumaciously refused to go there.*

Pip in Great Expectations-Charles Dickens, Chapter 4

*My sister's bringing up had made me sensitive. In the little world in which children have their existence whosoever brings them up, there is nothing so finely perceived and so finely felt, as injustice. It may be only small injustice that the child can be exposed to; but the child is small, and its world is small, and its rocking-horse stands as many hands high, according to scale, as a big-boned Irish hunter. Within myself, I had sustained, from my babyhood, a perpetual conflict with injustice. I had known, from the time when I could speak, that my sister, in her capricious and violent coercion, was unjust to me. I had cherished a profound conviction that her bringing me up by hand gave her no right to bring me up by jerks. Through all my punishments, disgraces, fasts and vigils, and other penitential performances, I had nursed this assurance; and to my communing so much with it, in a solitary and unprotected way, I in great part refer the fact that I was morally timid and very sensitive. I got rid of my injured feelings for the time, by kicking them into the brewery wall, and twisting them out of my hair…*

Pip in Great Expectations-Charles Dickens, Chapter 8

Primary relational trauma and disrupted attachment with the ensuing loss of family connections threatens the very foundations of all later development: a secure sense of self and identity, the ability to regulate emotion or soothe oneself, and the ability to engage in trusting, intimate relationships. Not only do primary relational trauma and disrupted attachment forever alter the normal trajectory of development, they also create an unhealed wound which becomes a deep reservoir of sadness, longing, fear, rage, guilt, shame, confusion and a sense of not belonging anywhere. Most importantly, it often resides in deeply dissociated and unconscious regions of the brain. I have emphasized the injurious impact of these early experiences throughout this work. The research is based on the research and contributions of many authors which supports these theories advanced by Allen Schore, one of the leading researchers in the area of infant development who phrased the issue very succinctly:

> Pathological dissociation—an enduring outcome of early relational trauma-is manifest in a maladaptive, highly defensive, rigid and closed system, one that responds to even low levels of inter subjective stress...this fragile unconscious system is susceptible to mind-body metabolic collapse and thereby a loss of energy dependent synaptic connection within the right brain, expressed in a sudden implosion of the *implicit self* and rupture of self-continuity. This disintegration of the right brain and collapse of the *implicit self* are signaled as the amplification of the parasympathetic effect of shame and disgust and the cognitions of hopelessness and helplessness. (Allan Schore, *The Science of the Art of Psychotherapy*, Pg. 83.)

Shame and disgust, the cognitions of hopelessness and helplessness, and the collapse of the *implicit self* are the enduring legacy of abuse. Levy phrased it more simply, "Traumatize a child and it becomes a life sentence."

Family, neighborhood, community, attachment to parents and siblings, school, and religious institutions, are the essential components of identity. The most essential of these foundational components are acquired in the first year of life and, according to Allan Schore, reside in the implicit unconscious memory of the right hemisphere of the brain. Early relational trauma and subsequent disruption of attachment may have a substantial impact on the developing self by affecting the entire developmental trajectory. He writes:

> Because the right hemisphere mediates the communication and regulation of emotional states, the rupture of inter subjectivity is accompanied by an instant dissipation of safety and trust. Stressful and painful emotional states associated with intensely high or low levels of arousal are not experienced in consciousness, but remain

in implicit memory as dysregulated, dissociated, unconscious affects. (*The Science of the Art of Psychotherapy*, Pg. 84)

This early and often devastating trauma, dysregulated, dissociated, unconscious affects coupled with the experience of disrupted attachment through placement and with a sense of loss of belonging, ensures that there is no secure base for attachment. Losses engendered by removal from family set in motion profound threats to the whole direction of a child's life. Removal from the home; the severing of family ties and all that entails is equivalent to uprooting a tree from its native habitat, and placing it in a foreign and possibly hostile environment and expecting it to thrive. In some cases this happens several times to children in foster care. Richard Rose cogently phrased the consequences:

> A child who has experienced poor care, life-threatening actions and/ or rejection at a young age may develop an impaired understanding of herself, her carers and the world in general. These beliefs can be deep-seated and act as the default concept for the rest of the child's life. The traumatized state is a potentially lifelong condition which is linked to learned behavior, reinforced by the experience of repeated trauma. (Rose, *Life Story Therapy with Traumatized Children*, Pg. 49)

I have written about the unrecognized and untreated effects of disrupted attachment in previous chapters. Well-known and documented data exists about the consequences. Research shows that young people in foster care are far more likely to endure homelessness, poverty, compromised health, unemployment and incarceration after they leave the foster care system.

- 54% earn a high school diploma
- 2% earn a Bachelor's degree or higher
- 84% become parents too soon, exposing their children to a repeated cycle of neglect and abuse
- 51% are unemployed
- 30% have no health insurance
- 25% experience homelessness
- 30% receive public assistance

- An unknown but suspected high number of children migrate to the state prison system

- 660 children have died while in foster care in Los Angeles County since 1990

These statistics do not even begin to tell the story of the hardship, pain, suffering, and helplessness and hopelessness of the lives of these children subjected to conditions that feel similar to the life lived by Pip under the care of his sister in England years ago. To live under a sense of threat and uncertainty profoundly cripples the vulnerable child's sense of self. Again, I turn to Allan Schore's remarkable insight into this entire process:

> The regulatory processes of affect synchrony, which creates states of positive arousal, and affective repair, which modulates states of negative arousal, are the fundamental building blocks of attachment and its associated emotions; and resilience in the face of stress and novelty is an ultimate indicator of attachment security. Through sequences of attunement, misattunement and reatunement an infant becomes a person, achieving a "psychological birth." This preverbal matrix forms the core of the implicit self. (Schore, Pg. 32)

In essence, what we are witnessing in the stories told are about individuals achieving "psychological birth." Statistics often have an empty, detached effect of distancing us from the harsher realities of these suffering children. Statistics need to be made flesh, given personalities. They do not tell the entire story, however. There are individuals, unique and admirable persons, whom I have encountered in my research and work in the past 10 years, whose stories I tell in this chapter. These are the stories of resilient individuals who have managed to survive their ordeals and create lives for themselves against all the odds and aforementioned statistics. It is the life process: attunement, misattunement and reatunement, perhaps these are their labor pains.

The unifying theme of this book has been *Shattered Lives*. I have examined the effects of early trauma and loss on the development of young children who entered the vast, impersonal system of The Child Welfare Department. I documented specific cases that tracked a child over time. The struggles of both the children and their families have been shown. Now it is time to look at the ones no longer in the system. These individuals entered the system, survived and emancipated. Their stories are told in their own words. From difficult beginnings, their lifelong struggles have been a search for *identity*, for an integrated, coherent, cohesive life story that makes sense to them. The very roots of our sense of self are in our families of origin and early attachments and if we are torn from that family, uprooted and displaced, how can we possibly find a secure sense of self?

> This powerful, regulating, rewarding quality of belonging to a group, a family, a community and culture is not just focused on the present. We each feel a need to be connected to the people of our past, and without being able to draw on this connection—this narrative—it is almost impossible to envision hopes and dreams for a connected and safe future. (Rose, p. 9)

During my research, I met an author, Patrick McMahon in an online discussion group. I became interested in his story, so I bought his book. In reading it I became impressed with his powerful use of metaphor to convey his remarkable story. Regarding being disconnected from his roots, he stated, "It is like beginning a book at chapter 10." In his moving and illuminating memoir, Patrick frames his search this way:

> Mom, what can you tell me about my adoption? The question is out. For all my life, it's been a hammer that could shatter a glass house with a tap. After approaching the brink many times during her visit from Chicago, after years of the relentless inner chant, *Who Am I?* I've sat her down in my living room and finally spilled it out." (*Becoming Patrick: A Memoir*, Pg. 3)

For those who have been adopted, this search has many levels and many obstacles. Also, for those who were placed in foster care first and then adopted, there are somewhat different issues. For those who remained in the system in long-term foster care, their issues are compounded. However, these groups have much in common. Their lives were all compromised by loss of family; they all have many issues related to identity and their identity quest has taken many forms. That quest searches in numerous directions, through immense data files, the internet, family photo albums, county birth records, and countless interviews. Each searcher is driven by the primal urge to discover their lost, secret roots. It is a longing to know who they are, to feel connected to family, to have roots, and in the process, try to build a coherent narrative. They are driven by an urge to create a life story that makes sense of a partially-told, partially-grasped reality of being given away, deserted, surrendered, abandoned, or involuntarily removed. In so doing, they are tasked with trying to sort fact from fiction, illusion and myth from reality. With each discovery, the story unfolds, and with each new discovery come feelings, often flooding and terrifying, feelings of shame and ambivalence, disgust, of wanting to know and not know. The mind, a beehive of feelings, thoughts, and memories, begins to assemble the narrative in search of, not only why, but also who they are. The elusive search for self is a universal phenomenon, but for those who experienced early interruptions of their life narrative, it is even more elusive, because it does not begin with the all-familiar family tree, the family of origin that is the foundation for our basic sense of self. To add a higher level of difficulty to the search (unknown to them) the quest must begin in their own unconscious, dissociated, implicit self. It may remain hidden and possibly fight against the physical search and attempts to discover and integrate these disconnected exceedingly painful experiences. In reality, their search for an identity is an inner journey. Though universal, it reflects the central experience of how we all remain a partial mystery to ourselves. Its beginning is the first encounter we have with another human being.

Erik Erikson, a developmental psychologist, described the early encounter between mother and child as a sacred meeting where the child experiences a sense of "Hallowed Presence." He goes on to note that if that sacred meeting is breeched, it creates in a child a perpetual sense of mourning. For the child who is removed, the search has an added layer of stigma. The shame and guilt of having been "adopted" or of being a foster child in our country is a mark on the forehead, a mark which signifies, stigmatizes the child as different and somehow inferior. Patrick describes the search as his "ache with no name, fascinated, saddened, furious, elated...[his] burning ache for connection with roots and a simmering rage for what [he] might have lost." (Pg 35) In essence, he wants to find a safe place he can call home.

These profound identity issues, revealed in the following stories, revolve around core dynamics: longing for home and family, the ambivalent nature of the search, conflicted loyalties, fear of what might be discovered, dealing with feelings of abandonment, the trauma of placement, the shock to self-esteem of not being wanted by the original family, grief and loss, the rising tide of powerful emotions of shame, guilt and fear, as well as the difficulty of making conscious the dissociated and unconscious implicit self and integrating the unfolding narrative into one's current sense of self.

The actual search for origins described so well by Patrick entails its own drama, the resistance of the bureaucracy, integrating the new information; each discovered new piece of the puzzle a veritable mine field. He deals with the emotional impact of each discovery: shame, secrets, lies, a "guilty hidden search." As the unfolding story is discovered, fantasies, myths, and expectations are incorporated into a working model of the world and his place in it. Who am I? Where do I fit? Why did they abandon me? The search takes on a life of its own and it has its own motif: the image of self--a cracked mirror, living with the ache with no name, fascinated, saddened, furious, elated...

> ...A ball of fire...a simmering rage for what I might have lost. The search is like living at the base of a dam that is about to break. The Grief would not stop. It seemed to come from someplace deeper than I've ever been. Someplace where there are no words, no thoughts, no associations with known people or things....I found myself wailing and kicking and flailing my arms, convulsing like a child, maybe like a baby, severely deprived." (*Becoming Patrick*, p. 58)

This struggle described in Patrick's story reflects the internal struggle of discovery and its deeply unconscious nature. It also deals with the double stigma of being adopted and gay, a problem that is not uncommon for children growing up in the system.

In addition to gay children, there are also a significant number of children who struggle with being transgender. Patrick writes that he felt exposed, vulnerable, and alienated. As he dug deeper into his roots, he felt an ever-increasing sense of shame: the shame of being gay, having an alcoholic father, being adopted, and knowing he was given away because he was not wanted or "defective." It was like searching for a path through shame in order to get the darker secrets loosened up and "out in the open. He rode the roller coaster ride of ambivalence into dark and scary places. Questions arose like "Who is my mother," and "Are you my mother?" and "How can I miss the mother I never knew?"

Patrick has documented and delineated the issues of identity quite well. The first issue is the life of perpetual morning described by Erikson, or a primal yearning for connection "just to know who I am." Second, there is the constant turmoil of feeling like there is a raging monster always lurking in the shadows, represented by periods of depression, confusion, and an uncertain future, like living in a dark haunted house. (This is a very apt description of struggling with what has been disassociated and remains largely unconscious; the implicit self) Third, all the feelings of shame and the embedded terror of having been given away are a child's constant state of being. Fourth, the child has to live with the deep unspoken unease that it might never go away even if the parents are found. Fifth, if the search culminates in finding the mother and her extended family, the next set of problems emerge, those being the integration of the new family into a new and fragile sense of self by getting to know them.

From this discovery there emerges a new gestalt, a merging of hidden identity, forgotten identity, imagined identity, and assumed identity. Which is the real, true self? Answering this question requires the creation, an amalgamation of different emerging selves. This is accompanied by shock, or dissociative periods where the sense of self feels unreal as all of the emerging bits of story are brought together. This is the very essence of an identity crisis which, when dealt with consciously, may lead to a transformation in which the child morphs into a new, coherent, integrated and redemptive narrative of the life story.

This period of the search is like editing a movie. There is so much that has to be assimilated and there are new realities which must be accommodated and integrated. This is an adaptive process where the self seeks equilibrium. It is a continual dialectic between the known and familiar and the unknown and frightening. Patrick described it as a "mind-blowing journey of dealing with childhood longings, discoveries, amazing change, a vast landscape of emotional storms, heartache and loss, of having to digest huge chunks of new material, of discovering too much way too soon, and of being overwhelmed. Experiencing dead zones and then coming alive again and discovering periods of bliss. It ends up being a story of discovery, of reconciliation, of a process of awakening and processing. Churn, spew it out, sift, go a little crazy and then find a kernel of peace and finally, of wanting to *know everything* but not wanting to *feel everything*. This is a classic exposition of what many trauma survivors reveal as their struggle to overcome traumatic injuries.

These are the identity issues revealed in one person's search for family. It is a search within a search; "in finding family hopefully, I find myself." What is remarkable is that while this search is going on, the individual is also dealing with all the normal problems of growing up. Patrick was fortunate in that his search did not officially begin until he was in his mid-thirties. For many children in the system, their search is often an unspoken question, a lived-with knowledge of being different from the moment of placement. Nevertheless, regardless of circumstance, theirs is a singular search, an imperative to discover the what, how, why and finally, who, in the elusive search for identity: to make the implicit self a more conscious and whole self.

What is remarkable is that as one courageous person tells his story, it shines a little more light in the darkness, and illuminates the path for others who find themselves on a similar quest. Then, as I discovered, these individual adventurers find each other and for them it becomes like finding lost family; someone who understands what it is like.

Speaking of finding lost family, recently I had the privilege of attending a support group for individuals who belonged to a triad—Adoptees, Foster Care children and Parents. This group is provided by a former colleague with whom I have worked for the past 10 years. It was hosted by Vista Del Mar, a residential facility for adolescents and children in the system.

Jeanette Yoffe, the sponsor of this group, is a survivor of the New York child welfare system. She grew up in foster care and was adopted. She has an understandable passion for her work, and it is no surprise that she has devoted her career as a psychotherapist to dealing with foster-adopt issues. She has created a public forum that meets once monthly called *Adopt a Salon*. At this particular meeting (during National Foster Care awareness month), she decided to share her story, which she previously presented as a one-woman stage show. She developed the show when she was an actress and with the help of her husband, a videographer, developed it into a video.

Jeanette Yoffe is an adult adoptee and former foster youth adopted at the age of 7 1/2. As a psychotherapist, author, blogger, educator and speaker, she shares her personal and professional experience on adoption and foster care across the country. She is passionate about training and teaches parents how to raise confident and well-adjusted children through adoption. She earned her Master degree in Clinical Psychology, specializing in children, from Antioch University in June of 2002. She has specialized for the past 12 years in the treatment of children who manifest serious deficits in their emotional-cognitive development.

Jeanette has worked with the following organizations: The Los Angeles County Department of Child and Family Services and the Department of Mental Health, Children's Bureau, Julia Ann Singer Center at Vista Del Mar, UCLA Ties for Families, Adoption Support Center, Kinship Center, Jewish Family Services, Valley Trauma Center, Antioch Counseling Center, Holy Family Services in Pasadena, and Southern California Foster Family & Adoption Agency as a Mental Health Therapist and a Foster Care Social Worker. (This last position is where I met her).

She was on the Advisory Council for Fostering Imagination, a mentoring program for at risk foster youth and a member of the California Adopted Youth Advocacy team. During her four years as a professional Social Worker and therapist, Jeanette developed innovative methods of working with foster and adopted children and currently presents creative workshops for parents as well as therapists and Social Workers in the Los Angeles Area.

She hosts a free support group for all members of the Adoption Constellation on the first Wednesday of every month in Los Angeles. In 2006, Jeanette received the Foster Care Hero Advocate award for the Foster Care Awareness Campaign from the County of Los Angeles for her outstanding contributions to the children and families served by the County Foster Care system. She lives in Los Angeles with her husband, Justin, and her son Nathan. Jeanette showed the group her video of her early experiences in foster care. She began her story as an 8-year-old that had been removed from her mother's care because the mother was schizophrenic and was in a psychiatric hospital, unable to care for her and her brother.

The story begins typically with Jeanette being brought to a prospective foster home in New York by a Social Worker to be placed with a potential family. She was introduced to them and subsequently placed. Jeanette reported that the foster father told her later that his impression was that Jeannette acted like she was auditioning for a part as a foster child in a play. He added, "You seemed to be trying to portray everything that you thought we would want in a child."

Jeanette's story is iconic, and she has agreed to let me tell her story because we both feel it has clearly defined issues so typical of the children in the system. It has all the elements of the struggle, issues and problems of being adopted and growing up with all the attendant residual problems in adulthood, (outlined so well by Patrick McMahon). The monthly group that she facilitates told their stories after seeing Jeanette's video. Like survivors of a ship wreck washed up on a deserted island, they told harrowing tales of abandonment, confusion, being lost in the system, living with guilty secrets, and seeking for a lost family and home with an almost primal urge to reunite with their original family.

Many were confused about their origins, trying to sort out myth from illusion and their own fantasies about the family they had lost. Searchers all, they struggled with the mixed feelings of wanting to know and not wanting to know. They live with a free-floating anxiety of uncertainty about themselves, their place in the world, a fantasy world of what might have been, and the illusions of finding paradise and reunification with a mythical family.

One woman described a group she had gravitated to as misfits, outsiders and aliens. Another divulged that he felt like an actor miscast in a play who did not know the plot or his lines. Each time they would gain a tidbit, glean a bit more of their history, it would have the portent of an information time bomb. Sometimes overwhelmed by what was discovered, they would shut down and try to integrate some new bit of information. One man found his father who did not want to be found. Not having family leaves a person feeling guilty, ashamed, and severely conflicted about their right to find their families. The bottom line of the search is a search for coherent identity. Again, Patrick clearly describes the predicament. "My life has been a play, scripted, carried out... in order for me to be chosen, I had to be un-chosen... feeling deserted, surrendered, given away, abandoned, sinks into my bones."

A room full of survivors, some 30 individuals, responded to Jeanette's story with questions, and tears: identifying and telling their stories. As I listened to them talk, I had the feeling of coming upon a lost tribe, the remnants of a lost civilization who had all washed up on the shore. Unknowingly, they were unconsciously attracted by the Trauma Bond of the *implicit self.* They were survivors and refugees, all with amazing stories--a modern-day Gilligan's island.

Jeanette further surprised us as she told her story. She revealed that she had been on a search for her father and because of today's technology could do much of it online. She apparently did a search and found an obituary of her grandfather from back east. This led to a subsequent discovery of two first cousins living in her immediate area. She found their names and discovered they were living nearby in Marina Del Rey, a suburb of Los Angeles.

Feeling conflicted about whether to observe proper boundaries and not intrude on their lives, she sat with the information for a few weeks, trying to resolve the conflict. She struggled with the issue of whether she really wanted to know, and if she had any right to alter their lives by appearing on their doorstep. Feeling overwhelmed by the ambivalent quest for roots, family, home, and to be connected, she contrived several plausible schemes about how she could "accidentally" run into them.

She finally got up the nerve to contact the first cousins of her father's sister. She sent an email and set up a meeting. When one cousin got the message, she grabbed a bottle of wine late at night, and ran over to her cousin's house and said, "We've got to talk." They did, and decided to meet with Jeanette. It was discovered that they knew Jeanette's father, Artie, and that he had been a part of their family for years, but that Jeanette and her brother were his deep, dark secret that none of the family knew about. After much discussion, they finally decided to meet with Jeanette, and also agreed to come to the support group. Jeanette introduced her guests as part of her long lost family and a product of her search for father.

This powerful, tearful, touching discovery of family ignited a firestorm of questions, similar stories and underlined the common bond of these survivors. They were all connected by their histories, they had a kinship of the disenfranchised; they were refugees washed up on the shore at Vista Del Mar.

These survivor stories have much to teach us, and the survivors have graciously opened their lives and agreed to tell us their stories so that we may all learn how they survived in spite of the daunting odds. We may also learn what they had to go through to achieve the success they have had in their lives, and it may help us understand why so many, badly wounded, struggle just to exist as casualties of an undeclared war. It will certainly help us understand and see the need for help for all those who are marginalized, institutionalized, and casualties who continue that elusive search for a livable, sustainable, coherent, and meaningful identity. Through this process, I hope we may come to have some compassion for those who live out their lives governed by the power of the disassociated *implicit self,* a shadow self never made conscious or integrated into their adult identities.

Out of that eventful evening in Del Mar, the theme of this chapter emerged like a montage created by a group of artists. What poured out that evening was like molten lava. One mid-twenties woman whose origins were from a Cherokee Indian family lived on the streets with other 'misfits'-- outsiders, drug addicts, and homeless people. A vagabond, she felt like she did not belong anywhere, looking, searching for home, family, and connection. All of these individuals shared a common bond through their stories of having been given away, feeling the sting and stigma of that identity. They were all searching for family and feeling ambivalent about knowing that family. They all had guilty secrets and the fear of either finding or not finding their families. Some felt like they had wandered into a war zone and had stumbled on unexploded bombs. Questions, questions, and more questions arose: where am I, who am I, and what am I? They sought validation in asking these questions at all. Finding out they were not alone and not so different from others after all enhanced the bond.

Many of the attendees had only fragments of their story and were living with myths told to them by people in the system, they lived with fragments and felt fragmented. All of them were on an identity quest, driven by a primal urge to reconnect with family and roots, and, in the process, connect with themselves. All the while in their search, they were feeling incomplete, creating a fantasy while trying to sort out illusion from reality. It was as if their hope was that having all of the questions answered would allow them to feel whole and finally know who they were.

There are many inherent dangers on this search. One young woman had been adopted by an affluent couple who helped her reunite with her birth mom. Her adoptive mother told the story of finding her and going to meet her. "We went way out in the back woods to this trailer on cinder blocks and met her mom. The place was full of cats and was filthy and I didn't want to touch anything," the foster mother revealed with some embarrassment. "I was shocked. This was way out of my comfort zone." But she said that "it allowed my adoptive daughter to feel much better even if she did walk away with several flea bites."

All of these individuals are survivors of circumstances not of their choosing or of their own making. This has left them wanting to know who they are, where they came from and why they were not wanted, given up, abandoned, and uprooted--feeling at some level always illegitimate, stigmatized and longing to feel whole, safe with family in a place where they can belong, a home that is safe, and a place they are wanted. Part of their search is also motivated by realistic concerns to know about their genetic and medical history. Several of the stories revealed that there were serious mental health issues such as schizophrenia, bipolar disorder and alcoholism. The implications are profound for each individual because we know that these tendencies are inherited. The underlying concern is, "If my mother or dad was mentally ill or alcoholic, what are the odds that I will have to deal with this at some time in my future?"

These are stories of children who were in the Child Welfare System who in addition, have suffered early primary relational trauma that leaves its own unique stamp. All of these stories are told with the hope that they will illuminate basic issues related to the impact of early traumatic loss and being placed in the system. Through the unique prism of their experience, we see how children respond to the experience of being removed from their homes and families, as wellas the effects of growing up in a home not of their choosing. I happily take this opportunity to share stories of individuals I know and admire who have, in spite of overwhelming odds, managed to emerge from the system and go on to functioning adulthood.

The basic questions I have asked them to answer are: How did you come to be in the system? What impact did it have? How did you cope? What are you doing in your life now? The questions I have tried to answer have to do with understanding such basic psychological processes as Resiliency, Identity Formation, coping with unpredictable environments, being stigmatized, feeling a loss of control, dealing with family relationships, and recovering from old trauma. How is it that these individuals seem to thrive when more than 80% of children placed in the system become homeless, mentally ill, drug addicted, or incarcerated? The stories I am about to tell are about remarkable individuals who are leading 'productive lives.' How did they manage to achieve this?

To continue with Jeanette's story, it only seems fitting to let her continue telling us in her own words.

> My name is Jeanette Shareen (Cox) (Fargo) (Kopitowsky) Yoffe, and I've been asked to contribute about my experiences growing up in foster care, being adopted and now working as a mental health professional.

> I'd like to start by saying I hope these words will help inspire, uplift, transform and strengthen the understanding of your own journey, through the myriad of challenges "my voice" has experienced, beginning as a biological daughter, foster kid, adopted daughter, sister, wife and mother. I am also a Psychotherapist who specializes in healing children's grief/loss upon separation from their original families and help facilitate attachment within their adoptive families.

> I am one of those people who in the past would "stuff" and "abandon" my early experiences because of the "shame" I felt. I truly thought "I had done something wrong" to cause my birth family and foster family to leave me. After years of difficult soul searching, therapy and the love and support of family and friends I have come to realize that there is no running from this sense of shame. There is only understanding where it comes from, rising above it and moving past. I know now that my existence or who I am was not the cause of the turmoil in my birth family and that the situation was out of my control. I was just a child, wholly dependent on the adults around me and it was the difficult circumstances in my birth family's lives that led to the heart wrenching decision to surrender me--<u>circumstances were not my fault and I was not responsible</u>

> Ever since this epiphany I have challenged myself to dig even deeper, to pick up the pieces of myself I've abandoned or lost, rekindle the goals and dreams I told myself would always be out of reach, feel my losses—avoid, bury and deny nothing—to be objective and honest. But also to take into account the many successes and achievements

in my life, both personally and professionally in order to "adopt" my many selves, put them all together and "become whole."

None of this was easy and in truth it is an on-going process, but a healing one and something I hope to inspire others to do through sharing my experiences and thoughts. As I reflect back I think of three different "journeys" that were critical to my personal development. This part will introduce the "first journey" which began in New York City in 1971. That was the year I was born in Bellevue Hospital. After leaving the hospital I lived with my biological mother and father for 15 months in a small NYC apartment on the lower east side. At the time my parents were married. I was an only child and I'm told I loved to go to the park and play every day if I could. My father worked in New York Telephone as a lineman and my mother was in NYC with a work visa from Argentina to be a dancer. My mother became pregnant for the $2^{nd}$ time when I was 6 months old but I never had a chance to meet that baby brother because just before he entered the world I was placed into foster care at 15 months—2 months before my brother would be born.

This is the story of how I was "surrendered" as it was told to me 30 years later in Buenos Aires, Argentina after the baby brother and I had "found" each other and then our biological mother through the help of the internet.

On a sunny August day in New York City, while I was happily playing in a park sand box, my birthmother told a woman sitting on a nearby bench, how stressed out she was. She told this random stranger that being pregnant and caring for me at the same time was just "too much for her." The woman then told her to "go to the Jewish Child Care, a foster care agency. They will take care of Jeanette for a little while so you can get some rest."

Which is exactly what she did! Apparently she did not speak very good English, had only been in the country for a few years, appeared shaken, stressed and overwhelmed. She would tell me years later that at the Agency they had her sign a document but as she did so she was thinking, "I was only going to be taken care of for a few weeks." Not in fact, surrendered for adoption. Which of course, is what happened.

In a letter from Jewish Child Care, dated July 29, 2004 I received some non-identifying information about the circumstances of my early separation. It was stated, "Your birth mother was emotionally quite fragile and was apparently under additional stress during her second pregnancy." An agency psychiatrist felt she might be Schizophrenic but noted she had reported taking LSD, which of course makes such a diagnosis tentative.

So on August 10, 1972, I was placed into a foster home in Long Island about 40 minutes outside New York City with a nice Jewish family. (On a side note. It wasn't until I was 17, talking with my foster sister that I learned I wasn't really Jewish. I was born Roman Catholic. I was shocked! My foster family had apparently put me in a high chair, drew a Jewish Star on my head, and sprinkled water on my forehead and made me Jewish! At 13 I had a Bat Mitzvah and everything! I had no inkling this wasn't the religion into which I was born).

The records I've been able to see indicate numerous visits with my birth parents even after I entered foster care. I'm not sure exactly how many but the letter states "frequently." When I think about this today, it just tears my heart. How difficult and confusing it must have been for me to see my birth parents for a short while and then watch them go away every time. Leaving me over and over again. What is a baby to think? Over and over I probably thought they were not coming back and would never see them again. Only to have them come and all those expectations flood, and through it all I don't recall anyone sitting down and talking to me, explaining what was happening. . . I was alone!

Presently, I often think of that time period and how helpless I must have felt and vulnerable and guilty. . .But now as an adult and psychotherapist I find I am able to fill that hole and help explain to children and their families *exactly what is happening*. There is enough mystery in adoption. I feel we owe it to the children involved to keep them as informed as possible. My experience as a foster care Social Worker for four years gave me the opportunity to do this day in and day out inside foster homes of every sort. Every day of the week I would watch the babies have visits with their birth families and I would identify with each and every one of them. I understood their cries and I understood what they needed deep inside. I would take the babies to and from visits with my little Toyota all across Los Angeles. I would talk to them and let them know I heard their cry. I would be with them through all their tears and tell them "everything was going to be okay." I wanted them to know they were *loved and accepted.* I would give them what I so desperately needed as a child, the acceptance that my feelings were valid. The lack of having someone do this for me fueled many years of feeling rejected, unloved and unaccepted for having these feelings, and I am now certain each visit with my birth family reinforced these feelings of "being abandoned" all over again.

Before I entered this field and chose to work with kids like me, I hoped the experience of social work would become a "corrective emotional experience," because I would be in control now as an adult and no longer a helpless victim as a child. I could now make sense of my past, open up to my grief, feel my grief. . . and cry so I could let go, and it has to some degree, it has helped me reach this epiphany but the feelings are always there.

This is another important piece of that epiphany---that we cannot change the facts about our past, the reality will always be there, however cold or frightening. However we can change the way we feel about it. Because "being adopted" is not the condition, the condition is the lifelong process of working through our loss, mourning our loss and picking up the pieces we want to keep and discarding those that we don't want in order to reframe our lives in such a way that makes us richer and more resilient beings.

I believe each and every one of us deserves to have an opportunity to change their attitude about their past and get out from under the suffocating thought process of guilt and abandonment and to make a choice to not be a victim. To say to the world, *"I am not a victim anymore and I am not a reject. I am a hero and I am worthy. I can do something with this pain now because I am an adult. My life is no longer at the mercy of other people: It is at the mercy of me."*

This is my work. To help as many people get to that healthy place as possible. Simply being at the *"mercy of me"* and doing whatever they can do to help themselves lead happy, fulfilling lives and understand the past but live in the present.

After Jeanette wrote this piece for me, I then arranged for an interview with her at her office in West Los Angeles. She was clearly a little apprehensive about doing this, but once we got started talking, she talked freely and at times struggled with difficult feelings. She was able to acknowledge with considerable insight that each time she told the story it felt like she was gaining greater integration and was becoming more compassionate with herself. This, of course, confirms my belief that as we struggle to make sense of the story of our lives and recount the story with feeling, it becomes a transforming and healing experience. After doing years of psychotherapy with individuals with unhealed childhood trauma, I have had this faith in the process confirmed over and over again.

The specific identity issues that are revealed in Jeanette's story are the recurring themes of foster and adoptive children. The original trauma of being removed from the home at the vulnerable age of 15 months, and the secondary trauma of multiple placements, the failure of social services to provide supportive or therapeutic services to children and families undergoing placement trauma, and the lifelong residual effects of trauma. Also, unremitting longing for family, the unhealed wounds of abandonment, shame, grief, loss, anger, damaged self-esteem, anxiety, inability to trust, and residual attachment problems, and the perpetual unresolved identity questions: who am I, where do I belong, what am I to become?

There are several critical moments, as there are in any person's life, but it is even more apparent in the lives of those who have had their early lives disrupted by removal from their families. Jeanette's story begins with a happenstance. Her mother takes her to play in the park and strikes up a conversation with a random stranger. She has Jeanette who is 15 months old and is pregnant with a second child, a son.

This event happens over and over again to thousands of children, and in this case, it is caused by a mother who is mentally unstable. Jeanette's mother had many problems and it was these problems which made it impossible for her to be an adequate mother. It was also apparently destabilizing to her marriage as well. According to Jeanette, her mother was tentatively diagnosed as Schizophrenic (a serious, major form of mental illness and is characterized (typically) by poor judgment, erratic and often bizarre behavior and makes the individual intolerant of stress. This disorder would manifest itself in the mother leaving the home periodically and disappearing for days at a time. Jeanette revealed that she had memories of being left alone by her mother. She speculates that the home situation had many problems which were upsetting to her father as well, because her mother was probably a drug user and was also sexually promiscuous.

One can imagine the scene when she came home without Jeanette and announced to her husband she couldn't take care of Jeanette and left her with a Jewish Foster Care Agency. She was thinking it was only for a short while, but this decision led to Jeanette being placed with a family for 6 years. This is the first major trauma in Jeanette's life. As Jeanette learned years later, her mother is now a full time resident in a psychiatric facility in Argentina and has been there for years. Jeanette has visited her there.

The second major issue caused by the mother's mental illness is the disruption of the family by placement. As is often the case, it is not just one placement. In Jeanette's case, it turned into two placements six years apart. Jeanette remembers this time as being very traumatic. She felt abandoned, shamed, humiliated, embarrassed, and reacted to this trauma with a recurring dream of continuously falling. She also reports crying for months because of the abandonment. She states that she never knew she had a brother until one bizarre day when a Social Worker arrived to tell her that she and her brother were going on a long plane ride to visit their mother in Argentina (something happened at this point and the visit never took place).

During the first placement Jeanette thought the foster parents were her real parents and wondered why "her birth father (a stranger to her) would come to visit." His visits were sporadic and she does not remember them well. What she does remember was that they were traumatic. Every time he would come and then leave she felt repeatedly abandoned as each visit re traumatized her.

What was only to be a temporary placement turned into six years. For reasons unclear to Jeanette, a decision was made to place her in another home, and this time it was to be a 'permanent placement.' Jeanette recalls that there were no social services to help her adjust to the first placement. It was also during this first placement that she learned from her foster sibling that she was not Jewish. As mentioned in her story, they engaged in a pseudo-religious ritual that "presto" made her Jewish.

This second placement was another major trauma for Jeanette. When she was told she was going to another home, she remembers clinging, kicking, screaming, and fighting in protest. She did not want to go, and in the car ride to the new home she remembers dissociating; she shut down and sat and stared. Jeanette describes

270

herself as a "stuffer" because she was afraid to show her vulnerability. She put on a "happy, smiling face."

This second placement reinforced all of her feelings that she was flawed, that there must be something terribly wrong with her for being shoved out of her previous families. The transition to the new family was not handled well. During the transition, she had several trial visits with other families. She would be told she was going to visit a different family, would participate in the visit and then nothing would happen. She remembers trying to be perfect and trying to see if she could get a read on how this new family wanted her to be. She remembers asking her new adoptive mother, after being there a few years, "When are you going to give me away again?" This sense of shame is a major theme running through the narratives of foster and adoptive children. Jeanette remembers creating a "false self," in which she put on a happy, smiling face to cover how sad and scared she was. She was having a very hard time making sense of why she was placed a second time. She concluded that it was her fault, saying to herself, "I'm bad, and it's my fault." It was during this time she felt like she was in limbo. Behind the happy face she began developing all kinds of "strange behaviors." In reality, they are not 'strange', because they are reactions that most children have when they have disrupted placements. She began wetting the bed, had stomach aches, began sleep walking, and would hoard candy and keep it all over her room in secret hiding places. She also ruined her dolls, and wrote on the floor with crayons. It was through this incident of writing on the floor that she realized that she was trying to make her floor her very own by marking it. Also, she admits that she was so nervous that she compulsively picked her nose until she would have a nose bleed, which would result in a trip to the Emergency Room. Jeanette acknowledges that she very much wanted to return to her foster parents and arrangements were made for her to have occasional visits with them.

Memories of her adoptive home reveal that she wore hand-me-down clothes and was treated differently from her two siblings, who were natural children of the parents. She also remembers her adoptive mother being a perfectionist, rigid with control issues, and that she dressed her like a doll. "She was very hard on me and did a lot of shaming. At times, I felt so stupid when she would sit with me at the kitchen table and help me with my homework. I just felt like I couldn't do it. Even though she was hard on me, somehow I learned that I could do things."

In this story of Jeanette's early life as an adopted child, she views her journey as one that begins with being a helpless victim, alone, vulnerable, abandoned and ashamed. Her journey is one of gaining awareness, healing and power as reflected in her statement: *"I am no longer a victim anymore and I am not a reject. I am a hero and I am worthy. My life is no longer at the mercy of other people. It is at the mercy of me."* Now, as an adult woman, she is still dealing with the effects of early trauma and loss. She admits that she still longs for a reunification with her father and has actively pursued it. It has been met with a refusal on his part. This leaves Jeanette with overwhelming feelings of rejection, being abandoned all over again. She used the term in our interview as "being shackled to him." It is as if she needs him to "affirm" her as a person, and his refusal to have anything to do with her leaves her with a great deal of frustration, anger and unresolved grief. Her fantasy of reconciliation is met with coldness and denial. She recognizes that he has been struggling with alcoholism for years, still lives in the same apartment she was born in, and probably was also traumatized by his wife's illness, which resulted in losing both of his children to placement.

Jeanette also recognizes that her choice of occupation is directly related to her early trauma. She strongly identifies with the children she works with, as well as the adults who have taken the children into their homes. The therapy work takes its toll on Jeanette because it often taps into her personal memories and grief issues. In her struggle to find and heal herself, she recognizes that she is both healer and the one needing healing. Therapists are often characterized as "Wounded Healers." I am also one. This is why I am so fascinated by traumatized children and their stories; their trauma is mirrored in my own life.

The reader is by now aware that ambivalence is one of the most common traits of a traumatized child. Jeanette recognizes that it plays itself out in her marriage as well as her role of mother. Fear of abandonment and difficulty trusting are the legacy of early abandonment. It is a need for love and a need to fill the hole where the original family is missing, coupled with the unconscious expectation and fear that they will not be there for her and she will be alone. The resolution of ambivalence is very difficult. It requires processing very deeply-felt feelings of disappointment and hurt and unmet expectations. These losses must be grieved, and each one must be faced, felt and given expression. Fantasies and illusions of reunification must be squared with the realities of the current situation. For Jeanette, the ultimate loss was of the original family. That loss can never be regained. That fateful visit in the park cannot be undone. Jeanette's life, her unborn brother, her father and mother's future altered by her mother's chance conversation with a stranger on a park bench all went down a path that brought them to this present moment.

It changed all of their lives forever and so Jeanette continues to ask, "Who am I?" By her work, searching, and healing, she is defining herself. In her work, her marriage, and reaching out to others with similar wounds, she is creating a more secure base and is finding a surrogate family, one of her own making and one under her own control. This is her new identity: an empowered and enlightened adult bearing her wounds as she helps others with the wisdom she is gaining in her search, her quest for reconciliation.

The next story is quite different in some ways, but similar in others. It is about Alex. I came to know him when he was 15 years old. I was assigned his case and made regular home visits to his foster home where he lived with two gay foster parents and two other adolescent foster siblings. His time in this placement was not without drama because of many issues related to the relationship between his foster siblings and the foster parents. He subsequently graduated from high school and was emancipated from the system. He is now in his sophomore year at UCLA. Alex wrote me this when I approached him with my idea for telling his story in his own words.

I grew up moving around with my mother and brother at a young age. We finally settled in an apartment in Highland Park in Los Angeles when I was 4 years old. This was our home for the next 6 years. I lived here with my single mother and older brother who was 6 at the time. My father was out of the picture before I could remember. My mother and father filed for a divorce just after my birth and as a result, he was not involved in our life from that point on. I was informed that the divorce occurred because of mental illnesses that my mom had developed shortly before.

For the next 6 years, my mother, brother, and I remained in the one apartment complex. I attended Yorkdale Elementary School until 2002 (age 10) when I witnessed the first relapse my mother had experienced. She developed several mental illnesses at one point in her life due to traumatic occurrences. Her relapse led to our neglect and behavior that led her to be taken into custody for some time. During this period, my brother and I were taken to our grandmother's house, only to be taken away for reasons I still do not quite understand. Perhaps she was deemed unfit to care for us. Following this, we were placed into foster care for the first time.

My personal thoughts about foster care were not negative at the time. I knew that where I was beforehand was not the best place for me so I lacked the common feelings of homesickness or sorrow after leaving home. I was actually okay with being in care because I knew this was better for me. During this placement, however, my brother and I became very aggressive with each other and this consequently led to our separation for the remainder of our time in care, which was not too long. The case closed within 2 years and my brother and I were back with our mother just in time to start the second semester of my 6th grade school year. Things seemed to be returning to normal when the exact same thing happened after 2 months. We were placed into care again for the second time but this time the case was closed within 2 months. I didn't really know what the reasons were behind that but I wasn't complaining.

Skipping a bit ahead, we all lived together for the next 3 years without a hiccup. At the age of 15, yet again, the same thing occurred. We were taken into care for the 3rd time. After several months in the home with my brother, things got really out of hand between us and I resorted to seeking help at the local police department. This resulted in our separation again. The next home that I was placed in was where I lived until my high school graduation and emancipation.

After Alex wrote me his abbreviated autobiography, I invited him to spend the day with me talking about his life. Alex is a mixed race 20-year-old male. His father was from the Netherlands, and his mother is Korean. His older brother Alvin is serving in the Military and they stay in touch. Understanding Alex's journey into the system begins with his mother's mental illness. When a single mother is unable to care for her children and the children are removed, there are many extenuating circumstances. Alex told me his family history.

It begins with a huge tragedy. Alex's parents had two children before they had him and his brother, a 2-year-old boy and a 3-year-old girl. According to Alex, they were being cared for by a baby sitter when they both ended up drowning in a swimming pool. His brother was born one year after their deaths, and Alex was born two years later. Shortly thereafter his parents divorced and his father returned to the Netherlands and was never heard from again. I asked Alex how he felt about his father's disappearance. He stated that there were times when he was much younger that he wished for a normal family. He says:

> ...But since he was never there I don't know what I might have been missing out on... In terms of why he left us, I don't know. It may have been that the deaths of their two children and my mother's illness may have been too much for him so he went home to his family...In terms of the effect that my father's absence has had on my life, it cannot be pinpointed. My life is going very well in my eyes, despite the unfortunate circumstances that occurred. I sometimes think that things wouldn't have gone this well if my father was present. The benefits of having been in foster care are definitely something that I am grateful for. I am pretty much set financially in terms of higher education without having to place any financial burdens on anyone else. Additionally, I feel that my experiences have allowed me to grow in many different aspects and prepared me to be independent far earlier than any of my peers. This may not have been the case if my father had been present."

Alex describes his relationship with his mother before placement as close and caring and describes it the same way today. For the past five years, she has been living in a residential treatment facility and Alex visits her twice a month.

I asked Alex to elaborate on the circumstances of his placement. He stated that his mother stopped functioning for two weeks.

"She stopped cooking, was highly agitated, restless, and stopped sleeping. She developed paranoid thoughts, and began behaving strangely (gross symptoms of an apparent psychotic episode). One day she went to my school and talked to the principal." The principal apparently called and reported her to the police, who came and took Alex and his brother away and called Child Protective Services. CPS discovered that there was a relative, the maternal grandmother, and called her, placing the boys with her for two weeks. Then, for reasons unclear to Alex, the boys were removed from her home. This episode set off a chain reaction of unstable, multiple placements as mentioned in Alex's story. They were first placed with a single woman who lived in Fontana with two children of her own. Alex and his brother were there for a year and a half. Interestingly enough, he says he has no memories of that experience (This is a common experience due to dissociation).

They were then placed back with their mother for two months, and when she regressed, the police had to be called back and they again went into placement. As is often the case, the CSW could not find a home that would take two siblings so they were placed in a temporary home for a week until a suitable foster home could be found. They were then placed in a foster home in Long Beach with a family who had three other foster kids. This placement lasted two months followed by a return to their mother.

It should be noted that during all this time of upheaval, Alex reports that he was being physically and emotionally abused by his older brother; they would repeatedly get into physical fights. Alex states that each time he was reunited with his mother it felt good, and that each time he was removed it was very difficult.

After the Long Beach placement he and his brother were able to stay with their mother for three years in Highland Park. During this time, however, the conflict between him and his brother worsened. He became afraid of his brother because he was physically abusive on a daily basis. He described his brother as domineering and a control freak and that he wanted to get away from him. During this time, Alex was doing well in school.

One day things deteriorated again. He and his brother got into a physical altercation which led Alex to seek help at a local police station. He was placed in a Covina home for a month and moved to Glendale. (As a personal observation, Alex demonstrated much maturity and insight by seeking help, but interestingly enough did not report the abuse directly to his Social Worker). Finally, a social worker was informed about the physical abuse and separated them, finding a permanent placement for Alex with the two men with whom he lived with until graduation from High School. The brother remained in care in the Glendale home until he was able to get into transitional housing. From there he joined the Army.

Alex describes the home where he lived from the age of 15 until 18 as "OK." Personally, I thought it was "less than ok." The foster dads were very uncooperative and at times verbally abusive with me. They also had issues in their relationship with fidelity and drug usage. The other two foster siblings in the home had their own issues with a drug-addicted mother who died of an apparent drug overdose and conflicts with the foster parents. Alex describes himself as being on the periphery, watching all the drama and staying out of it (This seems to be Alex's primary defense, remaining insulated and detached). He did well in school and the foster dads had a friend connected with UCLA who was instrumental in helping him apply and get accepted. He describes his first year as very difficult, a kind of culture shock, being away from home and on his own without family, as well as being overwhelmed academically. UCLA has a program that helps foster youth make the adjustment to college which Alex found helpful. That program is called Bruin Guardian Scholars Program. Their resources include workshops on time management and study habits, staying for free in college housing between breaks in semesters. They also provide care packages when needed. It is a very good support program exclusively for students who have been in foster care.

Presently Alex is doing well at UCLA and his brother is in still the Army. They stay in touch regularly and Alex describes their relationship as much improved now that they do not live together and both have grown up. No doubt a large part of their friction was due to sibling rivalry, the instability of their lives and the stress related to so much loss of control when living with strangers. Today Alex appears to be content with his life. He is enjoying school, loves to play the guitar and get together with friends to "Jam." He has several friends and remains in contact with his former foster parents whom he describes as close and supportive. He writes, "I am blessed to have them in my life. We speak frequently on the phone and will occasionally meet and get together about once a month. They check in with me to make sure everything is going ok, and they are there to support me if I need it." As mentioned, Alex still visits his mother twice monthly. In fact, the day of our interview I took him to visit his mother and met her. They appear to be quite close.

Alex attributes his survival of the placement ordeal to being adaptable. He has the ability to socialize and makes friends easily. He also believes that even though his mother has serious mental health problems, before her illness they were close, and this appears to have given him an early foundation of security. Even though there was a great deal of disruption and multiple placements, he still managed to maintain a relationship with her. Alex's story is still unfolding. He plans to graduate from UCLA with a degree in biology and perhaps work on a Master's Degree. What is atypical of individuals with such a traumatic history is that he believes he has a future and the ability to control it. As part of his commitment to others, Alex continues to work with a foster family agency. He volunteers his time and frequently agrees to speak to groups about his story.

His reflections on being in the system focus on the way Social Workers failed to protect him from his brother and how they did not pick up on the severity of his mother's mental illness. He feels that a lot of the placements could have been prevented if the CSW would not have continued to reunify him and his brother with his mother for brief periods, only to have to move again when she regressed. Without the stress of having to care for the two boys, the mother has been relatively stable while living in a residential care facility. Perhaps if she had been adequately assessed for her mental competency, she would not have been tasked with trying to do more than she was capable of doing and the boys would have not been moved around so many times. This highlights the aforementioned issue of the pressure to reunify families and the resultant havoc of multiple placements that happens when reunification fails. When I asked Alex to reflect on telling his story, He replied, "It's all good. I've had lots of time to reflect about my past and I have gotten to the point where I am very comfortable sharing my experiences with others."

For Alex, the identity issues have revolved around his mother's illness, his father's desertion and the resultant divorce that precipitated instability in his life through the critical developmental years of early childhood to adulthood. Again, multiple placements and repeated reunification followed by family disruptions were major stressors in his life.

The transition from foster care through emancipation comes at a critical time in an adolescent's life. Development to adulthood for adolescents is typified by leaving home and finding a place in the world. This is a stage that, for many young adults in the system, becomes a failed milestone. Failure to successfully leave the system and transition into self-dependence is well documented. Alex has done a remarkable job of maintaining family connections and of transitioning to college and successfully creating a functioning support system for himself. Anyone who has left home, gone to college and dealt with all the demands of college life while living on their own for the first time knows the challenges thereof. Skills of self-regulation are required for success. Performing regular self-care habits, eating, sleeping, and personal hygiene, developing study habits, getting up and going to class, deciding whether to study or go to a party are all examples of self-regulation. Additionally, dealing with the pressure of deadlines and exams is a challenge that any kid going off to college must manage. For someone with less maturity, all of these challenges would be overwhelming.

In addition to responding to the challenges of college, Alex also has demonstrated another level of identity development: empathy and impulse control. His empathy shows in his apparent high regard for his relationships; he treats people well. He is also sensitive to their needs and has good boundaries. He does not use people and throw them away, but maintains his friendships. Impulse control is also a healthy marker of secure identity. Alex's success in college demonstrates that, as success in college is all about deferred gratification. I had one case, an 18-year-old girl from a very poor family, who came into foster care as an adolescent and stayed with one family for five years. She went away to college and had the same kind of support as Alex, but she washed out in two semesters. She couldn't handle the lack of structure, the pressure to do the work, and the temptations of being on her own without supervision. Overwhelmed and totally lost, she became very depressed, failed her classes and returned home. She was lucky, as her foster parents remained supportive and let her come back. For many foster youths who emancipate from the system, they have nowhere to go.

Achieving successful emancipation is a major achievement. It reflects a secure sense of self with an optimistic world view. Alex believes that he has a future that is under his control and that his goals are reasonable and obtainable. He has the social skills to draw people to him and the ability to move toward his goals in a reasonable fashion. He appears to have a realistic self appraisal and does not appear to be burdened by anxiety, depression, or regrets over his past. For someone who has experienced the kinds of losses, disruptions, and traumas in life that he has, he appears to have done a remarkable job of surviving a very difficult childhood and adolescence and is moving well into the next phase of identity development, early adulthood. His resiliency under many major life stressors indicates a strong core personality.

My next story shows an entirely different life circumstance. These circumstances would have destroyed most people, but she persevered in spite of horrific abuse and a system which did more harm than good. It is the story of a woman who is 36 years old, married, with a daughter who just graduated from high school. I have known her for several years, and originally met her when she spoke in a meeting at St. Anne's School for Girls in Los Angeles. I was so impressed with her courage and how she told her story that I immediately introduced myself and arranged a series of lunches to hear more of her story. I had originally envisioned telling her story through a series of videos, but then I changed my mind and decided to write this book. We lost contact and but one day, a few years later, I found a file I had made and decided to contact her again with my revised plan. She responded enthusiastically to my request to meet and wrote me this background piece. Here is Machelle's story.

> For some autobiographical material, I was born on 12-30-1977 in Trenton, New Jersey to my mother who was 18 and had 2 children before me at the ages of 14, and 16. She was a product of the foster care system starting at the age of 14 when she was taken from her parents because they abused her physically, sexually and mentally (incest). She became pregnant with my grandfather's child and gave birth to a baby boy who was given up for adoption. We moved to California when I was 2 or 3 years old (1979-1980) as my mother tried to get as far away from her past as she could. However, her past followed her. The emotional and psychological impact caused by her parents was too much for her to overcome. Her past caused her to go into a depression as she blamed herself and experienced feelings of shame and guilt that projected onto my brother and me, long after the trauma had been caused. She turned to alcohol, prescription drugs, and men to try and ease her pain. In doing so, she neglected my brother and mr and treated us no differently than she had been treated. We were physically and emotionally abused.

> She was institutionalized for the first time when I was 7 years old (1984) for a year. She sent my brother and me to the only people she knew. The same people who had made her life a living hell, her mother and father. My brother and I lived a nightmare in New Jersey that year being passed from stranger to stranger. Although they were relatives, we had never met, seen or even knew of these people. It was then I experienced being sexually abused repeatedly by cousins and family friends. My grandmother was the physical abuser. She would throw me around like a rag doll and pour food on my head if I didn't finish eating.

> When we moved back to California in 1985, it seemed my mother had gotten better, however it never lasted. She would always relapse. Our family moved every 6 months to a year because my mom was always running from something; be it men, financial troubles or whatever, my brother and I always suffered for it. I can probably name every city in the San Fernando Valley that we have lived in. Reseda, Sherman Oaks, Sun Valley, Sylmar, Panorama City, Sepulveda, Northridge, Encino, Studio City and I'm sure

there are those that I don't even remember. I was always subjected to numerous men coming in and out of the house and only once did she do anything about it. Her priorities of drowning herself to forget the pain was always more important. Most of the time my mother was nowhere to be found, so it was just me and my brother, which was fine with us because when she was around, we were terrified until she would pass out and we would be in peace. By the time I was 12 and my brother 14 (1989), we had been to at least 6 different schools, if not more. I can only recount so many. My brother and I had finally gotten fed up. My brother ran away one day while we were out with my mother. She had one of her violent alcoholic rages and threw a beer on my brother's friend and attacked her. She was only 16. I, on the other hand, had nowhere to run. That year was the worst year because I was the only one she could attack. Before, the attacks were split between my brother and [me]. I had finally had enough and one night she came stumbling in drunk as I was eating my French toast. One of the things I could actually cook for myself. She punched me in my face and asked why her bed wasn't made. We were always her maids, cooks, and at times it felt as if she looked at my brother and me as her mates. It made me sick. I told her if she hit me again I would stab her and she did it again and I stabbed her. I ran as fast as I could out the door. This was the first of many numerous times my mother and I would go to battle and the police would be called. From then on, I stopped taking her crap and I fought back. I stopped being afraid and became the violent aggressor myself. From 1989 to1991, I did as I pleased and stayed with friends, only sneaking into my house when I knew my mother wasn't there. She again had been institutionalized for trying to kill herself. I on the other hand started to hang out with the wrong crowd, ran the streets, got into fights and constantly skipped school. I always had all F's. Although I had been stopped by police numerous times on the street and when altercations would occur with my mother, I had never been taken away. I finally got caught stealing in 1992 and when my mother was called to come get me from the Van Nuys police station, she just laughed and told the cops to take me away, she didn't care, that I needed to be taught a lesson. For this I was thrilled. To finally be taken away from her, to have a place to sleep and not be afraid, to have 3 meals a day and a chance to actually go to school not just because I had to but because I wanted to. My trip to Sylmar Juvenile Hall didn't last long however. Only a couple of days in and my mom came to my court date and told the judge how she wanted me to come back home. I begged the judge not to send me back but he did anyway. As soon as I was released, my mother started right away in the car yelling and screaming about how dare

I want to stay there. As soon as we got home I left immediately and went to stay with my boyfriend at the time. Of course I was put on 6-months probation with community service and an ankle bracelet to monitor my every move. I had to bring my grades u, which I did. Academics was never my problem, it was my home life. My probation officer at the time was a wonderful woman who believed in me and knew my mother was a head case. She tried numerous times to prove that my mother was unfit but my mother would always turn it around on me [saying] that I was the one who had the issues and she had no control of me. She was afraid of me. It was during my time of probation that I had found out I was pregnant. That was the supposed final straw for my mother. She called the police to have me removed from the house stating that my boyfriend and I were threatening her. However I kept an answering machine tape with messages from my mother and her boyfriend threatening to hang me and my boyfriend, messages of my mother calling me every name in the book. My probation officer was able to use this proof and finally have me taken away for good and that is when I became a ward of the court. August of 1993.

I'm sure there is much more you need but I'm thinking that's a start.

Machelle and I did finally meet for an interview. We met at a park out in Canyon Country, north of Los Angeles. It was a fine, sunny morning. We sat at a park bench and talked. It seemed that no time had passed since we were last together. However, a lot has happened since our last meeting. When we last met, Machelle was working for the County of Los Angeles as an educational liaison worker who coordinated the services of Los Angeles Unified School District with the various regional group homes for foster children. She held that position for 16 years. She was recently laid off because of state funding problems. She said, "They just did away with the whole department and decided to leave the task to the County Social Workers, as if they will do it and don't already have too much to do." Now Machelle is unemployed and has returned to college to work on a degree at the College of the Canyons in educational counseling. She does not want to be a Social Worker!

As she brought me up to date, she filled me in on the last few years. In 2006 she married a man she had known since high school. Since then he went into the military and when he got out went to work as an Avionics Technician. They reconnected via the internet. She describes him as a genius who is very good at his job. He has been off work for several months due to a back injury incurred at work. He has had multiple surgeries and is in a lot of pain. Machelle was quite happy and proud of her daughter who just graduated from high school. She credits the birth of her daughter for the turnaround in her life. When her daughter was five years old, Machelle recognized that she had to make a decision: to be like her mother or go in a different direction. She decided to give up her crazy relationships and focus on giving her daughter a stable life. "My daughter is # 1," she said.

In looking at Machelle's life story, the incredible violence, instability, incest, family chaos, social dysfunction, inter-generational abuse and mental illness are what resonate. Because it is all intertwined it is hard to identify a focal point when telling this story. Therefore, the best thing to do is to follow the narrative. After all, it is her story and it is told in her own words. The questions about identity are only theoretical ideas--the preoccupations of a psychologist looking at a person's life from an intellectual distance. When I listen to Machelle talk and then read her story, it is a compelling narrative, but it became very personal and alive as I sat across from her and felt the impact of what she was saying and remarkably lived through.

Her beginnings, like Jeanette's and Alex's, begin with a mentally-ill mother with whom she had a violent relationship. This was the foundation of her personality, the woman with whom she was to have such an ambivalent, complicated and violent relationship.

> My mother was 18 and had 2 children before me at the ages of 14 and 16. She was a product of the foster care system starting at the age of 14 when she was taken from her parents because they abused her physically, sexually and mentally. She became pregnant with my grandfather's child and gave birth to a baby boy that was given up for adoption.

Her mother, a product of the foster care system, herself a victim of incest and abuse, subjected Machelle to a rerun of her history. This is a very old theme psychologically: parents subjecting their children to the same abuse they experienced. This is the identity foundation for Machelle: A mentally ill mother, running from her past, escaping into alcohol, and uprooting her children too many times to count. Filled with shame, rage, and despair, she takes out her anger on her own children. Imagine the psychological impact on Machelle. The plot worsens when Machelle is subjected to separation from her mother and sent to be with the same individuals who abused her.

> She was institutionalized for the first time when I was 7 years old (1984) for a year. She sent my brother and I to the only people she knew. The same people who had made her life a living hell, her mother and father. My brother and I lived a nightmare in New Jersey that year being passed from stranger to stranger; although they were relatives, we had never met, seen or even knew of these people. It was then I experienced being sexually abused repeatedly by cousins and family friends. My grandmother was the physical abuser. She would throw me around like a rag doll and pour food on my head if I didn't finish eating.

An institutionalized, mentally-ill mother sending her children back to a situation that was a living hell for her personally. Yet she did it anyway (Parenthetically, where were social services at this time, allowing a mother to send her children back to an unsafe environment?). This is a major failure of a parent: failure to protect and to provide a stable, secure and loving home in which to care for her children. She placed them in the same danger from which she was trying to escape, and history repeated itself. It is déjà vu. It is where the sexual and physical abuse started at age seven. Again we ask, what is the working model of the world, the attachment paradigm Machelle is internalizing, i.e. what is she learning about people? What is she learning about trust? What is the working model of the world that she is experiencing? And most importantly, what is Machelle coming to feel about herself? What of her self esteem as she is tossed around like a commodity, used, abused, cast aside, shamed and victimized by strangers called 'family.' This is occurring at a critical period in Machelle's psychological development: she is seven years of age. This is the time when a child is supposed to be developing a sense of independence, mastery, worth and confidence that she can do things. When the familial world does not support this phase of behavior and instead her parent victimizes her, renders her helpless, and uses her body for sexual gratification and subjects her to physical abuse, this is catastrophic to a child's sense of identity. Family life, instead of being a secure base for becoming a healthy person, is instead is a school of horrors with terrorists upon whom she is dependent. She is passed around, used, and then "thrown around like a rag doll."

The next 5 years were no better for Machelle. She was returned to her mother, who was out of the hospital and supposedly fit to care for her two children, but became another form of the continuing nightmare. Machelle and her brother were now being terrified daily by an unstable, violent, alcoholic mother who moved them all over the San fernando Valley. Again we ask, where was social services? Here are children exhibiting all the classic signs of abuse with red flags everywhere.

> By the time I was 12 and my brother 14 (1989), we had been to at least 6 different schools if not more. I can only recount so many. My brother and I had finally gotten fed up. My brother ran away one day while we were out with my mother. She had one of her violent alcoholic rages and threw a beer on my brother's friend and attacked her. She was only 16. I, on the other hand, had nowhere to run. That year was the worst year because I was the only one she could attack. Before, the attacks were split between my brother and [me]. I had finally had enough and one night she came stumbling in drunk as I was eating my French toast, one of the things I could actually cook for myself. She punched me in my face and asked why her bed wasn't made. We were always her maids, cooks, and at times it felt as if she looked at my brother and me as her mates. It made me sick. I told her if she hit me again I would stab her and she did it again and I stabbed her. I ran as fast as I could out the door. This was the first of many numerous times my mother and I would go to battle and the police would be called. From then on, I stopped taking her crap and I fought back. I stopped being afraid and became the violent aggressor myself. From 1989 to1991, I did as I pleased and stayed with friends only sneaking into my house when I knew my mother wasn't there.

This age, the beginning of adolescence, is another critical period of development. The developmental task for the teenager is to find a sense of independence, transition from dependence on adults through the way station of peer groups. Again, in normal situations, the parent is supporting and encouraging the development of good boundaries, self-esteem and confidence. The role of the parent is to model healthy expressions of emotion and resolution of conflict. The role is also to provide a stable environment and provide physical and emotional care for the child. Home is supposed to be a safe haven, a place where a teenager unquestionably belongs. For Machelle, it is very obvious that the opposite of healthy was taking place. Fed up, full of rage and terror, dependent on her mother, violence breaks out and Machelle stabs her mother after being struck in the face and humiliated. What can a young girl do? She is living the paradox of attachment: Take the abuse, retreat into depression and shut down, or violently break out of the bind. Machelle fought back and then ran away. This seems very adaptive to me. Machelle, a resourceful young girl, fought for her life and spent the next two years living with friends and staying away from her dangerous mother. Again we ask, where were the protectors? A child stabs her mother and runs away and is missing for two years. One can imagine the desperation, loneliness, confusion, fear and unhappiness she felt.

> [Mother] again had been institutionalized for trying to kill herself. I, on the other hand, started to hang out with the wrong crowd, ran the streets, got into fights, constantly skipped school. I always had all F's. Although I had been stopped by police numerous times on the street and when altercations would occur with my mother, I had never been taken away. I finally got caught stealing in 1992 and when my mother was called to come get me from the Van Nuys police station, she just laughed and told the cops to take me away, she didn't care and that I needed to be taught a lesson. For this I was thrilled. To finally be taken away from her; to have a place to sleep and not be afraid, to have 3 meals a day and a chance to actually go to school not just because I had to but because I wanted to. My trip to Sylmar Juvenile Hall didn't last long however.

Finally, there is intervention and the police become involved. This is what I find both illuminating, and sad. Machelle told me that she would rather be in Juvenile Hall than be with her mother because she felt safe away from the insanity and abuse. Sylmar provided three meals a day, a routine, and people who were in charge--structure and a place where she could go to school because she wanted to and could excel because she is so intelligent. However, Mother returns to her life and removes her from this safe environment. Machelle goes to court, she pleads with the judge to stay in Sylmar. What does the judge do? He returns her to the mother who has terrorized her for years.

> Only a couple of days in and my mom came to my court date and told the judge how she wanted me to come back home. I begged the judge not to send me back, but he did anyway. As soon as I was released, my mother started right away in the car yelling and screaming about how dare I want to stay there. As soon as we got home, I left immediately and went to stay with my boyfriend at the time. Of course I was put on 6-months probation with community service and an ankle bracelet to monitor my every move.

Adolescence is often described as a time of *sturm and drang,* or of turmoil and restlessness. It is a stormy and volatile period in the life of a child who is trying to find her way to adulthood. In fighting for her life, Machelle precipitated a crisis. Crisis can lead to resolution and growth, or at least change. This period of time was a struggle for Machelle. She knew she must get away from her mother, but how? Typically, troubled youths find other troubled youths because that is where they identify and feel accepted. Getting into fights and skipping school is a common pattern for abused kids. They are on the streets, have altercations with the police, shoplift, and fail in school. These are all very loud cries for help.

Again I question the court's judgment. With the mother's history of mental illness, frequent hospitalizations, alcoholism, failure to care for her children, suicide attempts and propensity for violence, as well as Machelle's stated preference against returning, the judge returns Machelle to her mother's custody. This is a decision that is very hard to understand. Given what happened next, it is clear that it was the wrong decision. Machelle, having no other choice, left home again. She knew it was a dangerous place and that she could not stay there. She ran away, and was then placed on probation with an ankle bracelet. Why not return her to Sylmar or a foster home? What typically occurs is that the child is blamed. "She is bad, uncontrollable, and violent. I am afraid of her."

This is one of the most compelling features of Machelle's story. She is always fighting: her mother, authorities and the system. She does what she has to do, as it is a fight for self-preservation. I see it as courage and evidence of her spirit that was not crushed by all the forces aligned against her. Her actions and behavior are quite adaptive and street- smart.

> ...that I was the one who had the issues and she had no control of me. She was afraid of me. It was during my time of probation that I found out I was pregnant. That was the supposed final straw for my mother. She called the police to have me removed from the house stating [that I] and my boyfriend were threatening her. However, I kept an answering machine tape with messages from my mother and her boyfriend threatening to hang me and my boyfriend, messages of my mother calling me every name in the book. My probation officer was able to use this proof and finally have me taken away for good and that is when I became a ward of the court. August of 1993.

Finally, Machelle connects with someone who does the right thing: Her probation officer. She is made a ward of the court, and since she is pregnant, she is placed in St. Anne's which has an entire program designed to help young women who find themselves in predicaments like Machelle's. This is the beginning of Machelle's transformation. In 1993 she found herself, for the first time in her life in a safe, protective environment. As mentioned, Machelle told me that having her daughter was the turning point in her life. "I decided to put her #1 in my life, give up all my crazy relationships and focus on giving her a life much different than the life she had been living." She gave birth to her daughter while at St. Anne's. It was there that she completed her high school education and formed a life-saving relationship with a therapist. This is remarkable, because so many kids with her history fight therapy because of their ambivalent attachment history.

Below is an excerpt from a letter Machelle sent to her therapist (published in a St Anne's newsletter):

> To my special person,
>
> I've decided on writing you this letter because I don't want to say goodbye. The time has come for me to move on with my life, but I have so much to say to you and so little time. We've known each other for about two years now and yet it doesn't seem that long.

We've grown to know each other very well and I can truly say, YOU HAVE BEEN AN INSPIRATION in my life.

You have helped me change my life and the way I look at things. You understand me and see me like no other person sees me. You know the real me, and I'm glad you do. I care about you and respect you. I care about what you think of me and am glad you are able to tell me what you think. You always believed in me when others would give up. That's what makes you so special. You don't give up no matter what, even when you know you are pushing. Ha ha.

It's not gonna be the same without you being there when I need to talk. You make me smile, laugh and in the end cry. Yeah I said it, cry. It's hard to say good-bye to someone as special as you. I remember in the beginning I wouldn't give you the time of day, and here I am, two years later not wanting to say good-bye. You have been a big part of my life.

Oh don't worry, this isn't goodbye forever. I'll be back when you retire. Ha ha. You're the best, and don't let anyone tell you any different. I know that there will never be another person that could fill your shoes, but when I leave, I'm taking you with me, in my heart, in my thoughts, and in my prayers. I will never forget you and how you've helped me. THANK YOU!

I thank God for bringing you into my life and now it's time for me to let you go. I will miss you more than you will ever know.

GOOD-BYE MY SPECIAL PERSON!

Love ya lots,
*Machelle*

The years at St. Anne's were clearly a defining moment for Machelle and dramatically altered the trajectory of her life. Those years brought structure to a life which had known nothing but instability and chaos. It stopped a cycle of abuse and resulted in her making a decision to be a better mother than the one who had so terrorized her life. According to Machelle and the Social Workers who worked with her at St. Anne's, she arrived as an angry, frightened, pregnant, self-destructive young woman who had few social skills and trusted no one. She remarked in an interview, "Before St. Anne's I was never in school. I didn't trust anyone, especially adults. St. Anne's has helped me grow. I am learning to be a good parent; to be patient. I'm planning to go to college and have a career. I have goals for my life. I am learning how to make better choices. If it were not for St. Anne's, I really think I would be nowhere."

An interview with Cathy Harwood, Program Director, reveals both Machelle's condition at the time and the changes she made while at St. Anne's. "Machelle came to St. Anne's prenatal program in August of 1993. She was very closed, untrusting and angry. She acted tough, not needing anything from us."

"What did you see in Machelle?" I asked."[I see] the results of no consistent, positive adult influence in her life. She had been neglected by her own mother and had learned that adults were not trustworthy. I sensed that within, there was a young woman longing to be nurtured and cared for." "What changes have you seen in Machelle?" I asked. "She is finally learning to trust those around her. It continues to be a struggle. She genuinely cares for Jazzmen, her daughter and makes Jazzmen her top priority. I think she is truly liking who she is. She is determined not to repeat the abuse with her daughter."

Three years of structure, consistency, support, care, and guidance made a huge difference in Machelle's life. As is the often case in the life of an adolescent, this is the period of the highest possible risk and so often the time when children of the system fail to transition successfully into adulthood. Leaving a safe harbor brings on entirely new challenges. She was a single mother, emancipated from a system that gave her an opportunity, but at the time did not have provisions for extending the support and aid in transition. In 2012, St. Anne's built a housing complex for young women in the process of transitioning from St. Anne's into the community. They get job training, child care, and a stipend. None of that was available for Machelle at the time she was there. Her next three years were a very difficult struggle. She moved into an apartment with a girl she had met at St. Anne's and tried to find a job. She participated in the GAIN program that helped her get some needed work/life training. But her roommate was unreliable and it was a tremendous struggle, which led to her contemplating suicide. She had no job, no food, no medical care, and saw herself as an "Epic Failure." A call to her old therapist saved her life and got her through the crisis.

Then she applied for a job with the County of Los Angeles as an educational community worker, a job she held for 16 years. Again, getting this job was a defining moment. It saved her life, helped her get financially stable and had an immensely positive impact on her self-esteem. It was during this time that I met her and was impressed by how much she cared about the kids and how dedicated she was to helping them. She knew the system, their problems, and was very competent in helping them "hook up" to school. Meeting her old friend and getting married also was another important step in her life. She longed for stability with someone to care for her and a safe place to live where she could take care of her daughter.

The next important step in Machelle's long journey has been her relationship with her mother. When children are severely victimized by their parents, it leaves deep and lasting scars. Healing these wounds is often made more meaningful when the child and parent can have a dialogue about their relationship. Machelle was remarkably able to reconnect with her mother. In her words, this is how it happened:

> The reconciliation between my mother and me happened 3 years ago, a year after I got married. She found out I had gotten married through my brother. She had tried to contact me when I got married but I was not ready to let her in. It wasn't until she got a computer 3 years ago and started contacting me on Facebook and through emails. We started out slow and I would only give so much information as I did not want to let her back into my life fully. We would have nice chats over email and in the chat box on Facebook. She began to tell me how she had sobered up since moving to Kansas in 2005 and found God. I did notice a change in her but still had up my guard because I had seen her change before, but it would never last. I finally started letting her in more, sending pictures and updates of what was going on in my life. We eventually exchanged numbers and began talking every so often until it turned into almost a daily phone call. I decided to forgive her when she had a conversation with me for hours about all of the things she remembered doing to my brother and mr. For the first time in 31, years my mom had admitted to all of her faults and apologized profusely for all she had done. Before this, my mother refused to apologize for anything, saying she did nothing wrong

and did the best she could. She would always make me feel like I was delusional and that I did not live the life I did. I had asked her throughout my life to just admit what she had done to me and apologize and I would forgive her but she never did until 3 years ago. I told her that her apology and her admitting to her faults was all I ever wanted from her and that now that she was sober, she was finally able to see clearly and I forgave her.

The past 3 years have been great between us. I can honestly say she is one of my best friends if not my closest best friend. She is my number one supporter and helps keep me going when I get down. We talk every day for the most part for an hour or so. We talk about her life, my life and just plain stupid silly stuff at times. Although I can't say that we will ever have that close mother-daughter bond that my daughter and I have, I am happy with the relationship we finally do have. I am proud of her for accomplishing what she has by gaining sobriety. We are both proud of each other for how far we've come in life. Things are so good between us, I entrusted her with the care of my daughter for an unspecified amount of time, really until my daughter says she's ready to come home or stay in Kansas with my mother. She's been with my mom now for almost 3 weeks and they are both having a blast. Jazzmen has started work at two ranches and my mom has what she calls "me" back. She says it's like having me at home again but I laugh and tell her well, not so much, because that clearly didn't work out for us. I believe she is getting a second chance at being a parent all over again, of course as a grandma this time. She would like Jazzmen to stay with her forever, but it's completely up to Jazz what she wants to do.

Mom spent the 5 days before they left to go back to Kansas with my family. I was worried that it wouldn't work out, seeing as how I haven't been in the same physical space with her in over 7 years but it actually turned out well. We had a great time together. For the most part we kept busy, so I'm sure that helped, but it was nice being able to have a normal family visit. No physical fighting, no arguing, just adults enjoying one another's company. At times, yes, I would lay in bed with my husband after a long day and say, ohhhh I just want my house back, but not because she was bothering anyone, just the fact of having others in your house. (I believe you know exactly what I'm talking about when your children come to visit you.) I was happy that she was able to share the experience of Jazzmen graduating high school and it will be a memory we all will cherish for the rest of our lives. Jazz surprised us and kept it a secret that she was graduating as valedictorian. It was such a proud moment and the speech she gave left everyone in tears. There wasn't a dry eye in the house. I am happy that life has come full circle for my daughter ad she can have a grandmother that I always wanted as a mother. That is how much my mother has changed. When I hear her have conversations with my daughter, I often tell my mom, god I wish you would have talked with me like that, but I try not to look at it as I missed out so much as how much my daughter is gaining.

I will be honest and say that I take everything one day at a time with my mother. As much as she has changed, there is still that fear that I hold deep down inside that she will relapse and we will once again be estranged. Will I ever be able to let that go. I'm not sure. All I can do is enjoy the relationship we have now and continue to move forward.

Machelle's journey is remarkable and illuminating on so many levels. We see her honesty, insight, self-awareness, and willingness to tell her story. We see first a young girl who is subjected to terrible physical abuse and neglect as well as sexual molestation at such a vulnerable age. We see the ravaging effects that a mentally-ill and alcoholic mother has on her children and the remarkable story of their reconciliation. We also see her ongoing struggle to survive, the failure of the system to protect her and then her big break-- her placement at St. Anne's. We also note how much wisdom and compassion she has gained in relationship to herself. She is one of the most resilient people I have ever encountered. Finally, in this story I asked Machelle *the big question* as I put it. Are you able to talk about the Incest? Not surprisingly, she wrote this about it.

Well, I was 7 years old when I first encountered incest from my mother's family when she sent my brother and me to live with them in New Jersey while she was institutionalized for a year. I found out that my cousin, Laura who was the same age as I, was being molested by her brothers (one younger than her and one older), her father and their neighbor, who I believe was around 15 or 16 at the time. She told me it was a game they all played and that they wanted me to join. Not knowing any better, or should I say not being taught from my mother what was right and what was wrong, I felt I had to be involved since I was living with them and that it was just a normal thing. My uncle never touched me, just my cousins and the neighbor boy. No penetration happened. I just learned at a very young age unfortunately how to give oral sex on a regular basis, numerous times a day, to all 3 boys. I think my cousin Laura was relieved that it was no longer just her. There was always touching and kissing involved even while grownups including my grandmother (my mom's mom) looked on. This went on for a year until we were finally sent back to California to be with our mom again. I'm not sure if anything happened to my brother while we were there, but I believe things did. I know he and my cousin Laura would kiss but I'm not sure how far they went. He never talked about it and to this day still has not. I never told my mom. I didn't even think about telling her. I can't say that I was afraid to tell her. I can only say I never trusted her enough to tell her.

It wasn't long after we moved back home with mom when a roommate of hers started creeping into my bed every night while she was away getting drunk or high. He was a disgusting, smelly, old Asian man. Every time he got in bed with me he reeked of alcohol like my mother did when she was blasted. He would put his hands in between my legs and I would squirm and squeeze my legs as tight as I could so that he couldn't touch me. He would kiss me on the lips and it made me sick. He didn't even care that my brother was above me in the top bunk. I would run into the bathroom and lock the door on the nights he would creep into my bed. I would sleep there until my mother came home. Those were the nights that I longed for her to be there, whereas other nights I wish she would just die and leave us alone. I don't know how long the episodes continued until I finally told my mother, because she always questioned why I was sleeping in the bathroom and I ran out of excuses. She threw the guy out but never called the police. She never got me any help either. You would have thought she was the victim as she sobbed for days to her friends and boyfriend at the time. Never once do I remember her hugging me, consoling me or talking to me about the situation. I never told her of the other after that, including her 4th husband who was another drunk creep that would touch me every chance he could ,even in front of my mother by acting as if he was just hugging me, but with the hugs came gropes and rubs and feels. I let it happen and didn't say a word. Why should I say anything, nothing would be done.

Being that young and experiencing incest and sexual abuse affected my sexuality in that I became promiscuous. Sex meant nothing to me, especially seeing my mom have sex all the time in front of us. Sex was just something you did, it wasn't a good thing or a bad thing and per my mom, you could always get what you want with sex. I started having sex on my own accord when I was 12. The guy was 21 I believe, although I told him I was 18. How does a 12 year old look like an 18 year old you ask. Well just look at the girls nowadays with the way they dress, their makeup and the way they act. I never practiced safe sex and by the time I got pregnant at 15, I had slept with at least 13 guys, all over the age of 18 and if I wasn't having sex with guys, I was giving oral sex or being groped and touched. Mom was right, I was able to get what I wanted and needed with sex, like a roof over my head and some food in my stomach. When I got older, I used sex to get my bills paid and to be taken care of. Did I ever hook on the street, nope didn't have to. Every man I ever got involved with even for a short amount of time were willing to give whatever I wanted as long as they got what they wanted.

Being at St. Anne's for those 3 years helped me cope with what had been done to me and that <u>it of course wasn't my fault and that I should have been protected.</u> My weekly therapy gave me the chance to actually talk about sex, the good and the bad. For 2 years after I had my daughter I refused to have sex with anyone and if the men I was with didn't like it, well they could F*** off. Most stayed, though I think for men it's a challenge when they can't get what they want. I do have residual wounds in that every day I walk out the door, I fear some man is watching me, stalking me, waiting to pounce. I fear every day my daughter walks out the door and take a mental picture of what she is wearing, how her hair is done, what shoes she has on, what jewelry, every last little detail. I think about what can happen to either of us but if that makes me more aware and more sensitive to my surroundings, I'll take that any day over being naïve and carefree. I pride myself on knowing I can kick some ass if need be and can protect myself now when I couldn't as a child. Some victims run and hide in fear. I say bring it on. I think some victims like myself get angry and fight back. That's how we cope. Others I feel for, those who become fearful of everything in life, not just what may or may not happen. My heart breaks for those who blame themselves and feel worthless because of what has happened to them. What happened to me was not of my doing and those sick people who took advantage of a helpless child cannot and will not beat me!!

As a married woman, my views of sex still have not changed, it's not good and it's not bad. At times it's hard because I could care less about sex. Sometimes I can be very sexual and want sex all the time and others, I can go months even years without it. I believe victims of sexual abuse will always have a hard time coping with sex and I am no different. Sometimes sexual experiences, even with the one you love, can bring up emotions or memories that you thought you had conquered or forgotten. Alcohol and sex is a memory that triggers bad emotions so that I have to tell my husband to stay away from me when he has had a drink because it makes me sick. It reminds me of my childhood, the smell of my perpetrators and my mother. At least I am able to know certain triggers and am able to discuss these with my husband. Some women have not had the opportunity to deal with these situations. I have heard from men who have had relationships with women who have been sexually abused and I'm told it is like a Jekyll and Hyde routine that I can certainly relate do. It's like walking on eggshells with us at times. One day everything is great and the next day we can be scared, rabid dogs.

I honestly wouldn't be able to suggest advice to a survivor as we have all had different experiences--some worse than others. I believe it's a lifelong process for any victim to go through. I choose to be ok with myself and what happened, knowing it wasn't me. Talking about my experiences with others has always been a healing process for me, whether it be the sexual abuse or the life I lived period. I am an open book and I believe that's why I have survived and what makes me who I am today. I am proud of who I am, who I was, who I have become and am not ashamed. I'm a love me or hate me kinda gal, nothing in between and am perfectly ok with either!

And so ends the narrative of four remarkable individuals. All of them have in common a singular life-changing event: hey were given up by their birth families. It launched them on a path not of their own choosing, but one we all have in common: the elusive quest for identity, a sense of who we are and of what we are becoming. Losing the primal connection at the beginnings of one's life, the very foundation of what makes us truly human, has effects far beyond the moment of relinquishment. As we have seen in all of these stories, each individual is haunted by the past, struggling in the present and uncertain of their futures. Bruce Perry frames the problem in this manner.

The powerful regulating, rewarding quality of belonging to a group, a family, a community and culture is not just focused on the present. We each feel a need to be connected to the people of our past, and without being able to draw on this connection—this narrative—it is almost impossible to envision hopes and dreams for a connected and safe future. (*Life Story Therapy with Traumatized Children*, Pg. 9)

The theme of this book, *Broken Systems- Shattered Lives* is clearly reflected in the lives of these remarkable individuals. They show the trauma of removal, the compounded trauma of multiple placements, violence, physical and sexual abuse. The failure of the protectors to assist, support and provide necessary interventions compounded the injuries. The enormous sense of loss that goes with removal is ever present. Loss of family, neighborhood, possessions, schools, toys and friends become secondary trauma. I have discussed at length the dynamic and powerful importance of attachment to human development and the many consequences of disruption of that development. In Patrick's story, we hear the poignant longing for his roots, and his family, the sense of shame and devalued worth as a person and the disenfranchisement of being both adopted and gay. In Jeanette's story, we see the themes of loss, the struggle to retain some sense of self through multiple placements, and the terrible cost of the trauma of being adopted after 7 and ½ years of uncertainty. In Alex's story, we see the impact of a mother's mental illness, and the failure of the system to assess the level of illness, resulting in continued reunification and failure of these placements. In Machelle's story there are so many tragedies, failures, violence, mental illness, incest, and placements, it is difficult to know where to begin to sort it all out.

To say that they all are wounded is to grossly understate the nature of their experiences. Yet, as they each struggled to survive, cope, and heal themselves, we are inspired and learn a great deal about resilience and recovery from trauma. Patrick said it very well when he described the process as "wanting to know and not know, to feel and not feel, as if [he] was living at the base of a dam that was about to fail." In these stories we see how attachment shaped their early world views. Each felt unsafe, unable to trust their caregivers, uncertain of really belonging to a family. Each struggled with feelings of shame, being flawed and unworthy, somehow responsible for their own plight. Each felt helpless and victimized by their situations. They all struggled with an over arching feeling of peril and dread. The consequence of children living in dangerous situations, as in the case of Machelle, is that they develop a pronounced sense of hyper-vigilance. Remember her statement that when her daughter left the house she took a mental picture of everything she was wearing? That is the result of violence and of being sexualized at a young age.

Another consequence of disrupted attachment is the failure to learn how to soothe themselves and how to modulate their feelings.

As a result, they all struggle with issues of anxiety, depression, complicated mourning and unregulated sadness. As a result, they did not learn how to heal themselves or how to heal relationship breaches. Also, a consequence of disrupted attachment is the very attachment paradigm itself. This internalized model of how relationships work left each individual with enduring feelings of uncertainty, distrust, ambivalence, and anxiety about their lovability and worth. Growing up in a world characterized by fear, instability, frequent changes, violence, and adults who cannot be counted on, what is going to be your view of the world? Who can you trust? More importantly, can you trust yourself? Fundamentally, I believe that our sense of identity is the sum of all our attachments. Difficulty in areas of attachment leads to uncertainty about who we are, what we are and who we are becoming.

### Healing the Wounded Inner Self

*Love is the master key that opens*
*the gates of happiness, of hatred,*
*of jealousy, and most easily of*
*all, the gate of fear.*

—*Oliver Wendell Holmes*

### Reflections

As someone who has been deeply interested in trauma, and life crises, I find myself to be both observer and participant. What I experienced when I sat in on the Adopt-a-Salon group was a feeling of admiration and empathy, as well as discovery. I realized that I was sitting amongst a group of individuals with unhealed wounds who were on a mission to get answers: sojourners, looking to be with people with similar experiences where they could feel understood, even if only for two hours on a Wednesday evening. Healing wounds from early childhood is a difficult undertaking, as I well know. What I observed was that there were individuals who were making discoveries and having feelings that broke through their defenses that "were too much, too soon." In short, they were not ready for the upsurge of old wounds and were having difficulty integrating memories as well as their feelings. Work with trauma,

I have found, needs to be slow, and careful. There needs to be a structured framework of support. There also needs to be time to integrate newly-discovered memories, fragments of disassociated traumatic experiences from long ago, and very painful memories of abuse, rejection, abandonment and loss. These experiences are the residual effects of early relational trauma and damage to the implicit self. As we have seen, these wounds are persistent and have shaped the entire course of their lives. This struggle I have captioned the elusive search for Identity.

It is a struggle that is ongoing and pervasive. As such, it is a reflection of who they are. In effect, the struggle defines all of us. There are many defining moments in life where the struggle reaches crisis points and it is at these times where specific issues become focal points. If it is grief then there needs to be time to grieve each and every loss. The individuals that night were sharing a lifetime of wounds as well as their struggles in the here and now. Many of these individuals have been struggling by themselves. That night, perhaps they discovered that meeting with others makes the struggle less lonely. The challenge for all in order to heal is find a way to integrate what is discovered and manage the often times overwhelming, deeply-seated feelings that have been buried for so long. They may discover that a more-structured process with a skilled therapist, to guide them on the path to recovery and self-discovery, to help them make sense of what was being discovered, is often helpful.

Richard Rose put it rather succinctly, "What we needed as children to become securely attached, i. e., safety, stability, warmth, security, and engagement with caring people, we still need as adults." We also needed to learn how to be self-regulating. However, the problem for children of the System is that they also have to overcome the trauma of being given away, the disruption of placement, violence, and abuse. And so, the task for Patrick, Jeanette, Alex and Machelle as well as all of the other children in Care, is to create within the boundaries of their own lives a sense of safety, security, control, stability, purpose, meaning, and a sense of worth through meaningful attachments. In other words they still need as we all do, to create a coherent narrative, a meaningful life story. Their lives need to make sense, need a secure base, a sense of belonging, and a place called home. Each step taken in that journey is a defining moment which takes us closer to home. Jeanette said it very well, "I am not at the mercy of anyone," thereby announcing that she had found a way to empower herself and establish a feeling of competence and mastery over her life.

While they are accomplishing this, they still struggle with old wounds and questions about their worthiness, and a primal longing for family. The miracle for all of them is that somehow they found just enough within themselves or found someone at just the right time, and were able to survive against rather overwhelming odds and circumstances. They also survived being in a system that more often hindered their struggles than helped them, and in so doing created a coherent narrative which preserved the fragments of their past, without being destroyed by shame, doubt, and fear. The many crises of identity they each weathered became a process of transformation resulting in a stronger sense of personal identity. Their stories, of course are still ongoing. They still struggle with their unhealed wounds, struggle to feel good about themselves, to forgive themselves by working through guilt and shame. They struggle to trust and establish intimacy with those they love and get to a point of acceptance. They struggle to channel the longing for home and family into the dynamic and vibrant present with opportunities for creating a home of their very own. They search for an organizing, empowering faith that enables them to create a world of their own choosing, a world of meaning and purpose they can call their own. This is the elusive quest for identity: Being able to affirm ourselves and say 'yes' to our lives in spite of all the circumstances which challenge our efforts and sustain us through difficult times. Finally it is my hope that this journey of hope and discovery will end for all the children with new caring-transformative attachments that provide a high sense of self awareness that brings fulfillment and joy. We do it in spite of all that gets in the way of a relentless pursuit of self-discovery. This is truly the arena of personal heroics.

# Chapter 12

## SUMMARY AND CONCLUSIONS

My personal odyssey as recounted in the beginning of this book began innocuously after a series of ongoing informal conversations with colleagues who shared similar concerns and frustrations about complex problems emanating from their cases. It takes place all over America in workplaces everywhere: commiserating, sharing daily problems, attempts to deal with an antiquated system, common frustrations and visions of a better way. My colleagues and I shared problems and stress, told stories, expressed a frequently felt sense of futility, raised questions, and debated solutions. Out of this dialogue a narrative evolved. The common folklore that we seemed to live daily was that yes, it was a terribly hard job, and we were operating in the theater of the absurd, but little could really be done about it. We were doing our small part as best we could and were kept in the game by an occasional win or successful case.

Ever the crusader, I looked at bigger issues and dreamed of being able to do something about the travesties we saw on a daily basis. As we talked, ideas began to come to me. Gradually, it occurred to me that perhaps there might be some way I could make a difference. My colleagues and I shared a compassion for wounded children. We had a desire to find a more effective way to fix some of the broken links and build some bridges between psychology, social work and the foster care system. I thought that because of my particular background and perspective, I could see the problems from outside the system and do something for the children caught in the middle between the system and their families. The irony for me was that in making a career change and going from the familiar "abnormal" world of psychiatry with all its problems to the world of foster care, I had entered a very different kind of institutionalized dysfunction. I certainly did not find it easier, it clearly had its own share of problems, and the problems were very different.

I initially began with a diffuse, rather global sense of frustration and an intense concern for the suffering I was seeing. I realized that with such a wide field of problems, issues, and concerns, I had to find a place to begin to unwind this tangled ball of twine. The title for this book spontaneously came to me as I was reflecting on my daily observations at work. Hence, I began this project with the governing idea that the children were not being protected and the flawed system to which they were subjected was having an injurious impact on them. Therefore, broken systems lead to shattered lives. I quote Bonheoffer's famous statement: "One measure of a country's character is how it cares for its most vulnerable citizens." In this case, the outcome of our brokenness is the abuse, neglect and violence perpetrated against our children.

The plight of children in Los Angeles, I discovered, is part of a greater context of broken systems across this country. For me, the crystallizing event was the discovery of how many children were dying not only from parental abuse, but also while in foster care. That unsettling realization provided the motivation to learn more. What started out as frustration and anger turned into a pursuit to understand the intricacies of a complicated network of interacting agencies.

As I learned more, I became fascinated by several things. The first was the enormity of the problems in the child welfare programs. I came to believe that the broken systems begin at the very top (nationally) in the way we fund our social welfare programs. Because of *trickle-down economics*, we have a resultant trickle-down pathology. The poison in the system stems from the federal government's dysfunction, brought about by individual and corporate greed in the form of lobbyists who dictate social policy and the allocation of funds to the primary programs affecting children: health, education, and welfare. The outcome of this policy has been a shifting of wealth toward the top and a net increase in children and families living in poverty.

The programs affecting people with mental health, drug and alcohol problems and children with special needs are starved for funds. Hence we have the vicious cycle of poverty, mental illness, domestic violence and substance abuse: broken government contributes to broken, impoverished families. The vast majority of our children in the child welfare programs come from impoverished families of color. Once they enter this broken system managed by the Children's Law Center and the Department of Children and Family Services, they are subjected to further abuse, neglect and maltreatment.

As I gained experience, my awareness grew as well. I sensed I had entered a strange and fascinating new world when the realization dawned. I was immersed in a massive dysfunctional system unlike anything I had encountered before. What was most concerning was that it seemed to be doing a lot of harm despite its best intentions. Encountering one strange situation after another raised all kinds of questions and compelled me to search for answers. I realized that first I must understand what I was seeing before I could find answers. My quest was driven primarily by my empathy for the distress of the children in the care of my foster care agency. Along with compassion came a growing sense of outrage as I saw what seemed to be unnecessary suffering. One shocking discovery came after another. The system seemed to be compounding its problems! This, I decided, is a story that needs telling!

My first shocking discovery was the abuse inflicted upon the children, and the enduring impact it had on their physical and emotional development. The second discovery was that once I dug beneath the surface, the system whose purpose is to protect these children was causing further trauma, which exacerbated preexisting developmental and behavioral problems. Part of this was understandable as it was due to multiple disruptions of their primary attachment. Each new placement decreased the likelihood of children being able to trust and successfully attach to a future caregiver.

In order to tell this story, I decided to document the problems a child encounters after placement through the presentation of several case examples. I described what I encountered every day: overburdened staff, enormous caseloads, and inadequately or poorly trained professionals who did not understand or recognize the emotional problems related to trauma and loss. Systemic failures such as lack of permanency planning, judicial delays, and inadequate mental health services all contributed to the growing numbers of children with unresolved trauma and attachment problems. These were not abstractions. I felt the need to ground what I was seeing by telling individual stories.

It was very distressing to see the profound effects of trauma on these children, and each child seemed to be affected in a different way: language delay, poor psychomotor skills, volatile mood swings, learning disorders, hyper aggression and rages, bizarre phobias and obsessions, self-injurious behavior, and incessant battles for control with caregivers. I observed children who were abandoned, neglected and horribly abused, I saw assaultive, aggressive children, out of control and injuring themselves and their caregivers. These were just a few of the complex disorders my foster parents and I encountered. The most shocking thing for me to handle emotionally was the level of violence, abuse, and trauma inflicted by adults on their children. As I searched the trauma literature, it became clear that the enduring detrimental effects of parental-inflicted trauma was well documented and being studied by impressive scholars. Because of abuse, neglect or abandonment, clearly these children not only need protection, but also better and more effective care. Due to the abuse and neglect leading up to their placement, these children are often difficult to parent and subsequently are moved from one foster home to another while the system slowly works out a permanency plan. This is another glaring sign of a broken system. What I encountered daily was foster parents struggling with behavioral problems in their children, problems far beyond their experience and skills. They lamented, "I didn't realize what I was getting into; I thought I was a good parent, but all the things I know how to do and tried just don't seem to work."

This book seemed to organize and write itself as I realized each case had a story to tell about some aspect of the systems' malfunctions. One case documents how the system worked, another illustrates how it failed to function, and a third resulted in the actual death of one of my cases. As this story developed, there have been numerous headlines reporting children dying of abuse while in the care of the Child Welfare System. As this story comes to an end, I have concluded that too many children are dying and the survivors and casualties are a sadly neglected, disenfranchised minority! The Child Welfare System is an overburdened, broken system mandated to protect its children that frequently fails, or is unable to meet even their most basic needs.

My professional background in trauma helped me understand these troubled and traumatized children. As I did my research, I came to understand the underlying dynamics of the system and the context in which the children were trapped. This was more complex and much harder to comprehend. It required me to look at how dysfunctional and abusive families and the system contributed to the severity of the behavioral problems I was encountering. What was so troubling to me was seeing children more disturbed than the population I was familiar with in the world of adult and adolescent psychiatry.

My psychological training taught me to analyze problems and to systematically research things I did not understand. My background in dealing with trauma also gave me a framework of understanding. But again, I discovered that the kind of trauma I had been working with was much different than the trauma these children were encountering. Theirs was very complex and ongoing, perpetrated by their parents, and often included multiple acts of abuse, neglect, and violence endured over a prolonged period of time. It was certainly not a single event trauma in adults which I had been accustomed to seeing and treating. The evidence of the effects of trauma on the children was all around me. Originally, the term I developed for this trauma was Placement Trauma or Placement Syndrome. However, my studies took me in a direction that was already being researched.

As the narrative of my discoveries unfolded, I found that Van der Kolk had already put forth the concept of Developmental

Trauma Disorder, a diagnosis intended to be used with children and adolescents, which reflected complex adaptations to prolonged psychological trauma in childhood. This diagnostic category brought into sharper focus the damage of neglect, physical and sexual abuse which stemmed from multiple, complex maltreatment. This brought order out of chaos, for me it was a big "Aha" moment.

This was a giant leap in my understanding of why all these children were fundamentally out of control. Current workers in the field of developmental *traumatology* now agree that the overwhelming stress of parental abuse and maltreatment in childhood is associated with adverse influences on behavior as well as brain development, especially the right brain which is dominant in coping with negative emotions and regulating stress.

Thankfully the research I had done earlier in my career on attachment became the key for understanding the larger picture, and the puzzle pieces began to come together. I realized what I was searching for was a model, a paradigm, which would allow me to piece together the seemingly disparate data I was accumulating. I looked for a comprehensive, integrated view, and I found it, surprisingly, in the work I had done in my doctoral dissertation years ago, which was based on the studies of John Bowlby's work on attachment and loss in children in World War II. Interestingly enough, it is still highly relevant. His pioneering work in 1969 has become the foundation of attachment theory:

That the infant's capacity to cope with stress is correlated with certain maternal behaviors, that the developing emotion processing limbic system is impacted by attachment transactions and that attachment outcome has consequences that are vital to the survival of the species (Attachment and Loss, Vol. III, p. 235).

What I was specifically concerned with at the time was crises of identity and the role anxiety and depression served in those crises, and here I am, years later, still looking at problems of the self in crisis. This was the comprehensive and integrative perspective I was looking for, and one I believed would be very helpful to others struggling with these same problems. It became a major connection for me. I learned that attachment is the foundation for children learning to connect with others, regulate their behavior and emotions, soothe themselves, and build a working model of the world. The good news is that there is a great deal of specific research on underlying factors linking attachment, trauma, and neurological development. Block after block, all of these scientists were building a model, a way of viewing all the disparate bits and pieces of the behavior of children under stress and struggling to adapt to their chaotic worlds. A crucial component of the child's dilemma, I learned, is the child's failure to find a safe haven in the maternal relationship, but instead is alarmed by the parent. This leads to low stress tolerance, disorganization and disorientation in the experience of attachment. The old *nature- nurture* question I had wrestled with seemed to be resolved. These new findings offered a new paradigm which integrated all of my questions and observations.

Schore, illuminated the problem when he wrote, "The question of why early events of life have such an inordinate influence on literally everything that follows is one of the fundamental problems of science" (Affect Regulation and Disorders of the Self, p.71). As I pursued this line of research, I found the next link, how the infant's brain becomes wired through experience as it develops. This was the link, the bridge between trauma and its impact on the development of young children.

Rose, Seigel, Perry, Lillas, and others contributed to my growing understanding of how developing brains and neuro-systems were shaped by experience and how they became malformed by abusive caregivers. This was a giant leap in my understanding of the reasons these children were fundamentally out of control. Current workers in the field of developmental traumatology now agree that the overwhelming stress of parental abuse and maltreatment in childhood is associated with adverse influences on brain and behavior development, especially the right brain which is dominant in coping with negative emotions and regulating stress. In fact, the capacity to regulate the stress response was found to be fundament to the very organization of the self. Therefore, regulation of emotion is at the core of what we call the self. Siegel concluded that how we experience the world, relate to others, and find meaning in life is dependent on how we have come to regulate our emotions. So it comes down to this: It is the ability of significant caretakers to safeguard the child by interacting with him in a consistent and caring manner that leads to secure attachment, self regulation, and an integrated self.

The further I traveled in my research, my fascination with and joy of discovery compelled me to widen and deepen the scope of my search. My comprehension of attachment deepened because of Schore's theory based on regulation of emotion and disorders of the self. He concluded that "Attachment style is functionally related to the mother's regulation of the infant's internal states of arousal." His model is an integration of psychological and biological models of human development which has shifted attachment theory to a *regulation theory*. This led to discovering a whole array of parental behaviors that contribute to attachment difficulties. These factors were found to be directly related to symptoms of emotional-behavioral dysregulation.

The profile below is part of the parental betrayal trauma theory of the parent who abuses her child:

Abusive caregiver characteristics:

- Shows less play
- Induces traumatic states
- Has weak attachment
- Provides little protection from other abusers, (eg. fathers or boyfriends)
- Is inaccessible
- Is rejecting
- Shows minimal participation—inconsistent participation in affect regulation
- Induces extreme levels of emotional arousal instead of modulating
- Ranks very high in abuse

- Ranks very high in neglect

- Does not participate in interactive recovery from distress

- Induces prolonged levels of intense negative states

Because of these behaviors, the continued survival of the child is at risk. The actuality of the abuse jeopardizes the primary attachment bond and continually challenges the child's capacity to trust and securely depend on new caregivers in the future. Hence, the child remains in a perpetual state of threat and is more difficult to manage in future placements. This constellation of parental behaviors led me to observe how the behavior of the mother became a means for the child to learn regulation of behavior. Ultimately, the focus shifted to an understanding of the process of emotion regulation. This led to understanding the critical role that regulation played in the development of personality disorders which are based in faulty development of critical brain areas.

In a review of the studies on trauma and attachment, what is disturbing is a study by Solomon and Main who discussed the "intergenerational transmission of trauma, or trauma imprinting." In this study of infant maternal interactions, they noted how the mother presents in her facial expressions the *fear-terror gaze*, which occurs when the mother withdraws from the infant as though he were the source of alarm. When they observed this interaction, they reported infant behavior as trancelike, fearful and dissociated. This study shows the link between frightening maternal behavior and disorganized attachment (Type D attachment). What is significant in these studies is that they link this type of maternal behavior—the mother's dysregulated states--with the critical firing patterns of the stress-sensitive limbic regions of the infant's brain (frequently called the emotional brain) during critical periods of the infant's brain development. Their conclusion is as follows:

> In light of the fact that many of these mothers have suffered from unresolved trauma themselves, this "imprinting" of the mother's chaotic alterations of a dysregulated state facilitates the downloading of psychogenesis, a context for intergenerational transmission of trauma. This represents a fundamental mechanism by which maladaptive parental behavior mediates the association between parental and offspring psychiatric symptoms. This parental

behavioral trauma exposure impacts the child's development of PTSD as feelings of horror and intense fear in a non-verbal infant (Solomon and Main in, Schore, Pg. 252).

The importance of these findings is in two areas. First, it underscores the tremendous effect of relational trauma on the vulnerable infant and how it is imprinted in the neural structures of the limbic system. Secondly, it shows how this becomes the mechanism by which trauma is transmitted inter-generationally. Schore concludes, "The cumulative effect of trauma is enduring in infants—states become traits and the early effects of relational trauma and the defenses against such trauma are embedded in the core structure of the evolving personality" (Pg. 252).

These ideas are foundational. Maternal trauma impacts a child in the most fundamental way. First, her trauma is transmitted and becomes the vehicle for intergenerational PTSD. Second, it is embedded—imprinted--on brain areas central to personality and emotional development, and becomes a part of the infant's core personality. This has many implications, one of which is the wisdom of birth parent visits that create the risk of further imprinting of the maternal behavior as well as reinforcement of the child's trauma-induced potential for remaining in a perpetual "fear-terror state." The cumulative effect of this research was to create a model that powerfully affected the evolution of my understanding of the impact of attachment trauma on development. This includes outcomes where attachment is disrupted by placement and how further regulatory and attunement failures by caretakers unfold following placement.

In the chapters on attachment, I presented a great deal of complex material. A model, the pieces of the puzzle, can be summarized as follows:

- Development is experience-dependent—physical, emotional and brain, development, as well as personality development are formed through interaction with attachment figures.

- The quality of the dyad determines the formation of the self for the direction of growth—either healthy or psychiatric disorders manifest later.

- The role of affective regulation is crucial.

- Complex brain regulatory processes are affected by attachment bonds, particularly how emotional regulation takes place.

- Attunement and regulatory failures are what underlie future psychiatric disorders.

- Disorganized attachment becomes the basis for future violence-prone, self-destructive and psychiatric disorders.

- Specific brain areas related to emotional processing and the stress response system mediate social-emotional functions.

- Removal from even the most abusive of situations entails significant losses: family, friends, neighborhood, familiar routines, clothes, foods, and pets.

- These losses are the foundation of identity and the child's place in the world; the narrative-life story is compromised.

- Trauma, loss and grief reactions, along with resultant social-emotional-behavioral consequences, must be ameliorated in the surrogate home.

- Recovery and healing must be based on an attachment model in order to facilitate a stable, consistent, secure and nurturing recovery environment.

The above data represents the foundation of a model for understanding both the effect attachment trauma has on human development and how complex social systems interact with the developing child. These agencies and their agents can either support and facilitate healthy growth or seriously impact and serve as serious risk factors or impediments to the developmental trajectory of children in the care of these systems that are supposed to protect them.

This research highlights the dilemma of the child whose attachment to an abusive parent is interrupted by court order and how what happens after a placement leaves the child in a continued state of threat. It is ironic how the child's dilemma within the family is replicated by the dynamics of the system. It is the classic impossible situation. First the child is born to dysfunctional parents and then they are replaced by a dysfunctional system. In both cases, the child is in a dependent and helpless position with the parent, needing the parent for protection, safety, and daily caregiving. He can only accomplish this through seeking proximity. The problem, of course, is that the parent is unreliable and/ or dangerous, so what is the child to do? He cannot seek proximity and she cannot run. The answers to the abused child's predicament reside in the paradox of the attachment conflict, which Allen Schore stated so well:

> Because it is natural to seek proximity when alarmed, any parental behavior that directly alarms an infant should place it in an irresolvable paradox in which it can neither approach, shift its attention, or flee. At the most basic level, these infants are unable to generate a coherent behavioral coping strategy to deal with the emotional challenge (Pg. 250).

This sort of trauma in which the child remains in an irresolvable situation occurs in about 80% of infants in the first year of their lives. Unfortunately, if this continues, the child's progress is stalled.

> When infants are not in homeostatic balance or are emotionally dysregulated they are distressed, they are at the mercy of these states. Until these states are brought under control, infants must devote all their regulatory resources to reorganizing them. While infants are doing that, they can do nothing else (Schore, pg. 247).

Obviously, in the case of the child's placement in the system, the child is still vulnerable, helpless, and dependent in another unreliable and potentially abusive predicament. There is no way for the child to ease the threat or restore the failed attachment so there is no resolution of the problem. Hence the child suffers from complex and serial accumulative trauma. Either way there is either failed attachment or disrupted attachment. Perhaps some of the harm of placement comes from unintended consequences. We do not want children to live in dangerous situations, but we have failed to recognize how much harm is caused by removal, and furthermore could not envision how the system could also participate in causing and perpetuating more harm.

The cumulative effect of what I learned about trauma and attachment led me conclude that disrupted attachment creates serious developmental delays and a variety of psychological, learning, and behavioral disorders, compounded by the failure of CLC and DCFS to coordinate a program with the best interests of children in mind. There is no debate that adoption and foster care are necessary for the care and protection of children who are living in unsafe environments. It clearly is not a question of if, but how the child is removed, and formulation of a plan for transition and placement. Once we clearly see the effects of placement, all of the related problems will be put in perspective, and an entirely different discussion must take place.

As a society we cannot permit children to be abused and live in dangerous homes. If they are to be safe, they cannot live with their birth families. It is imperative that we acknowledge this reality, which means we must come to a thorough understanding of the effects of placement on children and their adoptive or foster parents, as well as find a more humane solution to their dilemma. In other words, we must ensure the mental health and safety of the child through safeguarding their tenuous attachment needs. The system must not continue its dysfunctional ways; the costs to the children are too great. This growing awareness of the problems facing child welfare is not localized to just Los Angeles. Others have written extensively regarding these same issues. Paula Pickle, in *Handbook of Attachment Interventions*, writes about community-focused attachment services and documents the many problems facing children placed in foster care such as:

- Prolonged delays in permanency plans
- Unspecific requirements for parents to retain parental rights
- Lack of matching children and families
- Failure to disclose important information to adoptive or foster parents
- Faulty screening of adoptive or foster parents
- Failure to adequately evaluate the child's needs for specific services

- Failure to provide specialized services for children and inadequate assessment of the child's needs

- Failure to demand that mental health service providers have experience and training in adoption, foster care, abuse, neglect and attachment issues

- Failure to adequately support foster and adoptive parents experiencing difficulty with the children placed with them

- Gross lack of assessment, providing mental health services and training in the areas of adoption, attachment, and care of behavioral disorders

- Failure to adequately assess birth families for their "realistic capacity" to be able to care for their children in a healthy and stable manner before reunification (p. 226)

This is an extensive list of problems and failures. Nevertheless, it seems to me to be a very concise analysis of the problems found in Los Angeles, and in systems throughout the country. The magnitude of the problem is a strong indictment of how we are failing to protect our most vulnerable children. We can only conclude that our system is not adequately prepared to serve the best interests of children in custody disputes, challenged adoptions or other critical decisions relative to child placements.

I am enough of a realist to realize that there will be no magical transformation of governmental social policy leading to "The Great Society." Rather, I believe that change can only come from enlightened legislators and an awakened citizenry. We have seen how this country is divided on these issues and polarized over ideology to the point that nothing is accomplished, so I can only conclude that we will have to find ways to improve and manage the systems we already have in place and deal with the realities facing us at the local level.

Here are some concepts I have been working with while undertaking this project. It is done in recognition of the complexities of the problems but I do believe that things could be improved if some of the following problems were to be addressed. First, whatever changes are made, it is essential that we place children in an intentional and caring way in the most appropriate circumstances where they may thrive. Since I began by looking at how children get into the system through the portal of the Children's Law Center, I would like to begin by looking at issues I encountered while working with children placed by court order.

The issues concerning The Children's Law Center are as follows: It is a sad but true fact that legal decisions often are not in alignment with the mental health and well-being needs of children, and that this misalignment often results in tragic and sometimes lethal outcomes. It would seem that legalities and parental rights take precedence over the child's needs for a safe and stable environment and the child's mental and emotional well being, and, as I have stated, it also appears that there is greater concern for the child's physical safety than the child's "mental health as related to secure attachment."

I do not envision this problem going away any time soon. The courts continue to press for family reunification, and they reunify children with dangerous parents and remove them from stable surrogate homes, even against the advice of mental health professionals, case workers, and sometimes over the protests of the children themselves. As a result, young children are being tearfully removed from their foster and adoptive families where they were healing and developing healthy attachments, only to be returned to a toxic environment with their birth families. When parental rights are given precedence over the well being of children, it leads to a variety of problems that in my view, are solvable.

With regard to Family Reunification, I have advocated for more extensive assessment of birth parents, in terms of their capacity and skills for parenting as well, as their mental health and ability to provide a safe environment. Too often, reunification is based on proof of completion of a parent training program, drug rehabilitation, or an anger management program. These programs are notoriously ineffective, because the problems they seek to address are deeply rooted and resistant to change. As someone who has worked with individuals with serious mental health problems, I have found that a few classes where cursory information is handed out in a classroom does not have any significant impact, nor lead to meaningful changes in personality parenting behavior. Drug rehabilitation programs are fraught with frequent relapses. Domestic violence is also a big problem and is often the result of a combination of personality disorders and drug and alcohol addictions. Moreover, it is often perpetrated by the single mother's boyfriend, who often is not in the reunification plan. None of these programs even address the issues of unemployment, mental illness and poverty that form the back story to these problems.

A second factor to consider is the Reunification Plan itself. At best it is disruptive and at worst it is traumatizing to the children and destabilizing to the surrogate family. The visits are often ordered to be on a 3-times-weekly schedule of two or more hours per session. A reunification plan this intense should be ordered only if there is a *realistic* chance that this family may be rehabilitated. The parents must demonstrate through carefully monitored visits that they have the capacity to parent in a way that leads to healthy attachment, instead of perpetuating intergenerational trauma and dysfunction. Connie Lillas has been working on a pilot program which attempts to tutor birth parents in developing stronger, more competent parenting skills. This is one example of how to improve family reunification and ensure better child safety.

I believe that reunification outcomes could be significantly improved if these visits were monitored by a trained person who can observe the parent-child interaction for evidence of attachment behaviors in both parties. Birth family visits, as they are now conducted, are often horror shows where the child is terrified and the birth family interacts in ways that are ineffective and damaging. This kind of information should be recorded and provided to the monitoring court representatives, and it should be given consideration when determining reunification.

Several things would have to change with regard to the visits. Assessment of parenting potential, and strictly-observed visits, with observations documented and provided to the courts regarding parental behavior and the child's response to the visits are essential. In order for this to happen, it should be instituted in conjunction with changes related to parental rights vs. children's mental health needs and rights to be in a stable, safe and healthy situation. There also needs to be a spirit of cooperation and openness regarding input from mental health experts, FFA workers, foster parents and minor's attorneys. In other words, what is required is a spirit of inclusion, teamwork and communication dedicated to the wellbeing of the child. In chapter 10, I documented what happens when the system operates as it does now. Children die.

When the system operates well, it has more positive outcomes. To illustrate these complex and vexing problems, I utilized examples from several cases with which I worked. The first example I used illustrated what happens when the system functions well and has a satisfactory outcome. I refer to the discussion of my case in Chapter 6 in which a two-year-old girl was severely abused by her father and subsequently removed and placed in foster care. She had a mentally-ill mother, and was ordered to have monitored visits with her. She was later reunified, and as events unfolded, the mother became very unstable and contacted the foster mother regarding her willingness to adopt when the mother found she could no longer care for her daughter.

This is a brief synopsis of a complicated case, but I refer to it because in it I see elements which point to ways the system could work better, since it worked very well. I believe it went well because all members of the system collaborated and, because of this cooperation and collaboration, everyone was included and shared information through constant communication. Also, it worked well because we had team meetings in which representatives from CLC, the minor's attorney, DCFS, CSW were present. As the FFAA worker, I represented the agency as Kathy's case worker. The foster mother and even the birth mother were invited to discuss the case disposition.

The case was thoroughly reviewed. Because she and the foster mother had a good relationship, the birth mother was willing to have Kathy adopted by the foster mother, and the DCFS and CLC worked together to affect the adoption based on my recommendations and experience as a psychologist. Collaboration, inclusion, communication, and coordinated team work saved this placement and preserved Kathy's attachment to her foster mother. Later, we worked with the child and foster mother to help Kathy deal with the trauma of being placed, replaced, and placed again, as well as heal from the original trauma of her father's abuse. Furthermore, Kathy's therapy was integrated into the entire process along with her foster family.

All of the elements of the problem were addressed and solved by teamwork, collaboration and inclusion, and everyone did their job well! In order for this to take place, several things had to happen. CLC had to be open to recommendations from the CSW, who had to work closely with the FFA caseworker and be open to my recommendations about the mental status and welfare of Kathy. The foster mother had done her part by arranging for needed medical and psychological services for Kathy and worked with me to provide a safe, stable and consistent environment in support of her. In spite of erratic and often strange behavior on the part of the birth mother, the foster mother managed to maintain a relationship with Kathy through cards and phone calls so that when the birth mother decompensated, she felt safe enough to realize that she could not take care of Kathy and subsequently offered to give her up for adoption.

CLC had to render a judgment that adoption was better for Kathy than trying to keep her with a mentally ill mother, even though the mother changed her mind later and filed abuse charges against the adoptive mother and then filed an appeal for suspension of adoption. The CSW did a good job by staying with the case and staying informed in order to give the CLC attorney good information and convey my recommendations about what was best for Kathy. My recommendations were based on continuous contact with the foster family, Kathy, and developed knowledge of the birth mother over four years. Again, Kathy's case illustrates what can happen when all concerned work together and place the best interests of the child first.

Conversely, in chapter 7, the Smith case illustrates how the incompetence of a Social Worker can thoroughly throw a case off track and cause the children great suffering by continually exposing them to pathological birth parents with 37 counts of abuse filed against them. It was well-documented that the father was a sexual predator, and the mother was a mentally ill prostitute who burned one of her children with a hot plate and tried to drown another in the bathtub. As documented in the case, the Social Worker delayed the placement and disposition of the case for four years, subjected the children to traumatizing birth family visits, totally ignored my reports regarding the erratic and bizarre birth family behavior and did not communicate any of my objections and warnings to the minor's attorney. The CSW continued to advocate for family reunification in spite of overwhelming evidence that the parents were totally unfit to take care of their six children, and during the interim four years of proceedings, the mother managed to have two more children fathered by a convicted felon.

The case was finally resolved when a meeting was held, the CSW's malfeasance was exposed and my information and reports from the therapists of the children were finally heard. The children's lawyer then conveyed this information to the court and parental visitation and rights were promptly terminated. But the damage was done. Four years of traumatizing uncertainty, limbo, inappropriate birth family contact, and continual bombardment by parental pressure to come home did a great deal of unnecessary damage. In fact, ten years later, the youngest boy is still involved in litigation regarding his placement with the original foster parents who had allegations of abuse filed against them as well. The harm done to him has set his development back several years and he still has trouble functioning in school and in most social situations.

In chapter 8, I discussed the most egregious example of a case gone wrong because of a rogue CSW. Several examples of the CSW's behavior were detailed in this chapter. It is important to understand the damage one CSW can do to a case and ultimately to the mental health of both the children and the foster parents, who were put through four devastating years of trying to protect and safeguard the children to which they had become deeply attached.

The most egregious aspects of the CSW's behavior revolved around several issues, the most obvious of which was her incompetence and failure to do her job. She did not visit the two girls for over six months when they were replaced with the foster parents of record. When she did, she abruptly removed them and placed them in an inappropriate home. The RA refused to hear protests and requests for a team meeting. Then, the CSW interfered with continuation of the relationship of the children with their therapist, and to make matters worse, the two girls were subjected to unwanted visits from their mother, whom they repeatedly stated they did not want to see. When the birth mother decided she preferred the previous foster parents over the current placement, the CSW relented and re-placed the children with the original foster parents. The children's condition at that time was poor; they appeared to have lost weight and had regressed.

This drama took place over a period of 4 years. The motivation for the CSW's behavior is unclear. The original reason for placement was because she believed a 16-year-old girl could not care for them. At the time of the original placement, the two girls were emaciated, unkempt and in poor health: concrete evidence of maternal neglect. Fast forward to 4 years later, the girls were still being subjected to visits with the birth mother whom they repeatedly refused to see, but were forced by the CSW to visit anyway. These visits were very upsetting to the girls and stressful for the foster parents. The final act of cruelty was that the CSW filed a court petition, and the CLC granted it, even though the foster parents had *de facto* parent status. With no warning, the foster parents were ordered to return the girls to their mother who was living in a shelter at the time with her other two children.

There are no adequate words to describe how devastated the girls were by being removed from the home where they had become securely attached, were gaining daily in their recovery from previous trauma, overcoming their learning and speech delays and doing well in school. It looked like at last they might have a normal future in this secure, safe, financially stable and nurturing home with a married couple who loved them and were able to provide the necessary services for their continued therapy and other supportive services.

All of this was taken away with no time for preparation or transition and no warning. Their attachment to the only stable adults they had known for four years was terminated by court order and the action of a CSW who clearly had no understanding of the consequences of her behavior. She pursued an agenda quite at odds with the well being and mental health needs of the two girls. Even more disturbing is that the CLC supported this activity even against the protests of the girls, reports of mental health experts, their therapist, FFA worker, and the potential adoptive parents. This is what happens when the system fails; children suffer, not only in the present moment, but probably for the rest of their lives. It was senseless, preventable and lamentable.

This particular case illustrates all of the things that could go wrong and did: no teamwork, no collaboration, unilateral decisions, no communication, total disregard for the attachment the children had with their foster parents, unnecessary disruptive, multiple placements, decisions made by the court that went against the wishes of the children, recommendations of therapists and foster care Social Workers, total disregard for the mental health of the children and a CSW who violated the protocol and rules in several of her decisions, lack of review process, and just plain incompetence. The good news is that the children were not killed after being reunified. Other children have not been as fortunate.

In Chapter 10, my critique about children dying in the system reflects some of the major structural as well as functional problems still present today. Problems in data reporting, inappropriate family reunification, poor case management, poor technology and gross negligence contribute to continued abuse and even the deaths of children. Several hundred children have died in the last 10 years. This is happening to a disenfranchised, powerless, victimized minority: our children. Beverly James writes of the scope of the problem:

> The problem of children's severe attachment disturbances and trauma-related disorders are too big and too important to be

relegated to the care of the mental health community alone. We need help from everyone. The children need to belong, and they do—to all of us (*Handbook for Treatment of Attachment-Trauma Problems in Children*. Pg. XII).

Throughout this work, I have documented the problems in the Social Services Sector which is over-burdened and whose task it is to protect the most vulnerable children. I have documented with several cases how the system is unable to meet the most basic needs of the children it serves. All too frequently when children are removed from their families because of abuse, neglect or abandonment, they languish in temporary placements while the system slowly works out a permanency plan. Thus the system whose purpose it is to protect children frequently compounds the problem. Enormous caseloads, staff that are untrained to recognize mental health problems, delays in getting needed services and failures in communication and cooperation between all the agencies involved contribute to the growing number of children with lifelong attachment problems. In short, we have a very flawed system seeking to solve the endemic social problems which produce damaged children: Poverty, drug abuse, homelessness, mental illness, and domestic dysfunction and violence.

As I wrote this book and struggled with the complexity of the problems, I continually asked myself, what would a more child-friendly model look like? In my view, this new approach must come to grips with the severity of the injuries sustained by these children and it must recognize that the consequences of abuse, trauma, and disrupted attachments have long-lasting, potentially lifelong effects.

Numerous volumes have been written about the effects of early abuse on children. Most researchers and therapists agree that trauma at any age, particularly trauma inflicted by caregivers at an early age, has a profound, usually lifelong effect. Early trauma affects children by disrupting, distorting or delaying their development trajectory which interferes with their ability to attach, trust, and participate in their own recovery. With respect to the foster system, as a result of these early learning failures, they age out of the system and become social liabilities and perpetuate a cycle of repetition, creating another generation of impaired and marginalized citizens. These are just the ones who though impaired, were fortunate to have survived. There have been others who did not make it through the system.

The challenge we are facing is 1) the degree, complexity, and severity of the abuse history, 2) damage to the child's capacity for attachment, 3) a fragmented and often adversarial system judicial system, 4) a child protective services system that often contributes to multiple placements and serial abuse, and (5) the uncertain quality of the entire recovery environment. It is this cumulative effect that creates factors that severely limit the child's return to stability and normalcy when he/she become wards of The Child Welfare System.

I have come to recognize that adoption and foster care are necessary for the care of children whose life circumstances make it impossible for them to live with their birth parents. It is a reality which we must confront. But it must also be based on a thorough understanding of child development. It must have a strategy based on a comprehensive assessment of the needs of each child in order to enact a more thoughtful and targeted placement. This "Plan" should reflect the real emotional needs and realities of the children with their best interests in mind.

If the causes of Developmental Trauma Disorder are based in abusive/failed attachment and by definition are exacerbated by disruption of the parental bond, then it follows that this failed model must seek to restore the conditions under which attachment is taking place. Therefore, it must be an attachment-based treatment model. What would that look like? In order for this to be at all functional, there must be better training for foster parents and a great deal more funding for programs that support the placement and directly address the various developmental problems of the children.

I believe reforms must have the following critical elements. First, they must recognize that children, particularly abused children are resistant to change and they must take into account that multiple disorders co-exist in most children and are the reason that placement is challenging. Add to that the difficulty of the disorders and the damaged capacity to benefit from relationships and we have a very intricate and complicated problem facing us as professionals involved with these children. Moreover, as we have seen, children often react to the well-meaning attempts of caregivers with violence, aggression, and defiance (resistance).

This often results in caregivers reacting with bewilderment, confusion, and hurt. The uninformed and naïve caregivers (foster and adoptive parents) often take these bewildering reactions personally and react by giving seven-day notices or giving up on these children. This is such a critical issue that one researcher concluded that the capacity to derive comfort from the presence of another human being was essentially the most powerful predictor of successful outcomes in treatment—more powerful than the severity of the trauma history itself.

Bowlby first postulated that the major negative impact of early traumatic attachments is an alteration of the child's normal developmental trajectory. That was 40 years ago. These factors must be accepted before we can realistically deal with approaches to changing the way we address the needs of children in placement. Think first about the reasons the child is in placement and how the most basic fundamental needs of the child are violated. In order for anyone to grow up with some degree of normalcy, he/she must have the most basic and necessary requirement met: he need to develop in a *secure, safe, stable, consistent* and *loving* environment. The most common reason a child is removed from the birth family is because the child is in an environment that is abusive, unsafe, unstable, and places the child at physical and psychological risk.

Since the most important factor in healthy development is a secure attachment, it stands to reason that children growing up in unsafe-traumatizing environments, deprived of the most basic necessity--a loving relationship--would be severely at risk. Again, there is consensus in the research on this issue. The primary function of parents is to help children learn to modulate their emotional-physical distress by attuned and well-timed offerings of play, feeding, comforting, touching, looking, bathing, and sleeping—

in short, basic parenting. In so doing, they are teaching skills that will gradually help them to be self-regulating, self-comforting, independent citizens.

Secure attachment bonds serve as primary defenses against trauma in both children and adults. It cannot be stated strongly enough that the quality of the parental attachment bond is arguably the single most important determinant in a child's reaction and to eventual overcoming of both simple and complex trauma. *Consistent external support appears to be a necessary condition for most children to learn to comfort and soothe themselves, as well as the ability to derive comfort from the presence of others.* Again, Allen Schore frames the lasting impact of trauma this way:

> All traumatized persons seem to have the evolution of their lives checked; they are attached to an insurmountable object. Unable to integrate traumatic memories, they seem to have lost the capacity to assimilate new experience as well. It is as if their personality development has stopped at a certain point, and cannot enlarge any more by the addition of new elements. (P. 240)

In other words, the traumatized child is frozen developmentally and needs extraordinary circumstances in order to get back on track developmentally. This is why the quality of the recovery environment is so critical to the process of recovery in children of placement. It is also true for traumatized children who do not have the additional complication of placement. Unfortunately the placement environment is often sporadic, inconsistent, and unstable, and rather than being a factor in healing, it may add secondary trauma to the original problems. With this in mind, let us look at potential changes that would lower the risk factors for children in placement.

First, it is imperative to include the foster-adoptive parents in the therapy equation. Treatment is so much more powerful when it is done in an environment that is safe, secure, stable and consistently caring. Too often the new parents are not included in treatment and may even be seen as obstacles to working with the children. These parents are busy and overburdened by the demands of their lives and often resent the demands of a "special needs child" or the "reunification plan" as outlined by the courts, as well as the frequency of visits to the home by all the professionals involved. They may be resistant to efforts to include them in treatment and may not have the time or the inclination to modify what they may perceive as their own "perfectly good parenting style." They may also be suffering from the disappointment and frustration of having their best efforts to help a child go unrewarded and their love unrequited. In fact, one of the most difficult jobs of fostering "special needs children" is parents having to deal with their own emotional reactions to the child's behavior.

When I led foster parent training, I realized that the picture I painted was somewhat dark when I discussed the impact of trauma on the development of children. Yes, it is complicated and frustrating and fraught with many failures and disappointment. In spite of the system and the degrees of difficulty, there are many surprising successes and triumphs. However, the unfortunate statistics for children leaving the system are that too many of them end up homeless, unemployed, and or incarcerated with an inordinately high degree of mental illness and substance abuse problems.

Having a stable, powerful, consistent, safe, secure and caring recovery environment is only the first step. I believe we need to do much better, and can do much better. It must be recognized that placement is a crisis in a child's life. We need to do a better job of mitigating this crisis. It must be the primary step of intervention. The treatment must be prioritized in the following order: Use a crisis management model to deal with placement issues and make sure the child is in a safe, stable, secure, consistent, and caring environment. Then, we must take seriously the degree of disruption and impact this event has on a child's emotional and physical well-being. We must try to preserve the child's sense of dignity and self-esteem. When we do this, perhaps we will have a chance to break the intergenerational cycle of abuse.

I have already documented the need for a review of the placement procedures from CLC. There needs to be a serious look at the arena of birth parent rights in regard to the safety and mental health needs of the children. Also, there needs to be more teamwork and means for feedback from mental health experts and other professionals when it comes time for consideration of reunification. Additionally, the birth parents need to be assessed for their realistic abilities to effectively and competently take care of a child. Clearly programs designed to support reunification need strengthening and evaluation of their effectiveness. A performance-based model should be considered when looking at the outcome of drug and alcohol rehabilitation programs as well as those dealing with domestic violence and parenting classes.

Then there is the issue of birth family visits. These also need to be changed so that they are conducted by trained professionals who use their observations to determine whether or not there is any attachment between the parents and the child, as well as the effects of the visits on the child. This is all a part of the reunification process which needs significant changes, because there are too many children being returned to their parents with disastrous consequences.

I have also discussed the failures and problems of DCFS with regard to the need for better training, mentoring, reduced case loads, and communication with other agencies. As one County Supervisor put it so bluntly, "People need to do their jobs."

Additionally, I have explored the whole context in which the system operates and the daunting social problems contributing to abuse, neglect, and trauma to our children. Poverty, mental illness, drug addiction, and domestic violence are perennial problems. Lack of adequate funding and failed social policy add to the degree of difficulty when it comes to protecting our children.

I do not honestly know what can be done about the problem of mothers continuing to bring children into the world when they have already demonstrated an inability to care for them. It is overburdening the system and even worse, they are producing damaged children on a serial basis. Women who have 13 children in the system should be seriously evaluated for their suitability for parenthood. Do they have the right to produce as many as they can? Do we as a society have the right to limit their having children?

These are difficult moral and philosophical questions. They need to be addressed. We need to realistically find ways to educate and support single women who perpetuate their own misery as well as that of their children.

In conclusion, given the above-stated problems and issues, within the entire context in which CLS, DCFS, foster parents, FFAAs, and mental health professionals function, there are some things we can do to improve the quality of service and bring to bear our concentrated efforts at changing and revolutionizing the whole system. I call my proposal an *Integrated Service Plan*. It is based on the fundamental idea making the welfare and mental health of our children our primary goal. This controlling value will inform all of our decisions. When a child is placed, it must be done with as much humanity and compassion as possible. When the Reunification Plan is formulated, the impact on the child must be given priority. In my Integrated Service Plan, a comprehensive assessment of the family's circumstances and parenting capacity would be performed. This would realistically evaluate the chances they have of providing a safe, stable, secure, consistent environment, free of abuse, neglect, domestic violence, drugs and alcohol, and without major mental health issues. This is done by integrating mental health professionals and others to give feedback to the CLC while the child/children are in a safe harbor. During this evaluation period, the children would also be evaluated to determine the amount of initial damage done to them, the kinds of services needed to facilitate their recovery, and assess whether it is in their best interest to be reunified.

It must be remembered that a major feature of trauma and loss is the shame and humiliation that often accompanies abuse, intentional infliction of pain by a trusted adult, and the tendency of children to blame themselves for their misfortune. These powerful experiences damage self-esteem and create major obstacles to healing. We must find ways to help children regain a sense of worth, hope, and trust in themselves as well as others. There needs to be a model with these values as its framework.

This particular model requires 1) collaboration, 2) cooperation, 3) communication, 4) teamwork, and 5) a philosophical change which puts the needs of the children first. In this model, foster parents are given greater training and support in order to help them to realistically deal with problems attachment-disordered children bring to the placement, and in this regard there will need to be more targeted services tailored to the specific needs of each child. The "Needs and Service Plans" as they now function are useless. They are perfunctory, no one reads them, and they do not effectively state the goals of treatment. In addition, a plan must evolve to address the issues, and such plans seldom involve all parties concerned who work with the child and family. When a child dies, more action needs to be taken than the formation of another committee and audits of paper trails and agencies. Each tragedy must be given a complete evaluation and determination of what happened exactly in order to learn from the tragedy.

The Formation of the Integrated Service Plan should be created in team meetings where CLC and DCFS and other team members meet to determine an actual treatment plan. This is where the inclusion, collaboration, cooperation, and communication are a functional and dynamic activity. This will solve many of the problems created by a fragmented system where no one is talking to the other and each tries to do its job in isolation, more often than not while at odds with the others. The net result has been serial trauma to the children.

Adoption foster care advocates should be used when evaluating each case that comes before them so that the number of tragic outcomes may be dramatically reduced. If not, then this broken system will continue to shatter lives.

I noted that structural changes also need to be made, including better training of Social Workers, mentoring, improved supervision, and accountability when a child is injured by malfeasance, incompetence, or ignorance. Also, the Social Workers need to be assigned realistic, manageable case loads. I have had situations where one case took all of my time and others where the usual seven cases were quite manageable.

As I worked in the system, it appeared to me that the greatest number of problems centered on reunification and birth family visits. I saw these activities as the points of greatest risk and vulnerability for the children. There needs to be a better framework for preventing high levels of new trauma being added to the original traumatizing circumstances. The least that shouldould happen is to put the needs of the children on par with the rights of their parents.

If we do nothing, we will continue to see adults emancipated from the system struggling with the lifelong effects of unrecognized and untreated early disrupted developmental trauma. The shelters are full, the prisons are full, and the streets are populated by casualties. The casualties are children of the system who have failed to negotiate the treacherous journey of placement for their "protection and safety" while an indifferent society drives right by them wondering where all of these derelicts came from. Again Beverly James has said it very well when he said, "The work needed to help future generations of our global village is everyone's problem and must be addressed on all levels. We must recognize that children's mental health issues are a priority for their survival and ours." (Pg. XII)

Finally, to my heroes who participated in my chapter on survivors: Patrick, Alex, Machelle, and Jeanette, I say a profound thanks for your taking the risk to tell your stories. You have taught me a great deal about resiliency. You inspire me with your courage, and revealed a great deal about hope and the strength of the human spirit. For in your triumph against all odds, and in spite of a system that did more to hinder than to help, you found a way to preserve a sense of integrity and struggled to find and live out your best sense of yourself. You seem to have been able to create what you were looking for: a home in the world. You have also been able through your experience to find ways to give back to those who are still struggling with their wounds. I celebrate and congratulate you. There is a great deal to be learned in the narratives of survivors. You have given much to me and to all the others who have trod similar paths.

In your lives we see the persisting effects of your early trauma: the unhealed wounds, depression, fear, uncertainty, old doubts, and difficulties with intimacy, a struggle with your own identity and the shame of not being wanted. You have struggled to affirm your right to be and found ways to legitimize your lives. We met on our journeys, we shared our stories, and felt a similar passion and concern for all who still suffer in the system, as well as those who graduated but are still struggling. Children of the system, broken, wounded, dependent and vulnerable need an awakened society to hear their cries, see their suffering, and marshal a response that will truly protect them by creating a more secure base and a safety net--a viable compassionate system which heals instead of injures.

Since I have relied heavily on the comprehensive work of Allan Schore, it seems fitting to me to end this narrative with a quote from him:

> The mental health field must move from late intervention to early prevention in order to address the problems of violence in children, a growing concern of a number of societies. In these cases, the seemingly invisible "ghosts from the nursery reappear in horrifyingly sharp out line during the ensuing stages of childhood, where they haunt and destroy not only individual lives, but negatively impact entire communities and societies. The "ghosts from the nurseries that are associated with the early roots of violence...are in essence the right brain imprints of the non-conscious intergeneration transmission of relational trauma. These individuals represent about 15-25% of our prison population.
>
> The answer to fundamental questions of why certain humans can, in certain contexts, commit the most inhuman of acts, must include practical solutions to how we can provide optimal early socio-emotional experiences for larger and larger numbers of our infants, the most recent embodiments of our expression of hope for the future of humanity. (Pg. 306)

# References

Carroll, Lewis. (1941). *Alice's Adventures in Wonderland.* Norwalk, Connecticut: The Easton Press.

Bowlby, John. (1980). *Attachment and Loss, Volume III.* New York, Basic Books.

Brohl, Kathryn. (2007). *Working With Traumatized Children, A Handbook for Healing.* Arlington, Virginia: The Child Welfare League of America Press.

Dickens, Charles. (2012). *Great Expectations.* Lexington Kentucky: Popular Classics Publishing.

Doka, Kenneth J. (1989). *Disenfranchised Grief, Recognizing Hidden Sorrow.* New York: Macmillan, Inc.

Goldberg, Susan, Muir, Roy, and Kerr, John. (eds). (1995). *Attachment Theory.* Hilsdale, New Jersey: The Analytic Press.

Gray, Deborah, D. (2002). *Attachment in Adoption.* Indiananpolis, Indiana: Perspectives Press.

Hughes, Daniel, A. (2006). *Building The Bonds of Attachment, Awakening Love in Deeply Troubled Children.* New York: Jason Aronson.

James, Beverly. (1989). *Treating Traumatized Children, New Insights and Creative Interventions.* New York: The Free Press.

Johnson, Kendal. (1989). *Trauma in The Lives of Children.* Claremont, California. Hunter House, Inc.

Kagan, Richard. (2004). *Rebuilding Attachments with Traumatized Children.* Binghampton, New York: Haworth and Trauma Press:

Karen, Robert. (1998). *Becoming Attached.* New York: Oxford University Press.

Lillas, Connie & Turnbull, Janiece. (2009). *Infant/Child Mental Health, Early Intervention and Relationship-Based Therapies.* New York: W.W. Norton.

Levy, Terry M. (Ed). (2002), *Handbook of Attachment Interventions.* San Diego, California: Academic Press.

McMahon, Patrick. (2011). *Becoming Patrick.* San Diego, California: Deep Root Press.

Rando, Therese A. (1993). *Treatment of Complicated Mourning.* Champaign, Illinois: Research Press.

Reece, Gary W. (1999) *Trauma Loss & Bereavement, A Survivors Handbook.* Eugene, Oregon: Wipf and Stock Publishers.

(*Schore-Dysregulation of the Right Brain*, Published in the Australian and New Zealand Journal of Psychiatry).

Schore, Allan N. (2003) *Affect Dysregulation & Disorders of the Self.* New York: W.W. Norton & Company.

Schore, Allan. (2012) *The Science of The Art of Psychotherapy.* New York: W.W. Norton & Company.

Siegel, Daniel J. (2012) *Pocket Guide to Interpersonal Neurobiology.* New York: W.W. Norton & Company.

Siegel, Daniel J. (1999). *The Developing Mind.* New York: Guilford Press.

Solomon, Marion F. & Siegel, Daniel J. (Eds). (2003). *Healing Trauma-attachment, Mind, Body, and Brain.* New York: W. W. Norton, and Company.

Wainrib, Barbara Rubin, & Bloch, Ellin L. (1998). *Crisis Intervention and Trauma Response, Theory and Practice.* New York: Springer Publishing Co.

Williams, Beth and Sommer, John F. (Eds). (2002). *Simple and Complex Trauma, Post- Traumatic Stress Disorder.* New York: Haworth Maltreatment and Trauma Press.

Van der Kolk, Bessel A., McFarlane, Alexander C. & Weisaeth, Lars. (Eds). (1996). *Traumatic Stress, The Effects of Overwhelming Experience on Mind, Body, and Society.* New York: The Guilford Press.

# Internet Resources

- www.first5la.org
- www.childrensinstitute.org
- www.attach.org
- ww1.aapublications.org
- www.facam.org
- www.attachmentcenter.org
- www.childtraumaacademy.com
- www.zerotothree.org
- www.developingchild.harvard.edu
- www.childwelfare.gov
- www.childtrauma.org
- www.fosterfocusgag.com
- www.trauma--pages.com
- www.ntcsn.org
- Robert Pynos, M.D. National Center for traumatic stress network
- www.icfd.net
- Institute for child and family development: Connie Hornyak

# Appendix A

"The county's foster care system makes Charles Dickens' descriptions look flattering,' said Mark Rosenbaum, legal director at the American Civil Liberties Union of Southern California. David Sanders, who took over as director of the Department of Children and Family Services in March, said experts estimate up to 50 percent of the 75,000 children in the system and adoptive homes could have been left in their parents' care if appropriate services had been provided. He said DCFS comes into contact with nearly 180,000 children each year."There were probably issues the kids and their families were facing, but if they had some kind of support services, the kids could have stayed home,' Sanders said. "At the extreme, there are clearly parents who never should have had their children. They torture their children and everyone in the community would agree that they should not have their children. "On the other end, you clearly have situations where families have done things, but may be under stress one day, have every intention of taking care of their children and are not dangerous, but involvement by child protective services ends up being much too intrusive.'

The newspaper group investigation of the child-welfare system, which is shrouded in secrecy by confidentiality laws, involved the review of tens of thousands of pages of government and confidential juvenile court documents, studies, computer databases and several hundred interviews.

As the investigation progressed, state and county officials acknowledged that the financial incentives built into the laws encourage the needless placements of children in foster care, and officials have started taking steps to reform the system.

Social Worker Anthony Cavuoti, who has worked 14 years for the county, said DCFS employees use the most liberal of guidelines in deciding whether to remove a child from their home. Some parents have had their children removed for yelling at them, allowing them to miss or be late to school or having a dirty home. Sanders said he thinks caseworkers have sometimes been too eager to remove children from their homes a practice he is trying to change. "I think children should only be removed when there is an imminent risk. I've said consistently that we do have too many children who have been removed,' he said. "We need to provide the kind of supports to keep these kids at home.'

As early as 1992, the state's Little Hoover Commission cited experts who estimated that 35 to 70 percent of foster children in California should never have been removed from their families and have suffered deep psychological trauma as a result. On any given day, a total of 175,000 children are now in the state child protective system.

In recent months, parents in several states have filed class-action lawsuits and testified before Congress, alleging that thousands of their children have been wrongfully taken from their homes.

State and county officials admitted recently that they have placed too many children in foster care, especially poor and minority children. California has 13 percent of the nation's total child population, but 20 percent of its foster children, statistics show.

Minorities make up 85 percent of foster children in the county and 70 percent statewide. Experts say so many minorities are placed in foster care because the federal government pays for most of the costs of caring for foster children from poor families while states and counties are expected to pick up most of the tab for foster children from wealthier homes."That's exactly right,' Sanders said. "The eligibility for foster care reimbursements is poverty driven.'

State and county officials say not enough has been done to help troubled families and the system has deteriorated into an "adversarial and coercive' one that places too much emphasis on investigating families for alleged mistreatment and removing their children.

About 80 percent of foster children in the state and county are removed for "neglect,' which experts say is often a euphemism for poverty-related conditions, such as dirty or cramped homes, a lack of money to provide enough food, clothing and medical care to children or a single mother who works more than one job, can't afford child care and leaves her children unattended.

The Reason Public Policy Institute, a Los Angeles think tank, released a report in 1999 that found the current child protective system undermines parental authority, wrongfully accuses hundreds of thousands of innocent families and leaves many children at risk of mistreatment.

The study's author, Susan Orr, a former U.S. Department of Health and Human Services child-abuse researcher, said too many unfounded allegations drain the system's resources. She noted that nearly 50 percent of child-abuse deaths occur in families that have had some contact with children's services agencies. That statistic, say experts, shows the system is failing in its basic mission of protecting children from truly abusive parents.

A review of more than $25 million in foster care lawsuit settlements and judgments in Los Angeles County since the early 1990s found about half involved the unnecessary removal of children and their subsequent mistreatment or wrongful deaths, according to the county's own admissions of wrongful seizures in county Claims Board documents or assertions by the families' attorneys.

In a newspaper group review of 139 claims against the county an action that usually precedes the filing of a lawsuit against the county 26 of the claims involved allegations of wrongful seizures of children. In two cases, parents alleged their children were seized by the county for financial gain because local governments receive revenue for every child taken into the system.

Parents also have alleged in dozens of recent appeals to state appellate courts that their children were needlessly taken from them. "It's legal kidnapping to make a profit,' said Lancaster resident John Elliott, a 54-year-old former Warner Bros. special-effects technician, who filed a claim alleging Social Workers made false allegations against him and placed his daughter in foster care.

After he spent $150,000 fighting to get his daughter back, the county ultimately admitted it was mistaken in taking his daughter and returned her to him. "They tell lies to keep your kids in the system,' Elliott said. "My daughter was abused the whole time she was there. It's a multibillion-dollar business. It's all about profit.'

Santa Ana attorney Jack H. Anthony, who won a $1.5 million verdict in 2001 in a case involving the death of a foster child burned in scalding bathtub water, said parents often call asking him to file lawsuits over the unnecessary placement of their children in foster care. But, Social Workers are generally immune from liability for the wrongful placement of a child in foster care, Anthony said. "It's very difficult to hold anybody responsible for making a negligent decision to take the children,' Anthony said. "In most of the cases I see, the children would have been better off had they not been taken from their parents.'

For years, DCFS had no clear standards defining what child abuse or neglect was. The decision whether to remove a child was often left up to overworked Social Workers' hunches about how safe children were in their parents' homes, Sanders said.

Bruce Rubenstein, DCFS deputy director from 1991-97, said the department intimidated Social Workers into removing children for little or no reason after a couple of high-profile cases where children returned from foster care to their parents were murdered. "The word was, 'Remove everybody. Remove all the kids.' It's pretty fundamental that the county was breaking up families that didn't need to be broken up,' Rubenstein said. "Only new leadership giving clear messages can free that department from this sickness.'

DCFS recently began training Social Workers in a research-based tool called "structured decision-making,' that Sanders hopes will help them make better decisions about when to remove a child. The method has been successful in reducing unnecessary foster care placements in other states and counties.

The stakeholders report found the vague definition of neglect, unbridled discretion and a lack of training form a dangerous combination in the hands of Social Workers charged with deciding the fate of families. Despite a quadrupling in reporting of child mistreatment cases since 1976 due to greater awareness of the child abuse problem in the nation, the number of actual cases of abuse and neglect annually has remained flat.

Unfortunately, experts say in explaining the large number of false accusations, the DCFS Child Abuse Hotline has become a weapon of choice for malicious neighbors and angry spouses and lovers in child custody disputes. "A lot of people use child protective services for revenge,' Cavuoti said. "About half of the cases we get are completely bogus. They are just people calling to get back at a neighbor.'

While about 7,500 children enter the county's foster care system each year, only a small percentage are reunified with their families. A recent study found that nationwide 76 percent of children are returned home from foster care within a year. But in Los Angeles County, only 19 percent are returned home within a year of entering foster care.

Coming Monday: Following years of scandals and heartbreak in the nation's largest child-protective system, Los Angeles County officials and child advocates hope a new director and innovative ideas will dramatically improve the lives of local foster children.

# Appendix B

## *PLACEMENT ASSESSMENT PROFILE*

### *GARY REECE, PH.D.*

Name _____

Sex _____     Age_____

Date of First Placement     _____

Reason for Placement     _____

Birth Family _____

Disposition _____

Number of Placements     _____

Primary Attachment Figures_____

## TYPE OF ATTACHMENTS:

Secure _____ Anxious _____ Disorganized _____

Environmental/Situational/Stressors _____
_____
_____

## ABUSE SPECTRUM:

Rate on scale from 1 to 10 (one being low and 10 being extreme) _____

## TYPE OF ABUSE:

Domestic Violence _____ Neglect _____ Abuse (Physical) _____

Abuse (Emotional) _____ Abuse (Sexual) _____

## FREQUENCY OF ABUSE:

Single Event _____ Occasional _____ Frequent _____ Chronic _____

Perpetrator _____

## CHILD'S RESPONSE TO TRAUMA:

Cognitive_____

Behavioral _____

Affective_____

Relational _____

Somatic _____

Self-perception _____

_____

### MOOD:

Anger □   Numbness □   Rages □

Anxiety □   Sadness □   Phobias □

Depression □   Emptiness □   Helplessness □

### AUTONOMIC NERVOUS SYSTEM AROUSAL:

Irritable □   Easily Startled □   Sleep Disturbance □

Appetite Disturbance □   Intrusive Thoughts □   Hyper-Vigilance □

### ESTIMATE OF CHILD'S STATUS
### IN THE TRAUMA-RECOVERY PROCESS:

Impact □   Aftermath □   Denial □

Disconnected □   Active □

Coping □   Overwhelmed □

Depressed □   Angry □   Acting Out □

(reenactingtrauma) _____

Accepting □   Reattaching □   Stabilized □

## SECURITY/SAFETY OF RECOVERY ENVIRONMENT:

Rate on scale of 1-10, 1 being low and 10 being high the safety of the recovery environment _____

Current risks and threats to recovery:

_____

_____

Child's Assets/Strengths:

_____

_____

Recovery Environment Strengths And Assets:

_____

_____

Caregiver's Strengths:

_____

_____

Recovery Target/Behavioral Areas:

_____

_____

Recovery Strategies:

1. _____

2. _____

3. _____

4. _____

5. _____

CPSIA information can be obtained
at www.ICGtesting.com
Printed in the USA
BVHW082128250819
556756BV00010B/554/P